INSIDE
HOOVER'S FBI

INSIDE HOOVER'S FBI

THE TOP FIELD CHIEF REPORTS

Neil J. Welch

AND

David W. Marston

DOUBLEDAY & COMPANY, INC.
GARDEN CITY, NEW YORK
1984

Library of Congress Cataloging in Publication Data
Welch, Neil J.
    Inside Hoover's FBI
    Includes index.
    1. Welch, Neil J. 2. Police—United States—
Biography. 3. United States. Federal Bureau of
Investigation. I. Marston, David W., 1942–   .
II. Title.
HV7911.W42A37   1984   363.2'5'0924 [B]

ISBN: 0-385-17264-8
Library of Congress Card Catalog Number 81–43563

To those who, in the words of one of them, have elected to spend their lives between the sheep and the wolves—the working field agents of the FBI.

ACKNOWLEDGMENTS

The fast-breaking action of federal law enforcement, like that of infantry combat or sport fishing, is generally sandwiched between large layers of tedium, and plain, unvarnished waiting is a rarely recognized ingredient in many FBI successes. While they wait—for a suspect to appear, or a jury to return—agents trade anecdotes, and it was the rich store of FBI legend and lore which inspired this book.

We thought that field agent anecdotes hold a story which has not been told, and offer fresh insight into the FBI as an institution. Many observers have examined the FBI from Washington—Hoover's dominance almost required that viewpoint—but we have chosen to look through the other end of the telescope, depicting headquarters from the perspective of the field. And in doing so, we have relied heavily on anecdotes and vignettes, the favorite idiom of agents in the field.

Their story, which is our story, is true. At points, this truth from the field runs counter to what most Americans, for most of this century, have thought about the FBI. At points, our account is contrary to what J. Edgar Hoover—and his spiritual heirs in the Bureau—thought they knew about FBI field operations. Accordingly, to make certain that these truths—rather than the truth-tellers—are the focus of debate, we have disguised the names of most FBI agents quoted in this account. We have also, in a handful of instances, masked the identities of non-FBI people or places—in the interest of safety or fairness.

Fortunately, the aliases we have assigned will not withstand professional scrutiny, so we are confident that working FBI agents will recognize their truth-telling colleagues quickly, and join us in thanking them.

Agents will also understand that every FBI career requires commitment and sacrifice by the entire family—which Geraldine McLeod Welch, and sons Chip and Brien, have offered in full measure. We also acknowledge with gratitude Geri Welch's systematic collection, over three decades, of virtually every newspaper and magazine article concerning the FBI. It was a chore which she performed faithfully from Boston to Buffalo, from Jackson to Detroit, and in Tampa and Washington and Philadelphia and New York—and this account would not have been possible without the archive she created.

For a much shorter period but with comparable enthusiasm, Linda Zacherle Marston contributed much to this project.

Michael Pakenham, Associate Editor of the Philadelphia *Inquirer,* made an enormous contribution of time and energy to this effort. His insight into the workings of law enforcement and justice in our society was invaluable, and he challenged us to address issues which we had not considered.

We also acknowledge the contributions of researcher Eileen Flatley and agent Gerry McCauley, and thank especially our editor at Doubleday, Lisa Drew, whose advice and enthusiasm literally inspired this book.

NJW *and* DWM

Contents

INSIDE
HOOVER'S FBI

Prologue

Among FBI agents, one of the favorite Hoover stories was J. Edgar Hoover's apocryphal veto of Clyde Tolson's proposal that they purchase adjoining cemetery plots, Hoover being unwilling to pay for a plot he expected to use only three days. Like most irreverence, the anecdote betrayed nervous uncertainty about the true powers of its subject, and even after Hoover's death, in 1972, agents had no difficulty imagining him looking down (or, as his detractors claimed, up) at the FBI, still somehow dominating his Bureau.

From either vantage point, Hoover would have enjoyed President Carter's press conference on June 13, 1977, at which the President announced the five finalists selected by a blue-ribbon committee to succeed Clarence Kelley as FBI Director.[1] Replacing Kelley, of course, did not require a presidentially ordained national search committee. It was obviously Hoover, five years dead, that Carter was struggling to replace, hoping the committee's prestige would imply a national mandate for its choice. Hoover's ghost would have instantly perceived the whole selection process as an exercise in exorcism and been amused by its futility. Dead or alive, it was still Hoover's FBI.

Indeed, the departed Hoover might have reflected on that June day in 1977 that death had, if anything, confirmed his supremacy. With the irritating exception of war protestor–baby doctor Benjamin Spock (who had pronounced Hoover's passing "a great relief"),[2] even Hoover's critics, exemplified by former Attorney General Ramsey Clark, had, at his death, turned almost laudatory or at least remained tactfully silent. Forgetting or forgiving Hoover's demeaning (and redundant) reference to him as a "spineless jellyfish," Clark said he was "saddened" by the Director's demise, adding, "He has been a major figure on the American scene for a long time. He loved this country and we shall miss him."[3] It was a charitable statement which, if heard by Hoover, would likely have evoked a dubious snort.

Two months before death, Hoover had adroitly deflected growing criticism by explaining to a congressional committee that he was honored by his friends and distinguished by his enemies;[4] in death, despite the forbearance of his enemies, his distinction was indisputable.

Congress voted that his body lie in state in the Capitol Rotunda, only the twenty-second person, and the first civil servant, so honored in the history of the Republic.[5] Thousands came to pay their respects, and an indeterminate number came to make sure he was really dead, an assurance denied them by the closed casket. (The night before, however, the casket had been open at the funeral home for family and FBI agents. Viewers had been surprised how small and tired he looked.)[6] Chief Justice Warren E. Burger eulogized him at the Capitol memorial service as "a man who epitomized the American dream of patriotism, dedication to duty, and successful attainment."[7] President Nixon, at the funeral, called him "a peace officer without peer."[8]

After Hoover was finally laid to rest in Congressional Cemetery beside his parents,[9] Congress passed Senate Concurrent Resolution No. 64, authorizing the Government Printing Office to publish materials eulogizing Hoover "in the format currently used for memorial tributes to deceased members of Congress."[10] It was the legislative version of immortality. The resulting volume, solemnly bound in Bible black with gold lettering on the cover, contained tributes from nearly half the members of Congress and memorial editorials from 140 newspapers around the country[11] (thereby pinpointing, with unintentional precision, Hoover's twin constituencies).

If reading for pleasure was one of the approved activities wherever he was, Hoover could have enjoyably passed a fair portion of eternity simply basking in the book's accolades, reading and rereading the editorials calling him a giant, a legend, incorruptible, Mr. Law and Order, Master Crime Fighter, Mr. Integrity, Super Patriot, Mr. FBI, and more.[12]

But if Hoover's soul was condemned to eternal torment, his tormentor might have asked why, if he was really Mr. FBI, the 329-page volume did not contain a single tribute from anyone in the FBI.

Hoover would have had a snap answer: The book was prepared by Congress, not the FBI; everyone knew his agents had idolized him, had named their children after him, had cried at his funeral—big, rugged men crying.[13] Certainly if anyone had asked for tributes from the FBI, tributes would have been forthcoming, down to the last agent, all neatly typed with copies to headquarters and to file. Hoover had taken the FBI from 441 agents in 1924 to 8,000 when he died,[14] meticulously building the organization which would be his monument, and he had built it to endure. Of course he was Mr. FBI, and always would be.

Certainly President Carter's 1977 press conference did not hold any threat. Hoover would have liked the notion of having a citizens committee choose the FBI Director—it signaled reassuring presidential weakness, and a weak President would never undo what Hoover had built. Hoover understood Presidents. He had served under eight of them, which was about like a ball player hitting .600, a record no one would ever even approach, and he had had his way with all of them.

Looking back, it had actually been easier with the strong ones. Roosevelt, Johnson, Nixon—like Hoover, all consummate Washington politicians, and they had always understood each other. Harry Truman had been a little different, stubborn and unpredictable. He had not been much interested in Hoover's titillating political intelligence, the Director's standard presidential icebreaker, but then he had been equally incurious when someone brought him gossip about Hoover's personal life. In the end, Truman had simply not paid much attention to the FBI.[15] Neither had Jack Kennedy, but Bobby had more than made up for that.

Even in heavenly contentment, Hoover would have

gnashed his teeth at the recollection of Robert Kennedy. Bobby had thought the Attorney General actually had authority over the FBI Director, an understandable misconception since it was embodied in federal law. Worse, he had had the temerity to try to exercise that authority, and their ensuing conflict had been punctuated by Kennedy's repeated affronts to Hoover's dignity. Once, Bobby had his children with him in the office on a Saturday morning when he was unexpectedly called to the White House, and as he rushed out he had casually asked the Director to keep an eye on the kids. Hoover had sputtered about "those brats" for weeks afterward, and while his subordinates at headquarters had gravely concurred ("Yes sir, brats!"), agents in the field had roared with laughter at the notion of Uncle Edgar, baby-sitter.[16]

Agents in the field. Hoover would enjoy watching the new committee-picked Director try to handle them. Washington observers had always assumed, with characteristic myopia, that any threat to Hoover would come from a political challenge in Washington, a fallacy Hoover had encouraged, confident that on his worst day he was more than a match for any Washington politician. But FBI cases were made in the field, which made field agents indispensable. That in turn meant, as Hoover had recognized intuitively, that the field was the ultimate threat to any Director.

Melvin Purvis had proved it. As agent in charge of the Chicago office, he had mistakenly assumed he was entitled to some of the credit when agents gunned down John Dillinger on an East Chicago street. Suddenly Purvis was granting interviews, and his picture was on Wheaties boxes offering "Junior G-Man kits" for two box tops and a dime. Then he was writing a book about the Dillinger case.[17] Purvis's fame had seemed assured until Hoover named Sam Cowley, an obscure agent who had been sent *from headquarters* to coordinate the investigation, as the real Dillinger hero.[18] In the confusion between Purvis and Cowley, the clear winner was J. Edgar Hoover. The public never doubted his claim that the

Dillinger case ranked among his greatest personal triumphs. Purvis died a broken man, discredited and dispirited.[19]

Hoover had made certain there was never another Purvis. He moved field agents around the country, capriciously and often, so anyone who showed signs of developing a public identity abruptly disappeared. Once he transferred twenty-five special agents in charge simultaneously, national musical chairs, inspiring speculation that he had slammed his office door on the way out, jarring all the pins off the wall map, and the cleaning crew had replaced them randomly; it was as good an explanation as any.[20] He also reversed the normal inspection process, ordering junior agents to inspect their seniors, an ingenious stroke which insured that seniority did not mean security. Ambitious young agents always had a career incentive to be ruthless inspectors.

Remote and anonymous, that was what field agents should be, and after Purvis, Hoover's had been. In the final years, even his jealous assistants at headquarters, each scheming to succeed him, had recognized that *their* prospects might be threatened from the field, and their vigilance had, in the end, exceeded his. Shortly before his death, Hoover remembered with relish, his assistants had insisted that another field agent was becoming dangerous, deliberately defying headquarters, a more potent threat than Purvis.

Hoover had not been convinced.

The agent in question seemed quiet, respectful. Hoover had commented in a "Memorandum to Mr. Tolson" that "Mr. Welch makes a substantial, mature appearance,"[21] but based on their handful of meetings at headquarters he would almost have called Welch shy. There was nothing bashful about Welch in the field, however, if Hoover's inspectors were to be believed. Indeed, the man they described was so boldly combative it was almost as if there were two different Welches, and that puzzled Hoover.

There was something else. He had heard murmurings around headquarters about Welch's insubordination. But that was a puzzle too, because no one had more sensitive antennae for insubordination than J. Edgar Hoover, and he

had never caught Welch disobeying any of *his* orders. Unless
. . . no, certainly no one at headquarters would have issued
unauthorized orders in Hoover's name. Even in those last
years, when Hoover had been tired and Tolson sick, that
could not have happened.

Questions aside, the one thing certain was that Welch
made big cases—not one or two, but dozens. He had walked
alone into an apartment where the psychopathic killer of
Kitty Genovese held two hostages at gunpoint, walked out
again with the killer in handcuffs, and then shrugged off his
cold courage—just another case. For Welch, as it soon became clear, that was all it was. With unmatched regularity,
he mowed down mobsters, kidnappers, desperate killers—
cases like Hoover himself would have made if he had ever
been in the field, the kind of cases which had established the
FBI's reputation.

Suddenly Hoover remembered. Internal security, that was
Welch's problem. When an inspector from headquarters had
asked Welch why none of his agents in Detroit were pursuing
Vietnam draft evaders, Welch had snapped it was because he
would fire any agent who did; it was a waste of time. That
unthinkable response had earned Welch instant probation,
signaling the certain end of his career.

But two months later, responding to one of the periodic
congressional crusades against organized crime, Hoover had
publicly promised that the FBI would arrest one thousand
crime family members in the next fiscal year, and Welch had
volunteered to take one third.[22] It was an offer headquarters
could not refuse, but its brashness had infuriated Hoover's
staff. Even allowing for Welch's stubborn preoccupation with
organized crime, it was ludicrous to imagine that a single
agent could deliver that percentage of the national quota.

Welch's office had arrested over three hundred mobsters
that year,[23] and the headquarters staff liked that even less.
The man was clearly a threat, and worse, a temporarily untouchable threat.

A younger Hoover might have smelled danger in Welch's
accomplishment. It was too aberrant; Welch must be doing

something radically different in the field, something secret even from Bureau headquarters. But Hoover was a battle-fatigued seventy-six, and Welch's success was his success. The reassuring fact was that headquarters knew precisely what every field agent was doing, every minute.

Hoover had made certain that agents appreciated his omniscience. Briefing Welch on his first assignment as special agent in charge, Hoover had stated that agents in Buffalo were spending 12.6 percent of their time in the office, which was 2.6 percent too much, and working two hours and thirty-four minutes per agent per day overtime, which was acceptable if equitably distributed.[24] Those admonitions had been faithfully recorded for future reference in the inevitable "Memorandum to Mr. Tolson," and Hoover always had equally precise information on every office, every agent.

No, there were no secrets in the field. Hoover controlled headquarters and headquarters controlled the field. The formula was brilliantly simple, universally accepted, and Hoover died confident that it was true.

It was false.

Five years before Hoover's death, Special Agent Neil Welch had launched a daring covert operation in the field. Trusting only a handful of agents, each sworn to secrecy, he had successfully concealed the operation from other agents in his field office and from Bureau headquarters. Pioneered in Buffalo, the operation was refined in Detroit and would be perfected in Philadelphia and finally New York. It was spectacularly successful, and before headquarters realized what he was doing, Welch had irreversibly reshaped Hoover's FBI.

The full impact of Welch's revolution would emerge only gradually, however, and until June 13, 1977, it seemed probable that his influence would never reach beyond a few FBI field offices. But on that date, President Carter disclosed that of the five blue-ribbon nominees for FBI Director, only two had been unanimous choices of the committee, and of the two, one man had been the standard against which the committee measured other candidates.[25]

His name was Neil John Welch.

It was preposterous. Neil Welch had never been an associate director or even an assistant director. He was only a field agent, one who had somehow defied Bureau headquarters and survived, and now a blue-ribbon committee was telling the President of the United States that he should be Director of the FBI.

Headquarters went into immediate turmoil. J. Edgar Hoover, wherever he was, might have enjoyed it.

1

Hoover

His shoes were wrong.

Everything else was right. His nondescript gray suit, battered briefcase, and shapeless felt hat blurred him into anonymity with the other early commuters—businessmen waiting for the New York, New Haven, and Hartford train to Boston—and anyone studying the platform would need to be good to spot him because he had made himself as forgettable as everyone else.

Except his shoes. They were different. Well-polished shoes were common—it was 1952 and shoe-shine stands still stood in every train station—but his wing tips were more than well polished; they were perfect. Their hard glossy shine reflected endless hours with a soft cloth and a shoe-polish can lid of water—water exactly the right temperature, warmer than lukewarm but not quite hot. Dab on a little polish, rub, water, rub harder, more water. Drill a cloth-wrapped forefinger hard into a dime-sized piece of shoe leather until it was right, every tiny pore sealed, then start the next one. Gradually, finally, the black shoe leather was rubbed into a perfect glossy mirror. He had the only shoes like that, and anyone who noticed would know it had to mean soldier or cop.

But among the drowsy commuters, the FBI agent passed for another businessman, and when the train finally pulled into Providence, he shuffled aboard with the crowd.

Once inside, he moved quickly through the coaches to the

sleeping car, where an elderly black porter waited. The porter led him silently to a luxurious bedroom suite near the middle of the car and pointed.

The agent nodded. They had studied the man's patterns and knew it would be a comfortable mid-car compartment, never over the wheels. The agent examined the car briefly, mentally measuring distances to the doors, calculating which exit the man would pick. Then he slipped out and settled down in a coach for the hour-long ride to Boston.

It was all familiar. He knew the train, the porters, the scenery, every detail. He had been riding this train daily for a week, coming down from Boston on the late train, half dozing on a hard bench in the Providence station until dawn, then freshening up in the men's room to be ready for this train.

Practice. Repetition. All for today. There could be no risk of mistake.

Attleboro, Sharon, Milton, into the Boston suburbs. As the train approached Back Bay station, passengers collected their briefcases and moved into the aisle. The agent eased into the line when it reached his seat.

When the train stopped, the agent moved away from the cluster of commuters, walking quickly across the platform to a pay phone. Inside the booth, a waiting agent had already placed the call. He handed the receiver to the agent from the train, who spoke briefly and hung up as the train pulled away.

Four miles away at South Station, another agent left a phone booth and hurried over to the special agent in charge, top man in the Boston FBI office. His message was precise, brief: "Car three, rear door."

The special agent in charge, or SAC, nodded and moved across the platform. This train had been under surveillance for days, and agents had marked faint chalk lines on the platform, showing exactly where the train would stop and the location of each car. Followed by a cluster of FBI brass, the SAC positioned himself precisely where the rear door of car three would open.

They waited. Every man was armed. Since the $2.7 million

Brinks robbery two years before, still unsolved,[1] Boston had been the hottest FBI office in the country, and these men were the Bureau's best. Still, they were uneasy—the man on the train was unpredictable, explosive. They knew they would have only one chance.

Two minutes later the train arrived, sliding gradually into precise alignment with the chalk marks on the platform. When the door opened, the SAC knew instantly that his careful preparations had paid off—later, one participant would say that "only the FBI or the Marine Corps could have executed that operation."

The SAC was in perfect position when the powerful man stepped onto the platform, and he moved forward confidently. "Good morning, Mr. Hoover, and welcome to Boston."

FBI Director J. Edgar Hoover exchanged firm handshakes with the welcoming party, which immediately ushered him through the crowded station. Outside, four black Bureau cars were parked directly in front, motors running. Hoover and the SAC got into the first one, the others followed in the second.

As soon as Hoover was off the platform, a team of agents had collected his luggage from the train and had raced through the station to the other two cars. Their mission: get the luggage to Hoover's hotel, position every piece in its appointed closet, and be out of the room before the Director arrived.

It was an uneven contest, and starting second was only one of the baggage brigade's handicaps. Hoover's path to the hotel, a normally treacherous twenty-block gauntlet of Boston traffic, had been cleared of every movable obstacle, including other cars. Agents had painstakingly charted the fastest route for him, along with an emergency alternative, and the Boston police (even while waging open war with the FBI over the Brinks investigation) had agreed to reroute all traffic to clear Hoover's path.

Forbidden from marring the majesty of the motorcade, the

agents with the baggage struggled frantically through Boston's back streets, which were doubly congested by the rerouted traffic. It was a comic split-screen picture. Agents in the Hoover party cruised serenely through deserted streets, fast enough to look efficient but slow enough to give the others a fighting chance to get the bags to the suite first, knowing a failure by the luggage mission would wipe out any success by the escort mission. Meanwhile, a few busy blocks away the sweating, swearing agents blared their way through startled traffic.

The Hoover party appeared to have another stroke of good fortune as it reached the Sheraton. At that precise moment, four black cars pulled away from the curb, magically freeing four parking places directly in front of the busy hotel. Those cars and the agents in them had been there all night, saving the places.

The luggage detail battled its way in, arriving minutes after the Hoover party entered the hotel. The SAC bought them precious seconds by sidetracking Hoover into a brief tour of the opulent lobby; check-in had been completed in advance, so no delay was possible there.

Minutes later, Hoover was escorted to the lavish four-room presidential suite on the top floor, overlooking the Charles River. The SAC led Hoover into the suite, where he found a personal greeting from the mayor of Boston, fresh flowers and fruit, a fully stocked bar with his favorite, Jack Daniels— and every piece of his luggage, neatly stowed in the appropriate closet.

For the duration of his visit, Hoover was the only employee of the FBI who would enjoy such orderly tranquility. At the Boston field office several blocks away, deliberate bedlam prevailed—radios crackled, phones jangled, and harried stenographers churned out reams of urgent dictation. There was an unavoidable risk that he might judge too many—or too few—agents to be present in the office, but there was no danger of him seeing the wrong ones, since all overweight or otherwise unfit G-men had been banished to the streets. It was a carefully casted charade, which would continue round-the-clock while Hoover remained in town. Exhausted agents might nap nervously at their desks, but if the Director made a surprise inspection at 3 A.M., then his FBI would snap to attention, fully operational in an instant. And if, as was almost always the case, he did not bother to visit the field office, agents were invariably more grateful for the reprieve than annoyed by the wasted preparations.

On his departure, Hoover's hotel bill would be paid by the Boston field agents, who would also show their esteem by presenting him with a large silver bowl to commemorate his visit. Contributions were compulsory, but agent esteem for Hoover was still, in 1952, almost universally genuine. Ironically, although collecting evidence was their business, agents' opinions of Hoover were based almost exclusively on hearsay. A typical agent might see Hoover two or three times, totaling perhaps twenty minutes, over the course of a career, and hundreds of agent-hours were devoted to the task of avoiding contact with Hoover. It did not matter. Their credo was simple and unchanging: "We were FBI agents and J. Edgar Hoover was our leader—anybody else was down the line someplace."[2]

He was born, with characteristic orderliness, on January 1, 1895, in the District of Columbia.[3] His parents called the baby John Edgar; his classmates, mimicking his stuttering, fast speech, called him Speed;[4] and his lifelong companion, whom Hoover kiddingly called Junior, referred to him as Boss.[5] As a young man, he jettisoned the John, according to legend, because another John Hoover was a notorious Washington deadbeat,[6] but most people, for most of his seventy-seven years, simply called J. Edgar Hoover "Sir."

His father and grandfather had both worked for the U.S. Coast and Geodetic Survey,[7] making J. Edgar a third-generation federal bureaucrat, which was the only genetic predictor of his success (assuming that bureaucrats, like thoroughbreds, might be improved by breeding). Growing up in Washington, Hoover taught Sunday school and sang in the choir at the local Presbyterian church.[8] This suggested, as an

alternative, a theological explanation for his subsequent re-
nown, and on balance the predestination of Presbyterianism
was perhaps as satisfactory an explanation as any. Even
though a high-school yearbook editor would carve himself a
footnote niche in history by presciently describing Hoover as
"a gentleman of dauntless courage and stainless honor,"[9] the
plain fact was that nothing in Hoover's early life seemed to
mark him for national prominence.

His boyhood included the routine chores common to turn-
of-the-century town and city America, and the only character trait revealed by his performance of them was a sort of
earnest busyness, which would prove to be an enduring Hoover quality.

"I always had jobs to do," he recalled years later. "We had
an old-fashioned furnace and it was my job in cold weather to
keep the furnace going and remove the clinkers. From the
age of nine to twelve I was a [Washington] *Star* carrier boy.
On Saturdays I carried baskets for shoppers at the old Eastern Market."[10]

He was a bright but not brilliant student, a competitive
personality but too small for high-school football.[11] He was
remembered by younger relatives as a good-natured practical joker.[12] There seem to have been no serious teenage
romances,[13] no impulses to join the French Foreign Legion
or even the United States Navy, indeed no major excursions
beyond the District of Columbia. He turned down a scholar-
ship to the University of Virginia in favor of night classes at
George Washington University, which he paid for by working
days as a card cataloguer at the Library of Congress.[14] In 1917,
the United States entered World War I, and Hoover, armed
with a law degree and a draft deferment, entered the Justice
Department as a clerk.[15] He would work there for the next
fifty-five years, until he died.

His closest companion was his mother.[16] The descendant
of a line of Swiss mercenary soldiers, she was a rigid discipli-
narian and unquestionably the dominant force in the Hoover
household.[17] Amateur analysts attributed Hoover's inflexible
views on right and wrong to his mother's influence,[18] and his

relatives thought Hoover's lifelong bachelorhood was a consequence of his devotion to her.[19] (Hoover himself accounted for his bachelorhood variously, wisecracking during the 1930s that he had never married "because God had made a woman like Eleanor Roosevelt," whom he blamed for inciting racial unrest.[20] Years later he told a neighbor that the constant threats against his life would have made "sheer misery" for any woman living with him.)[21]

In any case, his affection for his mother was apparent, evidenced by unfailing thoughtfulness and regular gifts, including a canary Hoover purchased from the Birdman of Alcatraz, which turned out to be a sparrow dyed yellow, the only occasion on which he was ever admittedly conned by a con.[22] Following his father's premature death, Hoover lived with his mother until she died in 1938, when he was forty-three.

Hoover never moved from the District of Columbia, that peculiar political neutral zone created by the Constitution's placement of the nation's capital in "such district (not exceeding ten miles square) as may, by cessation of particular states, and the acceptance of Congress, become the seat of government of the United States."[23] He would adopt that constitutional phrase, designating his Washington headquarters as Seat of Government, and the accuracy of his description obscured its audacity; Hoover's claim never inspired the same derision as the State Department's location in Foggy Bottom, even though it came out SOG in Teletype abbreviation.

The District's population in 1900 was roughly equal to that of Milwaukee or Detroit (and more than three times that of Houston and Dallas combined),[24] but it had no industry except government and none of the melting-pot intensity of other Eastern cities, retaining instead the courtly flavor, and many of the racial views, of a small Southern town. It was an environment in which the courteous formality which would distinguish Hoover's FBI from all other American police agencies came naturally, and one which undoubtedly contributed to his lifetime reluctance to hire black agents.

Paradoxically, although Washington existed for politics, its residents, denied both self-government and full voting rights, had no direct political voice. As a consequence, the District had no definable political philosophy. Instead, Washington residents learned to accommodate the kaleidoscopic army of elected officials that perennially occupied their hometown, assimilating whatever political viewpoint the nation's voters imposed. That unconscious skill would account, at least in part, for the fact that J. Edgar Hoover, who as an adult never lived or worked in typical American circumstances, could nevertheless define and articulate the values of mainstream America.

It would also explain why, after many of the country's traditional values fragmented and then shattered in the 1960s, Hoover, the master assimilator, would end his career groping for a compass.

He would finally die, as he had been born, in a modest house in the District of Columbia, the only place where he was ever really at home.

"Palmer, do not let this country see red."[25]

President Wilson's statement during a 1920 cabinet meeting[26] seemed susceptible to several interpretations, hardly a blueprint for action, but scholar Wilson must have known his listener would find it as unequivocal as Henry II's exasperation with Thomas à Becket seven centuries before.[27] Attorney General A. Mitchell Palmer did not need encouragement. A devout Quaker,[28] Palmer's response to the anarchist bombings sweeping the country had been distinctly nonpacific. A bomber who understood anarchy better than chemistry had blown himself up along with a good portion of Palmer's Georgetown residence,[29] and Palmer ordered anarchists, Bolsheviks, and radicals picked up in a massive national dragnet.[30]

Palmer's raids were popular enough to make him a presidential possibility[31] and illegal enough to draw criticism from such respected authorities as Columbia Law School Dean Harlan Fiske Stone.[32] Thousands of persons were jailed without charges on the theory that anarchists could be summarily deported under the Alien Act of 1918.[33] Under scrutiny, however, the cases collapsed in wholesale lots. When only a few hundred were actually deported,[34] it gradually became apparent that Palmer's "Red Raids" threatened the Republic more than the Reds. Facing congressional critics, Palmer proudly admitted authorizing the raids, but he claimed the details, and the abuses, were the responsibility of Mr. Hoover.[35]

The Attorney General's attribution of a national scandal to a twenty-five-year-old Justice Department employee was perhaps the best measure of Hoover's rapid rise within the department. His appetite for hard work had immediately distinguished him, and after only two years Palmer had named him to head the General Intelligence Division of the Bureau of Investigation.[36] Continuing his habit of working evenings and weekends, the former card cataloguer pored over military enlistment records and alien citizenship applications and methodically supervised the compilation of 450,000 suspected threats on index cards.[37] Hoover's intelligence clearly begat Palmer's raids.

When the backlash hit, however, Palmer would learn—as would other Attorneys General over the next five decades—that Mr. Hoover was equally adept at taking credit and escaping blame. As an ironic consequence, Palmer's career was effectively ended and Hoover's launched by the same events; the raids which tainted Palmer marked Hoover as uncommonly able, and his professional advancement continued uninterrupted.[38]

In 1921, Hoover was named assistant director of the Bureau of Investigation,[39] by then a pervasively corrupt agency even by the wide-open standards of the Harding administration.[40] Bureau agents—some with criminal records of their own[41]—sold Bureau investigative files to criminals.[42] The Justice Department openly used the Bureau to investigate the Administration's political enemies,[43] a task the Bureau routinely simplified by employing illegal searches and "black-bag job" burglaries.[44] It was an organization spoiling for a housecleaning, and President Coolidge's appointment of Palmer-critic Harlan Fiske Stone to be Attorney General seemed to assure a vigorous one.[45]

Stone promptly launched a search for a man of "uncommon character and ability"[46] to reform the Bureau, signaling clearly his commitment to a sweeping reorganization. It was not surprising that the man he finally selected would accept the job only on certain conditions; indeed, his conditions seemed to reflect the man's acute recognition of the difficulties any outsider would face in trying to clean up the Bureau.

"The Bureau must be divorced from politics and not be a catchall for political hacks. Appointments must be based on merit," the man insisted. "Second, promotions will be made on proven ability and the Bureau will be responsible only to the Attorney General."[47]

The only surprise was that the man was not an outsider at all. He was the Bureau's assistant director, J. Edgar Hoover, and he was promoted to Director on May 10, 1924.[48]

It was a virtuoso display of bureaucratic agility, and one which accurately presaged Hoover's subsequent career. He would always, by some uncanny legerdemain, preserve a careful distance between himself and his Bureau. He personally would always appear to be part of the solution, even if the Bureau he embodied was involved in the problem. That skill, coupled with his connoisseur's command of Washington politics, would be the basis for Hoover's extraordinary longevity in office, but there was no reason to expect in 1924 that his office would ever be of paramount national importance. Catching car thieves and freeing "white slaves" were the two main Bureau missions,[49] and the public dread of a national police effort seemed to preclude any expanded jurisdiction. It did not appear significant at the time, therefore, that upon Attorney General Stone's acceptance of his conditions, young Mr. Hoover acquired an absolute personal authority over his Bureau which was unique in official Washington.[50]

The face had no eyes—just vacant sockets. It was a white plaster face, and it might have been a work of art or some kind of decoration, but the empty eyes said no, this face is real, real in some unreal, chilling way.

The macabre mask had been made by slapping wet plaster of paris on John Dillinger's dead face after five FBI agents gunned him down in 1934,[51] and its cold stare dominated J. Edgar Hoover's official reception room for the next forty years. It made visitors uneasy. Like the famous Uncle Sam recruiting poster, its lifeless eye holes looked everywhere at once, seeing everything, and visitors were constantly aware of it as they moved around the room. A Baltimore doctor, presumably not squeamish about death, wrote Hoover that he supported the FBI but thought the Dillinger death mask morbid, and he suggested its removal from Hoover's office. A furious Hoover did the opposite; he kept the mask and put the doctor on the "No Contact" list.[52]

Hoover would never have conceded it, but the fact was that Dillinger adorned his wall for precisely the same reason that Lenin reposed in an open casket in Moscow. Both men were dead, but those who directed institutions which survived them knew their credibility depended on the public memory, supported by tangible proof, that both had lived. From the days of the Red Raids, Hoover understood that his own importance was defined by his enemies, whom, by the 1930s, he had generally designated to be "Public Enemies" as well. For most, the metamorphosis from "Public Enemy" to Hoover trophy proved swift and certain.

The young FBI Director seemed to be a one-man answer to the national crime wave, which at its peak featured an estimated two thousand newly mobile, machine-gun–shooting gangsters operating across the Midwest. They had pillaged with impunity, eluding capture by simply driving across state lines, until targeted by Hoover's G-men, who blazed back with their own Thompson submachine guns and were armed with a national mandate to chase desperadoes anywhere. Sociologists would explain that the crime wave was a product of Prohibition-induced lawlessness exacerbated by Depression-era hardships, but what the public knew was that violent criminals like Machine Gun Kelly,

Baby Face Nelson, Pretty Boy Floyd, and Ma Barker and her boys were being systematically caught or cut down by J. Edgar Hoover.

Hoover had sensed, correctly, a surprising paradox in public opinion: Opposition to a national police force masked approval for a national police effort against specific types of crime. Individual liberty did not seem threatened by G-men capturing the "Ten Most Wanted," particularly since the top G-man was always, outspokenly and reassuringly, opposed to the concept of a national police force.[53] It meant that FBI jurisdiction could be expanded, a careful step at a time, always mirroring and never anticipating public opinion; it was an exercise at which Hoover would prove to be superb, but not perfect.

With public opinion the criterion, the second new FBI target was obvious—kidnappers. The desperation of the 1930s had spawned kidnappings for cash, nearly one a day,[54] but for a generation of Americans, kidnapping was only half a word, and the other half was Lindbergh. If Charles Lindbergh's dramatic success proved the American dream, the brutal kidnap-murder of his infant son shattered it, triggering a national nightmare which seared the public consciousness so raw that anyone alive when it happened remembered it vividly fifty years later. Hoover took personal command of the FBI's Lindbergh investigation and personal credit for its success. Treasury agents and the New Jersey State Police would variously and vainly contend that they had actually cracked the case[55] (and critics would later charge that no one had), but the FBI's undisputed capture of the ransom note undercut competing claims. The Lindbergh evidence became a proud and permanent exhibit in the Bureau trophy room, and the public never doubted that it was J. Edgar Hoover who had put the pieces together.

The Lindbergh case inspired the Lindbergh law, which gave the FBI clear jurisdiction in kidnap cases.[56] Hoover soon made jurisdiction almost academic. With FBI investigation a certainty, the number of kidnappings annually plummeted from hundreds to a handful, and the number of unsolved kidnappings was usually zero. It was a rare, perhaps unique, instance in which a serious crime was virtually eliminated by enforcement efforts, and the manifest moral was that what Hoover had done to kidnappers he might—if given jurisdiction—do to other criminals as well.

Over the years, Hoover's unfailing personal involvement in FBI kidnap probes produced casualties who were not kidnappers. During the 1953 Greenlease case,[57] for example, breaking developments from Kansas City were received at Bureau headquarters by a night supervisor named Hogan, who dutifully passed the information on to an assistant director. Hoover insisted on being informed immediately of every development in a kidnap case, which necessitated the assistant director calling him at home. During their conversation, Hoover asked numerous questions, and the assistant cautiously prefaced each answer with "Mr. Hogan says . . ." or "Mr. Hogan indicates . . ." Finally Hoover snapped.

"Just who is this Mr. Hogan?"

The assistant director instantly recognized the imminent disaster. Hoover thought he was getting firsthand facts from the field, and any assistant director who woke up Hoover to pass on the secondhand insights of a lowly Bureau supervisor would not remain an assistant director for long.

"Mr. Hogan?" the assistant stalled frantically. "He's a . . . he's . . . well, he's a close associate of Mr. Greenlease."

"Oh."

That solved half the problem but left open the dangerous possibility that the Director might encounter Hogan at headquarters and ask his name. Decisive action was required. Late that night, a bewildered Supervisor Hogan received an emergency transfer to Chicago, effective immediately. Agents drove him to the airport and promised to send his personal belongings later.[58]

"Bulldog" was the favorite cliché description of Hoover's appearance, but he did not resemble one until his thick, dark eyebrows had faded and his hairline had receded, and there was no hint of bulldog in the man who squirmed in the witness chair of the Senate Appropriations Subcommittee on April 10, 1936.[59] Tennessee Senator Kenneth McKellar, a persistent Bureau critic, was grilling the boy wonder Director, and he finally asked bluntly whether Hoover had ever personally made an arrest.

Hoover flushed with anger and embarrassment: "No."[60]

It was a rare public humiliation, and a furious Hoover moved swiftly to erase it. A few weeks later, agents finally cornered flamboyant gangster Alvin "Kreepy" Karpis (who had been sending Hoover death-threat postcards from all over the country) in a New Orleans rooming house. On the Director's instructions, instead of arresting Karpis the agents notified the Bureau in Washington, and J. Edgar Hoover grabbed a plane to New Orleans and *personally* led his men in arresting the desperado who, at the time, claimed the distinction of being "Public Rat Number One."[61]

(It was close, though. When Hoover commanded, "OK, boys, put on the cuffs," it turned out no one had thought to bring any. A resourceful agent who had grown up on a cattle ranch said he could tie him up with a necktie, so the notorious, nefarious Karpis was finally captured, hands tied with a necktie. Then Hoover and his posse got lost on the way back, and this time a solicitous Karpis saved the day, giving directions to the FBI office. It happened to be located in the post office building, which Karpis had been planning to rob anyway.)[62]

Despite Hoover's capture of Karpis, however, McKellar's question would follow Hoover to his obituary, and the handful of arrests actually directed by the Director were generally fiascoes. He made one final effort in the 1940s, dashing to New York with Clyde Tolson to arrest a notorious gangster who had been tracked down by city police. On his arrival, Hoover was advised that the police were waiting at the station house to commence the joint operation. He replied, "That's fine— let's go to the Bronx and make the arrest." He sped to the scene, sprayed the hideout with machine-gun tracer bullets, and the building promptly burst into flame. The New York Fire Department arrived at about the same time as the en-

raged police, who would remember Hoover's double cross
long after the flames were extinguished. In the pandemo-
nium, the gangster nearly escaped; and Hoover did—back to
the security of his Washington office, from which he would
preside over all future arrests.[63]

It was a rare lapse, soon forgotten. The impressive account
of what Hoover was doing, detailed almost daily by Hoover-
booster broadcaster Walter Winchell and a laudatory national press, muffled any quibbles about what he was not
doing. Always good copy, Hoover was a particularly colorful
figure during the 1930s, when he frequented the New York
nightclub circuit and major sporting events and was photo-
graphed with personalities as disparate as Jack Dempsey and
Shirley Temple.[64] The Director's reputation was by then already sufficiently secure that his regular acceptance of former bootlegger Sherman Billingsley's hospitality at the Stork
Club raised only eyebrows, not questions.[65] Later, after his
social preferences turned more private, the mementos remained, and Hoover's personal effects at death would include a large wooden stork[66] and three ashtrays from that
nightclub.[67]

World War II brought new enemies and new opportunities.
The defense industry mushroomed overnight, and the FBI—
responsible for the security clearance of every defense employee—grew with the industry. Hoover targeted spies and
subversives with characteristic zeal. He announced the FBI's
capture of German sabotage teams dropped off the East
Coast in 1942 before anyone realized they had landed.[68] That
coup inspired a move to award Hoover the Congressional
Medal of Honor, one of the few trophies he did not have and
would not get.[69]

(A 1980 newspaper account charged that it was one of the
saboteurs who actually delivered the German teams to a
reluctant FBI. The story asserted that no FBI investigative
work was involved and that Hoover's only role was to insure
that the saboteurs were tried and executed in absolute secrecy, so that the minor role actually played by the Bureau
would not be disclosed.)[70]

By the early 1950s, Hoover had become an international institution, courted by Presidents, acclaimed by the public. His agents not only respected and feared him, they accorded him an obeisance more suited to an absolute monarch than a federal civil servant, tolerantly cataloguing his every whim and foible. The Director presided over his empire by mail, using the salutation "Dear Mr. Jones" when he was angry and "Dear Jones" when he was not. He dispatched dozens of personal letters to his agents daily, crisp notes commemorating their successes and failures, deaths and births. Hoover's efficiency in recognizing each blessed event occasionally exceeded that of the parents who had produced it. When parents dawdled naming a newborn, it was rumored, the special agent in charge sometimes chose a name at random and notified headquarters, knowing that the timeliness of the Director's congratulations was far more important than the authenticity of the baby's name.

Even those accustomed to organizational discipline were awed by Hoover's mastery. Bishop Fulton Sheen, with a lifetime of exposure to the rituals of power, ecclesiastical and secular, stated his admiration bluntly.

"Edgar, I'm used to pomp and ceremony," he once told Hoover, "but I'm always impressed when I'm around you. Your FBI exceeds anything the Pope has ever done!"[71]

It was an apt comparison. Hoover had transformed the FBI into an article of the national faith, and its rigid hierarchy matched that of any religious order. Hoover's personal supremacy was as absolute as any pontiff's, and he wielded his power with the imperious assurance of one divinely ordained. (Some of his agents, however, enjoyed speculating about Hoover's own relationship with the Almighty. When Special Agent Joe Brock was gunned down in Manhattan,[72] the FBI supervisor escorting Hoover to the funeral, determined not to be late, had the misfortune to arrive at the church five minutes early. Hoover blew up and the supervisor's career nosedived. "It was just too much," one agent concluded. "Hoover and God alone in there for five long minutes—the church wasn't big enough for two super egos!")[73]

But if the FBI faith of the fifties meant pomp and ceremony and one-man autocracy, it was all built on the solid rock of accomplishment. To be sure, Hoover had certain advantages. He was able to select his own targets (which meant "Public Enemy Number One" would be a catchable, colorful "Public Rat" like Dillinger, not some amorphous foe like the multibillion-dollar organized crime industry), and since the only national crime statistics were those published by the FBI, Hoover was the only person who could keep score. Still, even critics had difficulty criticizing Hoover's assault on gangsters and kidnappers, and if his dragnet approach to internal security seemed dangerously unfocused, the remarkable fact was that the Bureau's wartime record against domestic sabotage and subversion was virtually perfect.

Ironically, while Hoover's reputation was based on his conquest of "Public Enemies," his mastery of public officials was consistently even more impressive. From his appointment as Director, Hoover had recognized, intuitively and instantly, that the best politics in law enforcement was no politics at all, and he made the Bureau's nonpartisan professionalism the first tenet of his catechism. He would never change the formula. A few months before his death, he told an interviewer, "I have never voted in my life. I don't like labels and I am not political."[74] It was a statement which, like hearsay evidence in a trial, was enlightening not because it was true, but because it was said.

Having depoliticized the FBI, Hoover then systematically detoothed the watchdog committees of Congress with a statistical razzle-dazzle unmatched in legislative manipulation before or since. Each year the Bureau appropriations request was supported by statistical tables captioned Convictions, Total Sentences (conveniently broken into Death Sentences, Life Sentences, Years, Months, and Days), Fugitives Located, Automobiles Recovered, and Fines, Savings, and Recoveries.[75] The right side of the chart indicated "Percent Increase or Decrease," a title apparently chosen to inject some suspense into it all, since decreases were virtually nonexistent (except, acceptably, in prison sentences measured by days and months). Hoover's statistics always went up, and somehow they simultaneously documented the FBI's dramatic triumph over crime last year and the compelling need for more FBI agents—and appropriations—next year. To Hoover, long before the term became part of the common language, massaging numbers was a vital source of power, both outside and inside the FBI.

As a consequence, FBI budget requests routinely swept through Congress untouched. For years they were deftly guided in the House by veteran Brooklyn Democrat John J. Rooney, who presided over the FBI appropriations subcommittee and put his views bluntly. "I have never cut [Mr. Hoover's budget], and I never expect to."[76]

Over in the Senate, eloquent Republican Everett Dirksen seconded the sentiment. Dirksen's assessment of the 1955 FBI appropriations request was typically critical. "Members are well informed of the current activities and splendid accomplishments of this great organization. In view of this knowledge and the fact that the hearings of the House Appropriations Committee [i.e., Congressman Rooney] contain ample justification of the Bureau's operations, it is felt unnecessary at this time to hear the Director and his associates."[77]

The deference of Congress toward the Bureau was only partially reciprocated. Hoover did make Capitol Hill a de facto demilitarized zone in his war on crime, and formal FBI investigations were normally not conducted there. Routine Bureau contacts with Congress were handled by liaison agents, typically tactful and uninquisitive, who could be trusted to check someone out for a Congressman—and not vice versa.

But Hoover also kept his ears open, and agents learned that "tidbits" they passed on to headquarters which intimated "deviant behavior" by any public official would be heard and appreciated by the Director himself. (Hoover also kept his eyes open, and in the era when pornography was not yet available at every newsstand he was said to have relished the obscene materials, which, when plucked by agents from interstate commerce, were rushed immediately to headquarters per his standing orders.)[78] Not all of the tidbits in Hoover's "Official Confidential" (OC) files were true; virtually none would be admissible in court. But Hoover methodically catalogued them with a librarian's care, keeping them in his personal office for ready reference.[79] The existence of the OC files was not publicly confirmed until shortly before Hoover's death, but the Washington-wide suspicion that such files must exist perennially chilled any congressional enthusiasm for investigating the Federal Bureau of Investigation.

For the previous twelve weeks, the class of June 1951 had met the challenges of FBI training, learning to identify fingerprints and Communists, mastering paperwork and weapons, acquiring equal proficiency with pen and pistol. But the final challenge was Hoover, and while he had been praised, quoted, described, and whispered about, the class members had never seen him. They could only imagine him, building a mental mosaic from bits and pieces—brilliant, tireless, charming, puritanical, decisive, vindictive, omniscient, likes dogs and horse racing and roast beef (medium) and Clyde Tolson (presumably), hates Communists and promiscuity and sweaty hands and weak handshakes.

The most relevant certainty, however, was that Hoover alone decided who would be an agent in his FBI, and everyone knew that even a superlative performance during the weeks of training was no protection against a last-day Hoover dismissal. FBI legend held that Hoover had once spotted an agent on the final day and snapped, "That man doesn't look like an agent, he looks like a truck driver!"[80] The man was dismissed. The story was passed down class to class. And since FBI exegesis of Hoover's decrees was always painfully literal, instructors from that day on had meticulously combed trainee backgrounds to be sure no one had ever driven a truck, which, of course, did not solve the problem at all, since a non-truck driver might still look like one, whatever truck drivers looked like.[81]

The class assembled in the Director's spacious anteroom, which was decorated with scores of framed editorial cartoons featuring Hoover triumphing over various evils. The room's ambience was defined by the arsenal of confiscated weapons on display everywhere. The straw hat and silver-rimmed glasses Dillinger wore when he died, along with the un-opened La Corona Belvedere cigar from his shirt pocket, complemented his death mask.[82] Dozens of other big-case relics, plus three decades accumulation of plaques and trib-utes to Hoover's FBI, completed the exhibit.

It was a fascinating collection, but the new agents were preoccupied, waiting, constantly wiping their hands dry on their trousers. They had been a difficult class. Mostly veter-ans, they knew their instructors had spent the war in the FBI while they had spent their war in the war, and they mutually sensed that this somehow reversed their roles. But their cocky confidence had evaporated in Hoover's anteroom, and now they fidgeted there, wondering why the determination to have dry hands made them moist and whether Hoover would notice.

Finally it was time for their audience. The instructor led them down the long hallway—it seemed to slant uphill as they approached his door. Even before they saw him, agents sensed he would be looking down on them, no matter how tall they were; the perception of his dominance was uncanny and unmistakable, their apprehension palpable.[83] Years later, one agent in the class who had by then captured dozens of dangerous criminals, would remember that first meeting with Hoover as the most tense encounter of his career, a view shared almost universally throughout the Bureau.[84]

It was a blur. Hoover was on his feet the instant his door opened, charging out from behind his desk to grab the first agent's hand, exuding supreme assurance and crackling elec-tric energy, chatting, greeting, talking nonstop, always mov-ing, absolutely in control. The agents flowed by, as compliant as logs in a river, surging past fast when his rapid-fire chatter

speeded the line and pooling up in clumps when he paused
to talk longer. Each of the fifty-two hands seemed to be the
one he really wanted to shake, and he looked every man
square in the eye and then it was over, over so fast they found
themselves dazed in the hallway outside, not sure it had
really happened.

(It was a common reaction. A veteran agent was once so
overwhelmed by a full-voltage Hoover performance that he
chose the wrong door out, walking into Hoover's closet and
closing the door behind him before he realized his mistake.
Then he agonized in the dark about whether he should come
out or hide there, hoping maybe the Old Man would go to
lunch, and of course when he finally emerged Hoover was
there, waiting for him.)[85]

All of the new agents passed the Hoover handshake test.
While none would have characterized it as a religious experience, all Hoover meetings were part revival baptism, since
agents typically emerged joyfully convinced that they had
survived by his grace rather than by their works. It was a
dynamic which Hoover understood perfectly and used mas-
terfully, requiring that every agent who sought advancement actually *ask*, in a personal meeting, that the Director
promote him (a risky request, since it sometimes triggered
demotion). Thus no agent would ever forget that Hoover
personally determined his fate. During audiences, Hoover
customarily monopolized the conversation while measuring
his man, alert for any hint of dissonance or dissent. While
Senator McKellar might question Hoover's experience in the
field, no one who had witnessed a Hoover meeting with field
agents would ever doubt his control.

Hoover's control was reinforced by the universal belief of
agents who made it through training that many others had
not. In fact, however, most trainees who were fired for looking like truck drivers or having sweaty handshakes seem to
have been "in the class just before ours" or in an anecdote
recounted by another agent. But that reality was largely irrelevant, since the perception of summary Hoover dismissals
was both unquestioned and pervasive.

In the end, it was Hoover's ability to evaluate individual agents which prevented surprises—and challenges—from the field. And Neil Welch, who looked like the quintessential FBI agent and was more comfortable listening than talking, seemed to be the member of the class of 1951 least likely to provide any.

2

Special Agent

Welch is smart. He works like a Mafia guy, always keeps himself insulated. He chooses one agent he can trust, and does everything through him.

-FBI Special Agent
Mike Landon[1]

Tom Crane had never aspired to be a Bureau official in Washington. In Philadelphia, he had no burning desire to be agent in charge and was essentially indifferent as to who supervised his squad. He was not, however, without ambition; to the contrary, Crane's ambition was to continue being precisely what he already was. As he waited for Neil Welch on Cameron Street in Harrisburg in August 1975, he had a vague premonition that his modest ambition was suddenly at risk.

Welch had called from Detroit the previous weekend, disrupting a lazy summer Saturday without warning or apology, and ordered Crane to appear with a Bureau car at the Avis rental office in Harrisburg on Monday morning. That was all. Crane had never met Welch, so he did not know exactly what it meant. But he could count on one hand the times he had been called by a SAC on a weekend over the past twenty-five years, and Welch was not yet officially the Philadelphia SAC. It was unusual enough to make Crane uneasy.

It was also contrary to the chain of command. Welch should have called the outgoing SAC, or the assistant, if indeed he had really needed to call anyone prior to reporting. Crane could not know that, even prior to leaving Detroit for his new command, Welch had made careful inquiries about the Philadelphia FBI personnel and reached tentative decisions. But Crane did know that, by calling him directly, Welch had placed him in an uncomfortable position with his current superiors, exactly the sort of bureaucratic danger Crane had years ago opted to avoid by not seeking advancement into the management ranks of the FBI.

Crane had arrived in Harrisburg nearly two hours early, standard procedure on his organized crime squad, to get the feel of the streets and a sense of who did not belong. He had carefully scanned the run-down buildings on Cameron Street for several minutes before he abruptly recognized the irony; meeting his new FBI boss had triggered the same automatic precautions as meeting the Mafia Godfather. Smiling to himself, he abandoned his surveillance and used the time instead to warn the Harrisburg FBI office that the new SAC might make a surprise inspection—a traditional courtesy, agent protecting agent.

A rental Plymouth crammed full of vegetation came into the lot, and Crane tentatively ruled it out. The voice he had heard on the phone would not arrive with potted plants and flowers. The driver emerged, grimacing in apparent pain, and that had not been in the voice either. But he was about the right size, and after studying him a few minutes, Crane walked over.

"Neil Welch?"

"Yeah."

"I'm Tom Crane. Welcome to Pennsylvania."

They shook hands, measuring each other. Crane's first impression was that Welch had someone else's hands—his should have been bigger. But when Crane glanced surreptitiously back down at Welch's hands, they looked proportionate to his body. This meant they were larger than average, which cancelled the first impression.

But it was a revealing misimpression, because it suggested that the physical force, evoking something close to awe, that

Welch projected was more a matter of personal energy or
presence than physical fact. Not that his size was illusory.
Welch's two hundred plus pounds were distributed, more or
less evenly, over a big-boned, six-foot two-inch frame, but he
was more businessman-big than fullback-big. And while
Crane sensed something vaguely menacing about him, it was
not his size.

Oddly, his wire-rimmed glasses offered no reassurance. On
someone else, they would have been professorial, owlish,
perfect for an accountant, but on Welch they looked like a
bad disguise. His facial features were too strong to include
weak eyes, and the level, brown eyes behind those lenses did
not seem to need any assistance. They were gambler's eyes,
Crane decided instantly, at once wary and audacious, calculating, challenging, weighing the odds, cut-and-deal eyes,
confident of winning no matter who picked the game—winning in the long run, whatever the quick turn brought. *Understanding* the long run.

Crane studied that poker face with a professional's skill; it
was not blank, but its clues seemed contradictory, canceling
each other. Welch's lips were sealed in what would have been
a grim straight line, except a flicker of humor behind his eyes
negated the grimness and the lines around his mouth could
only have come from laughing. His strong, serious jaw line
contrasted with his slightly upturned, almost puckish nose.
His full head of dark hair seemed almost boyish despite flecks
of gray.

"How about giving me a hand with Geri's plants so we can
turn in this car and get on to Philadelphia," Welch growled.

It was neither order nor question, and definitely not an
invitation for conversation. They silently transferred the
ferns and spiders, palms and rubber trees. Two lawmen,
armed and presumably dangerous, gingerly carried the
greenery from rental car to Bureau car, carefully placing
each pot in a secure position. Welch was suffering excruciat-
ing pain from a back problem inflamed by the long drive
from Detroit. He mentioned that tersely and carried only the

daintiest plants, while the barrel-chested Crane, a full six inches shorter, wrestled with the trees.

Welch broke the silence as they left the Avis lot. "Wait a minute. We have an office in this town."

"Sure do, Chief. Want to run by?"

"Yes."

Welch knew instantly that Crane had been there first. The office was inspection-clean, no coffee cups or cigarette butts anywhere, with agents sitting stiffly at attention as they studiously pored over case files. Welch glared at Crane accusingly; Crane tried, unsuccessfully, to look innocent, missing the faint trace of a smile at the corners of Welch's mouth. They stayed only a few minutes, then headed east on the turnpike, Crane driving, neither talking.

Affable and gregarious by nature, Crane pondered the silence. Welch did not seem unfriendly, yet he was totally content to sit there without talking. Welch's quietness did not seem exactly like shyness; neither did it suggest tranquility. Rather, Crane sensed it was the ominous calm at the hurricane's eye, likely at any second to explode.

"Pull over here. I'm going to drive."

Crane was startled. He had carefully kept his speed down and avoided sudden jerks which might intensify Welch's back pain, but he must have done something wrong because street agents invariably chauffeured SACs, not vice versa.

"Sure Chief. Is something wrong?"

"What's wrong is your legs are too goddamn short, and I'm tired of sitting here with my knees in my mouth the way you've got this seat moved up!" Welch replied, in a low roar.

"It's the way God made me, Chief, not much I can do about it," Crane replied lightly, relieved that his defect was physical and unfixable rather than something for which he might be more directly culpable.

Without warning, Welch's stern glare melted into a broad smile, which progressed into a quiet chuckle and then a warm, infectious, up-from-the-belly laugh. Crane was not sure what was funny, but there was an irresistible camaraderie in Welch's laugh and in an instant they were both laughing.

Tom Crane did not realize it, but at that moment he became Neil Welch's chosen agent in Philadelphia.[2]

The American Midwest and the FBI have traditionally enjoyed a special relationship in which each has tacitly exempted the other from prevalent suspicions. Conservative Midwestern apprehension about the overgrown federal bureaucracy never included the Bureau, though it was at once both the most visible local representative of the sprawling federal government and the most rigid of the Washington bureaucracies. For its part, the FBI implicitly recognized that the ideological threats to the nation—Nazi sympathizers of the thirties, Communist subversion in the forties and fifties, radical war protesters of the sixties—never took deep root in the rich soil of America's heartland. There were stubborn ingrown and imported heresies in the East and wild ideological lurches in the West, but the geographic center, for the most part, held.

The relationship was obviously partly historical, a product of the FBI's impressive success against the Prohibition-era gangs which had terrorized the area, but it was also part emotional. Hoover's men faithfully mirrored the values, attitudes, dress styles, and even speech patterns of the Midwest, which reciprocated with enthusiastic and uncritical admiration for the FBI.

And if the Midwest was the mold for FBI agents, Neil John Welch was a perfect fit.

He was born on August 9, 1926, in St. Paul, Minnesota. His grandfather had emigrated to America from Ireland's County Cork, eventually signing on with the Union Pacific. During the Depression, Welch's father extended the family's westward migration and railroading tradition, moving to Nebraska as a foreman with the Chicago & Northwestern.[3] The Welches settled in Omaha, and while young Neil would never live there again after he completed his education, neither would he ever spend as many years in any other single city. Omaha would remain his emotional hometown.

Welch had an older sister and younger brother before anyone had thought much about the implications of being a middle child, and he grew up untroubled, his rites of passage as stereotypically small-town American as Norman Rockwell's *The Saturday Evening Post* covers. The choir boy grew into an Eagle Scout who became a star pitcher, then navy gob. Welch returned from South Pacific combat with both body and idealism intact. World War II was a battle between right and wrong, and it reinforced, rather than shattered, the values Welch had learned at home.

It was a home in which stern discipline and regular attendance at the local Roman Catholic church were never questioned, and one in which work yielded its own rewards, which did not include prosperity.

"We didn't know we were poor because everybody was poor and no one told us," Welch later quipped.[4] But it was certain that without the war there would have been no money for college. The newly passed GI Bill changed that, and the unexpected opportunity it provided confirmed for Welch the connection between duty and success. It was not a quid pro quo—a man did his duty, no questions asked—but still a connection, one Welch had absorbed with the air he breathed. Every farmer who ever pushed a kernel of corn into the Nebraska earth knew good things were more likely to happen to people who worked hard and did their duty.

Welch completed his undergraduate work at the University of Nebraska in three years and promptly received a job offer from an organization which, despite its rigid hierarchy and dress code, held a powerful attraction for young men— the Boy Scouts of America.[5] He ultimately rejected the offer, but his consideration of Scouting as a career was notice that his boyhood values had survived, uncompromised, into adulthood. Indeed, Welch would never accommodate even socially acceptable deceits. On one occasion, years later, he embarrassed a companion who had slipped a Stork Club ashtray into her pocketbook by asking the bartender how much he owed for it, and of course the bewildered bartender had no idea, because everyone (including J. Edgar Hoover) had been openly filching souvenir ashtrays for years.[6] It was a value system which would put Welch on a clear collision course with politicians whose moral imperative was "go along to get along," and dozens of public officials would eventually be jarred—and jailed—by Welch's refusal to do either.

Still under the GI Bill, Welch enrolled in Creighton University Law School, a nearby Jesuit institution. Like many of his classmates, he entered law school without firm career plans, and the subject which most captivated his interest, the Nuremberg war-crimes trials, seemed a doubtful specialty. But Welch's fascination with Nuremberg would prove stubbornly enduring, and he carefully analyzed the conflicting duties of Hitler's generals, patiently studying the various rationales advanced in their defense. Long after he had forgotten the Rule Against Perpetuities and other sacred law school dicta, Welch would remember the Nuremberg arguments vividly, and they reinforced his conviction that no organizational imperative could relieve him of personal accountability for his actions.

After three years of studying Darrow and Holmes, nearly ten percent of the class of '51 found a more compelling role model in a local lawyer named James J. Dalton. As agent in charge of the Nebraska-Iowa FBI office, Dalton had recently captured notorious Kenneth Kitts and his bank robbery gang,[7] a sensational, page-one case. When he arrived at Creighton to recruit for the FBI, Dalton came armed with celebrity status. Crisp and organized, he stood in the ornate moot courtroom and confidently fielded student questions, sometimes taking half a dozen at a time and then answering them in order with perfect recall. After three years of labyrinthian Socratic questions, the law students found magnetic appeal in Dalton's clear answers, and there was a rush to sign up with the FBI.

But if Dalton was persuasive, he did not really need to be, because the students had been presold. They had been born in the same decade as Hoover's FBI and had grown up with

it, boys looking for heroes at a time when G-men regularly
were. "Gang Busters" had beamed the FBI's amazing ex-
ploits to a huge national radio audience, which had included
Neil Welch. After listening to Dalton, Welch concluded with
characteristic understatement that "it certainly wasn't going
to hurt anyone's career to have been associated with the
FBI."

In another government agency, notice of hiring might
have come from the administrative officer or personnel director, but FBI hiring (and firing) was the personal province
of J. Edgar Hoover. Western Union called Welch with Hoover's message on May 28, 1951. The confirmation copy came
the next day, neat strips of purple capital letters pasted onto
yellow Western Union paper, a memento the otherwise un-
sentimental Welch (and virtually every other Hoover-hired
agent) would carefully preserve.

NEIL JOHN WELCH
OMAHA NEB-
OFFERED PROBATIONARY APPOINTMENT SPECIAL AGENT
SALARY FIVE THOUSAND DOLLARS PER ANNUM PLUS
OVERTIME COMPENSATION AMOUNTING TO TWENTY
EIGHT DOLLARS FORTY EIGHT CENTS EACH BIWEEKLY
PAY PERIOD IN VIEW OF SIX DAY WEEK. REQUESTED
REPORT NINE AM JUNE ELEVENTH ROOM SIX THIRTY
THREE OLD POST OFFICE BUILDING TWELFTH AND PENN-
SYLVANIA AVENUE NORTHWEST WASHINGTON DC. IF YOU
HAVE BEEN PLACED ON NOTICE BY ANY ARMED SERVICE
THAT YOU ARE ABOUT TO BE ORDERED TO ACTIVE DUTY
IT IS REQUESTED THAT YOU ADVISE THIS BUREAU SO
THAT APPOINTMENT MAY BE CANCELLED. NO PUBLICITY
SHOULD BE GIVEN. LETTER FOLLOWS-
                    JOHN EDGAR HOOVER
        DIRECTOR FEDERAL BUREAU OF INVESTIGATION[8]

Despite its wording, Hoover's telegram was more order
than offer, which made Welch's response unthinkable. He
advised the Omaha FBI office that he had spent six years
studying to be a lawyer and planned to stay in Nebraska long

enough to take the bar exam, so the June 11 reporting date
would have to be postponed. The incredulous Omaha officials faced a dilemma. They could not fire a Hoover ap-
pointee, but they dared not modify a Hoover-ordered reporting date. They could only buck the Welch problem to
Washington, which created a dilemma within a dilemma,
since Hoover might consider that action indecisive. The ultimate cancellation of Welch's appointment, however, seemed
assured, because Hoover would never tolerate Welch's implied challenge to his authority.

Instead, incredibly, headquarters Teletyped permission
for Neil John Welch to postpone his reporting date in view of
the bar examination.

He passed.

Sixteen years later, in 1967, Special Agent Francis Ryan
received orders home,[9] a fortuity which provoked less than
usual jealousy among fellow agents, in part because home
was blizzardy Buffalo, but also because Ryan clearly deserved
good orders. For the past fourteen years the ruggedly hand-
some Ryan had worked internal security in New York City,
investigating the maddeningly elusive radicals and their endless conspiracies, both top Hoover targets.

Unfortunately for Ryan, his new SAC seemed mutinously
indifferent to Hoover's priorities and did not regard internal
security experience as a qualification for anything except,
perhaps, retirement. Exactly one day after Ryan reported to
Buffalo, he was demoted from the organized crime squad to
the standard rookie assignment—general criminal squad. It
was a stinging indignity, aggravated by the fact that Ryan's
Bureau experience matched that of Buffalo SAC Neil Welch
—they had been in the same FBI training class. Ryan accepted the galling demotion only because he already had
sixteen years invested toward an FBI pension. He had no
inkling that, having singled him out once, Welch would soon
single him out again for an extraordinary assignment.

Oddly, although they had spent fourteen weeks in the
same class in 1951, Ryan had no specific recollection of Welch

from training. When he dug out his old class photograph, he discovered, to his surprise, that Welch was not in the picture.[10]

In fact, Welch was nearly missing from his class as well as its picture. His cross-country train was delayed en route to Washington, and a firmly locked door greeted him upon his arrival, fifteen minutes late, at Room 633. His insistent pounding on the door was initially ignored, and when an angry instructor finally appeared, it was only to advise Welch that J. Edgar Hoover's understanding of 9:00 A.M. did not extend to 9:15.

It was an unfortunately conspicuous beginning, given that anonymity was a basic survival skill at FBI training (as indeed it was generally at Hoover's headquarters). Once he was reluctantly admitted, Welch discovered that the training was more boot camp than college, molding young men into organization men by demanding the discipline, uniformity of appearance, and paperwork perfection which distinguished Hoover's Bureau. The numerous examinations on subjects such as evidence and elements of crimes were tests of discipline rather than knowledge, being wholly subjective exercises which, Welch concluded, "anyone could pass or fail, no matter what you knew." Investigative technique, the presumptive heart of FBI training, was largely ignored, and agents picked it up later in the field, if at all.

Hoover was justly proud that one of the several factors which made his Bureau unique among police agencies was that no FBI agent had ever been proven to have taken a payoff (although a handful of sudden transfers and retirements, it was rumored, had been helpful in preserving that record over the years). But the training instructors made clear that agent morality meant more than honesty in money matters. Any overindulgence was taboo, and Hoover's enforcement was so stringent that it occasionally snared innocent victims.

One such occasion focused on the nocturnal activities at a Washington rooming house, owned by a Mrs. Barker, which was a favorite of agent trainees and dubbed, inevitably, "Ma Barker's." (Agents also honored that legendary mother of Midwestern bank robbers as a training crutch, using her name as a handy acronym for crimes chargeable under the Fugitive Felon Act: *m*urder, *a*rson, *b*urglary, *a*rmed *r*obbery, *k*idnapping, *e*xtortion, and *r*ape).[11] A busybody living near the house reported to headquarters that female visitors were regularly spending the night with agents there. Headquarters somehow garbled the address, and as a mistaken consequence agents living three blocks away were called in to account for their promiscuity. The Bureau interrogator advised the first agent that all would be forgiven if he told the truth; he reluctantly conceded that he had recently enjoyed the physical favors of a stewardess (though never in his rooming house), whereupon all three agents were summarily fired from the FBI.

One of the actual culprits from Ma Barker's, who survived to tell the story, remembered it as an educational experience. "It was like the first time your mother asked if you threw the rock and you said 'yes, mother' and she kicked hell out of you—you had to wonder if it paid to tell the truth. But the Bureau was constantly fighting the situation between boys and girls—I always felt Hoover figured that all of the children of FBI agents were adopted, because his agents would never do those filthy things with women."[12]

It was a recurrent theme, and lectures were punctuated with horror stories of agents whose appetites for alcohol or women other than their wives had destroyed their careers.

"They told us about the new agent who, riding the sleeper train to his first assignment in Chicago, met an attractive young woman bound for Cleveland.

"After dining together, they had a few drinks in the club car, and when that closed they retired to her berth for a nightcap. One thing led to another, and he ended up spending the night.

"When he finally decided to return to his berth the next morning, the agent was still preoccupied with memories of the evening's activities, and when he opened the door at the end of her car, he stepped off into the railroad yard.

"Dazed, he slowly picked himself up from the tracks. The first thing he saw was the Cleveland skyline. He rubbed his eyes.

"It slowly dawned on him that her car had been detached from the train during the night, and his car—with his clothes, gun, and FBI badge—was speeding on to Chicago.

"Needless to say, the instructors made it clear that agent was no longer with us.

"It reminded me of the stories the nuns told in parochial school. No one believed them either, but they always told good stories."[13]

Welch's skepticism was revealing but not, at the time, revealed. He sat quietly through the lectures, his strong, serious facade masking any sign of dissent, and he seemed to be learning the same lessons as everyone else. On one occasion, a nondescript visitor, presumably another FBI official, entered the room for a brief, whispered conversation with the instructor, then departed. Without warning, the agents were ordered to prepare a written description of the visitor, and Welch's was as fragmentary as the others. After collecting the papers, the instructor called the visitor back. He had one brown shoe, one black, a cuff link on one sleeve, button on the other, glasses without lenses, a pencil behind his ear, a Band-Aid on his left index finger, and a large grease spot on his tie. The charade instilled in Welch a career-long habit of systematic observation, a skill which typified Hoover's agents in both fact and fiction.

The class spent a week at the Quantico Marine Corps weapons range, the preeminent weapons training course in the country, perhaps the world. Hoover had determined early that his agents would not be outgunned by gangsters, and they drilled with .38 revolvers and .45 automatics, ordinary shotguns, and Thompson submachine guns. (The historic affection of field agents for the Thompson submachine gun was not easily ended. When Hoover eventually banned its use and in 1969 ordered all submachine guns returned to headquarters, compliance by the field was less than complete. It was generally known among agents in big-city offices that a leftover Tommy gun or two could be located if anyone really needed it.)[14]

Remarkably successful in minimizing both agent and civilian fatalities, Hoover's weapons policy was simple: Agents were permitted to fire only for self-preservation, never as a threat, but when they shot, they shot to kill.[15] Some agents flinched at their weapon's recoil, and some recoiled at shooting to kill, but Welch handled firearms with a professional's pleasure, shooting as surgeons cut—cold, clean, nerveless. It was a rare, instinctive ability, and one obscurely at odds with Welch's impassive demeanor, though not sufficiently incongruous to alert the instructors that Welch might be more threatening than he appeared, which was not at all.

(Later, Welch—and many other agents—would learn that guns were unexpectedly dangerous to those who carried them, in that their unbalanced weight often severely aggravated back problems. But agents had a simple prescription: "If you're going to carry one gun, carry two.")[16]

Welch readily accepted the Hoover dress code (business suits, white shirts, straw hats in the summertime, and snap-brims in the winter), which enabled agents to be simultaneously uniform and nonuniformed. Equally important, Welch conveyed the undefined impression which satisfied instructors that he "looked like an agent." One member of the class who did not had unusually large floppy ears and then was injudicious enough to appear in a pink shirt. It was never clear whether he might have survived one or the other, but the combination of ears and shirt was instantly fatal. The instructor promptly fired him. Agent acceptance of the dress code, universal in the early 1950s, was a reliable barometer of Hoover's control; by the late 1960s, agent shirts would become more colorful in direct proportion to their distance from Washington. Pat Gray's celebrated abolition of the white-shirt rule was actually, by then, only a ratification of reality.[17]

Pink shirts might have posed the most visible challenge to

Hoover's control, but as training progressed Neil Welch sensed a more subtle vulnerability. He did not doubt that a field agent's success would depend on the quality of his reports to headquarters, as the instructors emphasized, but he suspected that the opposite must be true as well. Once in the field, Welch would quickly confirm that he was correct; it was Bureau headquarters which was in fact absolutely dependent on reports from the field agents, and Hoover's grasp of events in the field would be limited to the information contained in those reports. It was a realization that would, in time, permit Welch to operate with unprecedented freedom from headquarters control, though there was no harbinger of that in 1951.

It was clear during training, however, that Welch's deliberate demeanor masked an impatient intelligence, as he demonstrated when an instructor asserted, during a routine lecture, that hearsay evidence is never admissible in court.

"A lot of us were lawyers, and it was becoming obvious that our instructors simply did not know what the hell they were talking about. I pointed out that hearsay is admissible for any nonhearsay purpose, plus there are at least twenty-one other exceptions to the rule.

"The instructor exploded. I shouted back, and we had a major argument. After class, I was yanked out and taken before a senior inspector, who said I was being fired.

"That would not have accomplished much, because I didn't have enough money to get out of sight.

"The inspector said the FBI's biggest training problem was that trainees were not aggressive enough, but that it was becoming clear that I was the most aggressive son of a bitch they had seen that year, maybe any year. He predicted that, if I made it to graduation, I would either be one of the best agents ever—or the worst.

"I finally persuaded him to let me stay, so he would get the answer to that question."[18]

It was not clear what standard the FBI used to measure aggressiveness, in view of the fact that one postwar applicant turned down for lacking it was named Richard M. Nixon.[19]

Much later, after subsequent events had revealed that particular rejection to have been ill-advised, Hoover would insist,
uncomfortably and unconvincingly, that it was actually a
budget problem which had prevented him from hiring the
twenty-five-year-old Nixon.[20]

James Sandler was an accountant with General Electric
who tolerated business cocktail parties until someone suggested that golf lessons might help advance his career. Then
he joined the FBI.[21]

Through the 1960s, he worked the labor squad in Detroit,
which was important (largely because of Bobby Kennedy)
and challenging (largely because of Jimmy Hoffa). By 1970,
Sandler was an acknowledged expert at what he did, and
Detroit was certain to generate enough new labor cases to
occupy him until retirement. He had avoided Bureau politics
as stubbornly as he had resisted GE corporate politics, and
the resulting limits on advancement were more than offset,
in Sandler's mind, by the fact that his law enforcement niche
was secure and predictable and likely to remain so.

But on July 13, 1970, a new SAC stood in the courthouse
auditorium and ordered every one of Detroit's 175 agents
into a new assignment.[22] He gave Sandler the promotion he
had never wanted, moving him up to supervisor, and ordered him to contact a Buffalo agent named Francis Ryan,
who had nothing to do with labor investigations.

For reasons completely mysterious to him at the time,
James Sandler had been selected by Neil Welch.

3

Novice

Becoming a Jesuit priest would have taken somewhat longer, but otherwise the disciplines had much in common. Hoover permitted his agents to substitute marital fidelity for chastity, but obedience was mandatory. And while poverty was not technically required, frugality was, given the pay scale. Both orders—the Society of Jesus and the FBI—were historical adversaries of Communism, and each would, in time, figure in domestic political controversy. The Jesuits may have been more peripatetic globally, going wherever God's greater glory required,[1] but Bureau foot soldiers also went where duty, or Hoover, sent them. During Neil Welch's first five years in the FBI he was assigned, successively, to New Haven, Stamford, Boston, Bangor, and New York.

While Hoover regularly used transfers for disciplinary purposes (though the General Accounting Office and finally a court would order him not to)[2] Welch's transfers were all routine, in furtherance of the "needs of the Bureau." It was never stated whether one such need was to demonstrate who was in charge, but Hoover had known for years that abrupt transfers had that useful effect. In the course of his migrations, Welch would uncover countless criminal secrets, earning several "Dear Welch" letters that conferred Hoover's trademark ceremonial blessing. "You should certainly take pride in knowing that you made such a major contribution to the favorable results achieved in this case. I wish to com-

mend you for your valuable services in this connection."[3]
Neither convictions nor laudatory letters, however, would
change Welch's true status.

He was a novice—a new convert in a period of testing. It
was not precisely clear which qualities were being tested,
although Welch would come to suspect that headquarters
valued passive obedience above the FBI insignia virtues of
fidelity, bravery, and integrity. It was absolutely certain,
however, that initiation into the higher mysteries of Bureau
headquarters would be granted only to the few agents
deemed by Hoover to have successfully completed the novi-
tiate.

Arriving in New Haven in September 1951, Special Agent
Welch promptly discovered that he was also First Office
Agent Welch, a designation somewhere between proba-
tioner and pariah. Veteran agents shunned him, minimizing
contacts, a practice which Welch would later learn was
nearly universal in small FBI offices—and nothing personal.

After years of unwanted transfers, the veterans were finally back home in their offices of preference, coasting into
retirement. They viewed new agents as doubly dangerous,
likely both to make mistakes and to tell the truth about mistakes made, either of which might incite Hoover to transfer
every agent in the office to remote corners of the country.
One rookie agent, after excusing himself from lunch with an
older agent, accidentally discharged his revolver while un-
zipping his pants in a bathroom stall, seemingly the most
personal infraction imaginable. Hoover nevertheless disciplined the veteran along with the rookie, even though the
veteran was sitting at the lunch table when the shot rang
out.[4] Although discredited in jurisprudence, the concept of
guilt by association was unquestionably central to Hoover's
administration of his Bureau, and prudent veterans limited
their association with disaster-prone rookies accordingly.

Even so, the veterans managed to inflict some generally
good-natured hazing on the First Office Agents (ordering
them on emergency missions to nonexistent addresses was a

favorite), even conspiring with local police in the effort. It was an uncharacteristic accord; ever since John Dillinger had shot his way out of a trap set by agents and Minnesota police in 1934,[5] Hoover had flatly barred police from all FBI operations, and his antagonism was generously reciprocated.

But rookie agents inspired a truce. The same police and FBI agents who had recently traded punches on a Boston street disputing who had been first at the scene of a bank robbery (while the robbers, sensibly, made a clear getaway)[6] managed to agree that the rookie agent working a stolen-car case would be given an incomplete serial number by the police, thereby producing both a futile investigation and a pointed reminder that their college educations did not necessarily elevate agents above police. Hazing was the field equivalent of the Hoover handshake—part test, part ritual welcome—and while it occasionally impeded investigations, no one felt obliged to include "Cases Lost in the Process of Initiating First Office Agents" in the myriad statistics reported to Bureau headquarters.

It was a rare exception. Statistics were Hoover's eyes and ears in the field—just as they were his sword and shield on Capitol Hill. Welch was astonished by the ingenious array of numbers demanded by the Director, not simply for his statistical conquests of Congress and critics, but more importantly for his internal Bureau purposes.

Welch quickly recognized that Hoover used statistics for control. He had an extraordinary facility for inventing numerical categories with a straight-line relationship to his objectives, and his command of numbers, it was generally assumed, translated into command of his agents in the field.

Without ever leaving his office, for example, the Director could insure that field agents did not waste time in their own offices, simply by carefully monitoring every man's "Time in Office." Hoover was convinced that crimes were solved on the street, and it followed naturally that agents in the office, whatever they might be doing, were not solving crimes. It was arguably overkill. Hoover had already provided persuasive disincentives for office-inclined agents by banning most

workplace pleasures (including coffee drinking). But "Time
in Office," Welch learned, was the most potent enforcer of
Hoover's policy. Each agent's total, to the minute, was faithfully reported to headquarters, and like a golf score, lower
was better.

Higher was better for the misnomered "Voluntary Overtime," which was mandatory and uncompensated. In 1955,
Hoover reported to Congress that his agents had worked
2,824,026 hours of "Voluntary Overtime" during the past
year,[7] an accomplishment to which the New York agent in
charge had contributed by suspending the laws of mathemat-
ics. Each of New York's 1,200 agents, it had been decreed,
would compile "Voluntary Overtime" statistics above the
office average, with an explanatory memorandum required
from any agent who did not. After a few days of guarded
snickers around the office, one audacious agent finally asked
the SAC, who was one of the FBI's legendary autocrats,
where he was planning to keep the six hundred memos; the
SAC snapped back that there were not going to be six hundred memos or any memos because every single agent was
going to be above the office average—or else.[8] It was the end
of the issue.

Being human, some agents were tempted to fudge their
numbers, a weakness which their leader, being Hoover, had
fully anticipated. Accordingly, when his inspectors from
headquarters visited field offices, their function was more
audit than inspection. Agents who had taken artistic license
with their statistics could expect exposure (and likely expul-
sion) through an intricate web of numerical cross-checks. If
there were flaws in Hoover's statistical scheme, Neil Welch
did not immediately find them; headquarters seemed to have
absolute control, by the numbers, over where field agents
went, how long they stayed, and what they did while they
were there.

In the early 1950s, those figures accurately told Welch that
bank robberies, stolen-car cases, and interstate thefts were
what most agents did most often in the field, unless they had
the misfortune to be assigned to internal security.

It was pouring rain, numbing November rain, sheets of water drilling a relentless tattoo into Long Island Sound. Bare trees whiplashed by the wind framed the desolate scene, everything a cold gray wet.

A black sedan emerged through the gloom on the Connecticut side, stopping on the shoulder at the point where the Rippowam River surged into the Sound. The driver stayed inside a few moments, hesitating. Then he stepped decisively into the storm, walked briskly over to the railroad trestle, and started to climb, overcoat flapping in the wind but hat curiously secure, sopping wet enough to be ludicrous but somehow not.

On the top of the trestle he paused again, peering carefully out over the shimmering New Haven–line tracks. At the limit of his vision, just where the tracks disappeared into the fog over the Sound, he could make out the outline of the drawbridge, and again he seemed to reach some decision. He started down the tracks, walking out over the Sound, oblivious to both the driving rain and the choppy raw water thirty feet below.

In a few moments, the man could see the operator's shack in the center of the drawbridge, hanging precariously over the deep-water channel. The point of light in the shack became larger as he approached. He picked his steps over the cross ties, periodically turning around to be sure no train was coming since he would never have heard it in the storm. Finally, he reached the tiny shack and rapped sharply on the window.

The man inside glared up from a man's magazine, annoyed, not surprised. Grudgingly, he moved to open the door a crack, determined to keep his room warm and dry.

"I know who you are and why you're here," he shouted into the storm, ignoring the badge the visitor pushed at him, "and the answer's the same as it was the last time."

Neil Welch was startled. "How the hell do you know who I am?" he demanded.

"Because you guys in the FBI are the only people who ever

come out here," the man roared back with flawless logic, "and I still haven't seen any spies. I'm not sure I'd know one if I saw one! No unusual ship movements, nothing strange to report!"[9]

In the history of the Republic, saboteurs had never attempted a hostile landing on the Rippowam River, and the nearby Stamford General Electric plant had ceased being a sensitive defense installation when the war ended six years earlier. But Bureau headquarters still required a security check on Long Island Sound every thirty days, a mission so obviously futile that the Stamford office had come to value it for training new agents. It was a perfect discipline, one which would produce subservience if not subversives. Since there were no spies to be found, the failure to find any would not trigger reprisals from Washington.

The assignment was Welch's introduction to internal security, Hoover's catchall description of Bureau activities designed to protect the nation from enemies within. Born of the prewar fear of fascism and Communism, internal security grew robustly through three decades while the threats it guarded against shriveled into anemia. Then, in the 1960s, when plotters of violent revolution finally showed signs of moving from advocacy into action, the Bureau's aged internal security program proved largely impotent in containing them. In the end it was perhaps more punishing to the Bureau itself than it had been to its targets in its entire history.

The program started discreetly. Twenty-two words buried in a 1936 appropriations bill nullified the condition set in 1924 that the Bureau be "limited strictly to investigations of violations of federal laws," by authorizing "such *other* [emphasis added] investigations regarding official matters under the control of . . . the Secretary of State as may be directed by the Attorney General."[10] It was tantalizingly vague language, but there was one person who knew precisely what it meant. His name was Franklin Delano Roosevelt, and his relationship with Hoover would define future President–FBI

Director relations as completely, and for nearly as long, as his New Deal would dominate domestic politics.

Confounding observers who had predicted that he would promptly replace Republican-appointed Hoover, Roosevelt had instead kept and cultivated him, inaugurating the Director's privilege of direct and private access to the White House.[11] In addition, FDR became the first President to regularly enjoy the gossipy tidbits from Hoover's secret OC files.[12] FDR ordered the Bureau to tap the phones of various of his top aides,[13] encouraged Hoover to investigate alleged nisei subversives (Hoover declined),[14] and generally demonstrated unusual enthusiasm for Hoover and his Bureau.

(Reciprocity was never assured with Hoover, however, and he persistently sniped at Roosevelt advisors and policies he believed too liberal. Indeed, according to former FBI Assistant Director William C. Sullivan, Hoover even considered running against FDR in 1936, an idea which was hastily abandoned after aides sampled the opinion of leading police chiefs—presumably the natural Hoover constituency—and reported that many did not think he should be FBI Director, much less President.)[15]

Even prior to enactment of the 1936 legislation, then, Hoover knew what Roosevelt wanted, and it was only a formality when the Secretary of State asked the Attorney General, who directed the Federal Bureau of Investigation, to investigate fascism and Communism in America.[16] Never inclined toward fine distinctions when defining his enemies, Hoover naturally concluded that his mandate included domestic subversion generally.

Suddenly, FBI investigations were no longer limited to violations of federal law. Hoover immediately transmitted the new orders to all field offices on September 5, 1936.

> The Bureau desires to obtain from all possible sources information concerning subversive activities being conducted in the United States by Communists, Fascists, and representatives or advocates of other organizations or groups advocating the

overthrow or replacement of the Government of
the United States by illegal methods . . . It is desired, accordingly, that you immediately transmit to
the Bureau any information relating to subversive
activities on the part of any individual or organization, regardless of the source from which this information is received.[17]

Subversive activity turned out to be like obscenity; no one
could define it, but Hoover apparently recognized it when he
saw it. By 1939, Roosevelt concluded that Hoover had spotted
enough subversion to deserve a monopoly in the field, and he
issued two presidential directives establishing the Bureau's
exclusive jurisdiction over espionage, counterespionage, and
sabotage investigations.[18] Roosevelt also officially requested
that local police turn over their espionage and subversive
files to the Bureau, an apparently innocuous request actually
intended to stop a sabotage squad formed by the New York
City police in competition with the FBI.[19]

(A 1976 report by the comptroller general of the United
States argued that, despite his 1939 request that local police
turn over subversive intelligence to the FBI, the Roosevelt
directives never explicitly ordered the FBI itself to collect
intelligence on subversive activities—a contention which
completely ignored the subsequent actions by Hoover and
acquiescence by Roosevelt. It should be noted, in addition,
that the 1939 directive was the foundation for two later executive orders, by Truman in 1950 and Eisenhower in 1953,
which clearly contemplated FBI control over investigations
of subversive activity.)[20]

Having conferred his mandate, Roosevelt next authorized
Hoover's method in a confidential 1940 memorandum to the
Attorney General approving the use of "listening devices"
against subversives and spies.[21] By then, the President was
fully acquainted with the independence of the judicial
branch, and court approval for his wiretaps does not seem to
have been considered. The 1940 action set the pattern: The
Bureau's internal security probes would continue, with presi-

dential approval and without judicial sanction, from wartime into peace, a healthily growing bureaucracy of listeners hearing ever more clearly as listening-device technology advanced.

Indeed, from Hoover's perspective 1945 brought cold war rather than peace, and his preoccupation with subversives never cooled at all. He was not alone. President Truman's creation of the Federal Employees Loyalty Program seemed to confirm that there were indeed dangerous subversives abroad in the land, and a previously obscure senator named Joseph McCarthy claimed to know how many.[22] The question, however, was how he had found out. As months passed and accusations multiplied, the suspicion spread that J. Edgar Hoover was more than marginally involved in the degeneration of McCarthy into McCarthyism.

(In 1971, when it no longer mattered, Hoover's disinherited heir apparent, William C. Sullivan, wrote a bitter letter to Hoover, charging that "you had us preparing material for [McCarthy] regularly, kept furnishing it to him while you denied publicly that we were helping him.")[23]

Hoover denied it. But as McCarthy's excesses accelerated, it became clear that his revelations and the Bureau's internal security probes had something important in common—both were vastly more effective in chilling political convictions than in supporting criminal ones. The problem was that espionage had blurred into subversion which was oozing into dissent, but it was all internal security to the Bureau, all headlines for McCarthy. And even as McCarthy's headlines turned increasingly capricious (he claimed to have found, variously, 205 or 57 or 10 or 116 Communists in the State Department alone),[24] internal security would remain the top Bureau priority. Critics might criticize, but J. Edgar Hoover consistently kept the approval of the only two officials who really mattered—the Attorney General and the President of the United States. And, always conscious of the frailty of human memory, he kept it in writing.

"I was assigned my first important internal security surveillance in New Haven, filling in for a senior agent who had
called in sick. After a quick briefing, they dropped me at the
pick-up point. The subjects appeared right on schedule, and I
started following them, adrenalin pumping, ready for action.

"They did not seem suspicious of anything, so I edged a
little closer. I finally got close enough to see who the hell I
was following—a little old lady and an elderly gentleman.
God, they must have been in their seventies! Traffic was
heavy, and they were struggling just to get across the inter-
section.

"They could barely walk, and these people were supposed
to be dangerous Communist Party members, a threat to the
internal security of the United States. Since I was standing
there, I thought I might as well do something—I went over
and helped them across the street."[25]

Apparently, Welch decided, subversives were a threat
which looked more dangerous from a distance, particularly
the distance which ended in that spacious fifth-floor office in
the Justice Department Building in Washington. Moreover,
the investigative scrutiny aimed at the handful of genuine
menaces among them was sharply diluted by the Bureau's
dragnet approach. If subversive X attended a meeting with
ten persons, agents opened ten new subversive files, all cross-
referenced, and when those ten in turn met others, the mul-
tiplication continued, uninterrupted by any evaluation of the
actual threat posed.

The plan was to maintain an up-to-date security index, a
comprehensive list of potentially perfidious persons who
would be immediately detained in time of national emergency (a concept not notably advanced beyond Hoover's
index cards from the Palmer Red Raid days). In practice,
however, the result was a steadily snowballing paper project,
its existence perpetually justified by its rising statistics, which
reflected the magnitude of the investigative effort rather
than the danger. Indeed, the menace of subversives may
have been most reliably measured by the one thing which

Hoover did not ascribe to them, which was nicknames; Kreepy Karpis and Machine Gun Kelly had no subversive counterparts, and those who would undermine the nation did not seem to qualify for the Director's "Ten Most Wanted" list or even his "Public Rats" list.

Nevertheless, Hoover's security troops trained for enduring ideological combat, studying Communist history, doctrine, and tactics. In sharp contrast to the FBI's case-by-case approach to criminal investigations, security agents studied the Communist Party and other groups deemed subversive as organizations, carefully analyzing and infiltrating them. Ominous "Messages from the Director" regularly updated the dangers, and those who read them realized that Hoover saw a 1950s America as ripe for revolution as Russia was in 1916. It was an apocalyptic vision more widely shared by those who had seen only the FBI's secret documents in Washington than by those who had seen the enemy in the field. Working agents rated any big-city tenderloin district, on any Saturday night, as more dangerous to both health and democracy than all the subversives combined.

But Bureau headquarters seemed perennially convinced that the nation's subversives were indeed combined, conspiring, and dangerous, mostly in New York City. By the time he was transferred to New York in 1953, Welch had learned (as had the radicals and subversives) that precautions were required to avoid the Bureau's huge internal security squad there. Welch reported armed with a letter from his Boston supervisor, highly recommending him for criminal work, and thereby escaped the security assignment meted out to every other newly reporting agent in the group. Welch's instinctive aversion to internal security would impress President Carter's blue-ribbon committee twenty-five years later; the committee asked every Director aspirant (including a number of bitter Welch enemies) whether Welch had ever participated in Bureau internal security abuses, and their answer was a unanimous no. The apparent reason for Welch's aversion, pieced together by one perceptive committee member, was clearly traceable to his early experiences in the field.

"Welch did not have a civil liberties approach or a lawyer's approach. I think what kept him away from that kind of activity," Charles Morgan, Jr., would conclude, "was the simple fact that he thought it was silly—there were more important things to do."[26]

In doing them, however, Welch would quietly borrow and refine Hoover's favorite internal security technique—the intelligence base. Not content to investigate crimes after they were committed, Welch would instead launch his own study of criminal organizations, using the sophisticated surveillance techniques which had been created for Communists, to compile intelligence on crime family members and methods. Eventually, he would be able to infiltrate powerful criminal organizations—as successfully as the Bureau had penetrated the impotent Communist Party—and anticipate crimes before they occurred, an accomplishment which would baffle mobsters and Bureau officials alike.

All of that was still years away, but it would nevertheless prove to be useful that when Tom Crane and Francis Ryan were also transferred to New York City in 1953 they were both assigned, routinely, to the internal security squad.[27]

"Petey Blue was a major crime figure in New York, top man in a gang which specialized in stolen luxury cars.

"We had an agent, call him Z, who was a genius at undercover work. Hoover never approved of undercover agents in criminal cases, but in the field we realized it was *the* most effective investigative technique. Our only problem with Z was to keep him from assuming total leadership of the criminal activities he infiltrated!

"Z quickly penetrated Petey Blue's entire organization and then decided to prove he was really big-time. He told Petey he was only interested in stolen cars as a means of shipping contraband machine guns to Israel—he filled the trunks with guns and shipped the cars overseas.

"A few days later, a whole shipload of armament was stolen

from the Brooklyn Army Pier, and two days after that he told
Z he could supply anything Z wanted for Israel—machine
guns, grenades, howitzers, anything.

"On delivery day, we had nearly a hundred agents scrambling all over Brooklyn and the Bronx, trying to keep track of
the cars, the weapons, and the payoff. Petey was smart
enough not to be personally involved in the details, and in
the excitement we almost forgot about him. But at the last
minute, word came over the radio: 'Leave Welch and his
partner there to pick up Petey Blue.'

"I had never actually seen him, but the boss said he would
be easy to spot—he had the biggest nose on Broadway, just
like Jimmy Durante, and he always frequented the same two
or three Broadway night spots.

"We had no difficulty finding him. He was with two girl-
friends in a bar, and we followed them through their evening
entertainment for the next several hours. Finally, after everyone else had been arrested, we received the order to pick
up Petey Blue.

"It was a warm Friday evening, sidewalks jammed, and he
was standing in front of Walgreen's Drug Store at Forty-
seventh and Seventh Avenue, near Father Duffy's statue. We
walked over, identified ourselves, and told him he was under
arrest.

"It turned out he not only had the biggest nose on Broadway, he had the loudest voice. He screamed, 'Kidnappers!
Assassins! Help me, I'm being kidnapped!' He fought like a
tiger when we tried to get cuffs on him—then a couple volun-
teers jumped in to rescue him, and in seconds we had a full-
scale brawl! It spilled out into Seventh Avenue, and police
moved in with clubs.

"By this time Petey had been knocked unconscious, and
we finally managed to tell the cops we were arresting a
federal fugitive. They still had their hands full fighting the
mob, so we dragged Petey out of the action, and at that
moment two other agents arrived. We grabbed their car,
dumped Petey in, and got out of there.

"My adrenalin was still going from the fight, and the only

thing on my mind was putting distance between us and that
mob, but I finally realized my partner was tugging on my
sleeve.

" 'Why are you pulling on me?'

" 'I'm trying to get your attention. Do you know why they
call this guy Petey Blue?'

" 'No, why?'

" 'It's his blue eyes.'

" 'So what?'

" 'They're brown.'

" 'Hell, you can't tell that for sure, let's get some better
light.'

"We stopped near a bright store window and dragged
Petey out of the car. Sure enough, his eyes were brown. And
by this time he was coming around, making noises about
round two, so we just left him sitting there.

"We worked through the night looking for the real Petey
Blue, without success.

"The next morning our squad was celebrating. They had
the gang of criminals, cars, guns, everything—except Petey
Blue. In the middle of the euphoria, the police precinct
called and asked what they should do with the 'federal pris-
oners' arrested during the riot. We told them it was all a
mistake, they should let them go.

"A couple nights later, we finally located the real Petey
Blue, which wrapped up the case, and subsequently we relo-
cated Petey Brown, who was a rackets figure himself and
eventually became a good source of information for us."[28]

Although Dick Tracy and J. Edgar Hoover touted the
magic of science as the ultimate twentieth-century crime
stopper, it had been quickly apparent to Welch that, fingerprints, ballistics, and two-way wrist radios notwithstanding,
unraveling criminal conduct had not changed essentially
since the Garden of Eden. Human informants still held most
of the answers, and fear remained a reliable incentive for
sharing them (though cash and revenge were generally acceptable alternatives). Those with useful knowledge about

crimes, unfortunately, were almost invariably criminals, which necessitated making certain that those told about were worse than those telling. And that, as novice Welch discovered in a South Boston tenement, was not always possible.

Welch had developed a relationship with an ex-convict who, determined both to make amends for his former transgressions and also to catch up financially from his years in jail, happily sold the FBI solutions to the crimes regularly committed by his former colleagues. It was mildly curious that a reformed felon could somehow maintain such productive criminal contacts, but the usefulness of his information had, by the time Welch sought his help on a cargo theft case in 1952, deterred critical scrutiny.

Approaching his informant's run-down row house, Welch heard hammering from within, the busy racket of a construction site.

Welch knocked on the door.

Hammering intensified, drowning the knock.

Welch rapped again, more sharply.

Finally the door opened a crack, and the informant peered out. "I can't talk now—I'm busy."

Welch looked into the hall behind him, where two men were continuing their furious sledgehammer assault on a commercial safe.

"Yeah, I can see that."

Returning to his office, Welch picked up a newspaper, which led with a front-page account of a daring downtown burglary. A flatbed truck had apparently been positioned below the second-story window of a finance company, and then the burglars had smashed out the window, glass and frame. The cash-filled safe was missing.[29]

Welch's FBI training had not prepared him for the disquieting possibility that criminal informants might simultaneously be both, largely because Hoover never conceded that such untidy dilemmas occurred. The Director prized informants, and he controlled them, as everything, with statistics. Every field agent was required to maintain a quota of "Potential Criminal Informants" (PCI's) who, after producing sufficient reliable information, were graduated to "Criminal Informant" (CI) status. The system was orderly and clean, and its results were often precisely the opposite of those Hoover intended.

In practice, the Bureau's informant quotas put a premium on stale information. Fresh facts might make a criminal case which could expose the informant or convict his criminal contacts, either of which would force the agent to develop a new informant to meet his quota. As a consequence, informant reports typically described crimes witnessed by only the informant (which never made cases because of the Bureau's ironclad refusal to identify an informant in court), crimes which lacked some essential element (such as the identity of the criminals), crimes so old that prosecution was barred by the statute of limitations, or even, on occasion, crimes fabricated by the informant simply to remain in good standing. Agents joked that every office had "files full of information on Ripples Ravioli."[30] For years, the FBI criminal-intelligence files were part fact, larger part street gossip, part pure fiction, and almost entirely useless. But every agent always had the requisite number of PCIs and CIs, which confirmed for Hoover that headquarters was still in control.

The plane was fully loaded for takeoff to Washington when agents received a tip that one of its passengers was a fugitive carrying an attaché case full of stolen securities. A quick phone call held the plane on the ground at LaGuardia, and Special Agent Don Ball boarded. He found the man matching the description almost immediately, attaché case clutched protectively on his lap. Ball flashed his badge and quietly ordered the man to deplane. Unaccountably, the man declined.

Renowned among agents for his hair-trigger temper and leather-lunged profanity, Ball exploded with both.

"Listen, you cocksucker," he roared, jerking the man by the shoulders, "you're gonna leave this goddamn plane with me, and I don't give a fuck whether you go standing up or lying down—take your pick!"

Terrified, the man quickly got up, and Ball hustled him off the plane and into an empty airport office. He seized the attaché case, then tore off the man's overcoat, starting a body search.

It was only then that he noticed the man's clerical collar, and only after he had looked at the man's wallet did he realize he had just arrested a prominent Washington clergyman who happened to include among his circle of close personal friends one J. Edgar Hoover.

Ball knew exactly what he had to do. He made an emergency call to the New York office, which immediately radioed Special Agent Kevin McMullin to report to LaGuardia ASAP. McMullin's mediocre investigative skills were compensated for by an extraordinary personal magnetism, and his recognized specialty was defusing potential disasters.

McMullin had chartered a private aircraft even before reaching the airport, and he had also decided on his approach. He apologized profusely to the bishop, explaining that agent Ball (who promptly vanished) had driven himself too hard, working night and day to solve a particularly heinous series of crimes, but of course no explanation could excuse Ball's egregious conduct. McMullin hoped that the clergyman would not mind going to Washington by private charter, and while he was certain a man of the cloth would not indulge in alcohol, perhaps, in view of the unpleasantness, a cocktail or two during the flight would have a certain medicinal value (after all, hadn't the Master Himself turned water into wine at the marriage feast of Cana?). And yes, McMullin would not only accompany him to Washington but would deliver him directly to Hoover's home, so that a full report of Agent Ball's unconscionable conduct could be made immediately. The plane was ready, and McMullin wanted to share with the churchman a hair-raising encounter during a recent investigation . . .

McMullin's Irish charm was formidable under any circumstances, but in combination with alcohol it proved irresistible. The result was that J. Edgar Hoover never heard about agent Ball's unfortunate mistake.[31]

Indeed, by the time Neil Welch neared completion of his New York assignment in 1956, it was apparent to him that Hoover was wholly unaware of much of the FBI's activity in the field, despite the unquestioned legend to the contrary. Hoover's penchant for punishing the messenger sharply constricted his access to bad news (or even accurate accounts) about FBI activities in the field, and the statistics he trusted never reflected the quality of law enforcement performance —and often distorted the quantity.

It was standard practice, for example, for agents with sagging arrest statistics to attend arraignments at New York City's night felony court. After the charges were read, if there was any conceivable federal connection (a simple robbery, for example, might become a theft from interstate shipment), the agent would rise and advise the court that the FBI wished to assert jurisdiction over the offender, a request with which the beleaguered New York City Police would happily concur. An alert agent could pick up multiple arrests and likely convictions on a good night (often relating to crimes which had not even yet been reported), and the statistics thus generated were indistinguishable from those reflecting exhausting weeks of investigation.[32]

There were other strategems. One New York agent, under pressure to meet his informant quota, simply listed the neighbors in his car pool as PCIs,[33] a deft deception which did not seem to have any particular impact on federal law enforcement.

Perhaps the most elaborate charade was one masterminded by Special Agent Clint Graham, a renowned prankster. Graham advised Bureau headquarters that he had opened informant files on one Sheri Newman, a high-priced prostitute who worked out of the Stratford Arms Hotel, and on one Alexander Green, a numbers banker in the same neighborhood. He neglected to mention, however, that both characters were purely fictional, as was the detailed criminal intelligence which they faithfully supplied. When Graham

finally tired of the game, he decided to circumvent headquarters again by eliminating both informants with a single
paperwork entry (even though policy required separate administrative action for each PCI). He laid the groundwork by
routinely noting that his two informants had become acquainted; then, after a respectable interval for courtship,
Graham solemnly advised headquarters that Newman and
Green planned to marry and give up their previous lives of
crime, thus ending their usefulness to the Bureau.[34]

At about the same time, Neil Welch discovered that it was
possible to eliminate subversives without marrying them.
Assigned to investigate the current political associations of
several suspected subversives, he simply scrawled "Regis-
tered Republican" on each of the security index cards and
sent them back to headquarters. They never came back.[35]

But if Welch had growing doubts about headquarters' ability to control what field agents did, no one questioned Hoover's absolute control over where field agents went. Duty
transfers were unpredictable and unappealable, and while
agents were required to keep their three "Offices of Preference" on file at headquarters, assignments to them were so
rare that some agents thought it more prudent to list their
last three office choices as insurance against assignment to
them. Hoover appeared immune to the normal political
pressures which might modify transfers in another governmental agency; in fact, his immunity was not absolute, but
the handful of persons who might influence him was well
beyond the acquaintance of most agents.

One young New York agent, homesick for Boston, decided
that weekend volunteer work in the Boston office might
somehow lead to an assignment there. After several weekends, a grizzled veteran finally asked what he was doing
there. When the rookie told him, the older agent said it was
hopeless—unless "the Speaker or the Cardinal" interceded
with Hoover. The former seemed more accessible, so the
determined young man shifted his weekend commute to
Washington, where he did volunteer work in the office of

House Speaker John McCormack. Soon thereafter, according to FBI lore, he received orders to Boston.[36]

Mothers were the only others who could sometimes modify transfer orders. Bachelor Hoover's well-known affection for his own mother seemed to extend to the mothers of his agents, and he was notoriously susceptible to reports of mothers in distress. Knowing this, agents spent hours concocting heartrending "mother stories" for his benefit. If a miraculous recovery followed the transfer home, Hoover did not always hear about it. It was a rare soft spot, strictly limited to mothers.[37] One Seattle agent, learning that his father had been critically injured in Pittsburgh, flew to headquarters and personally asked Hoover for an emergency transfer home. Hoover deferred decision, forcing the agent to return to Seattle, where he finally received permission to report not to Pittsburgh but to New York City, provided he paid his own expenses.[38]

But for most agents, most transfers were absolutely final, and they occurred with unfathomable frequency. Even by Hoover standards, however, Welch appeared to be approaching a record in November 1956 when he received his sixth transfer in six years, this time to Bureau headquarters in Washington.

He received the news with mixed emotions. While nothing in Welch's personality seemed to stimulate criminal conduct, he had nevertheless displayed an extraordinary facility for being in places where major crimes occurred. He had worked some of the FBI's biggest crimes, and splashiest successes, of the decade—Brinks robbery, Weinberger kidnapping, Victor Riesel acid attack. He had also solved scores of cases which never made headlines—car thefts, bank robberies, fugitive cases—and he thrived on the vast investigative challenges of New York City. Fellow agents there had nicknamed him Nails, admiring his combative determination, and the name itself portended dissatisfaction in Washington; it was difficult to imagine anyone called Nails enjoying shuffling paper at Bureau headquarters.

And of course Hoover had not consulted the former Geraldine McLeod about Welch's new assignment, though she was clearly a party in interest, having married Neil Welch in 1955 after meeting him while he served in the FBI's Resident Agency in Bangor, Maine, her hometown.

But orders to headquarters were a prerequisite for promotion above the rank of street agent. While Welch could not know he would return to New York as an assistant director of the FBI twenty-two years later, his new assignment meant he was on the advancement track and could expect, with reasonable luck, to eventually become an agent in charge. Welch had developed his investigative skills with studious determination, quietly perfecting his craft, and his Washington assignment meant, more than anything, that J. Edgar Hoover had decided Neil Welch might qualify for elevation above the rank of novice.

There was no reason at the time for Hoover to suspect that Welch would one day emerge as a dangerous heretic, disputing the doctrines of Bureau headquarters.

Welch's departure from New York was commemorated by an agents-only farewell party, an established Bureau tradition. (One legendary New York farewell party had modified the agents-only format slightly by including a bouncy young lady who emerged from a large cake clad primarily in icing. Word of the affair had leaked back to Hoover, who furiously ordered an intensive internal investigation which produced so many witnesses who claimed to have been out of the room at the critical moment that agents would later remember the event as "the night six hundred agents were all in the men's room.")[39] After the usually sober FBI men were not, a fellow agent rose to recite a poem prepared for the occasion—"Tales About Nails."

> Listen my children and you shall hear
> The saga of Petey Blue.
> Most all of us worked that caper
> I did—did you?
> Tracking down the criminal, a subject
> With eyes of blue,

Our hero Nails bagged Mel with the nose,
His eyes were brown—and that's a clue
That a grievous error had been made,
Our hero was quick to surmise,
So he saved the day with a master stroke—
He developed Mel as a PCI.[40]

4

Agent-Killer

They did not know that the Florida records had been destroyed.

As a consequence, Bureau officials assumed that what they knew about Neil Welch—who would report for headquarters duty in late 1956—was approximately the same as what was known about every other agent, namely everything of any significance. Certainly the Bureau files were reassuring. Welch's complete personnel records were available, supplemented by his health data, and there were mountains of memoranda he had written and reports he had prepared. They knew all about him.

Indeed, with bureaucrat patience, it would even be possible to know precisely where he had been on every duty day during his five years in the FBI. The "Travel Authorizations and Expense Vouchers" were there, so it could all be reconstructed—except the Florida trip.

A few months earlier in 1956, Welch had penetrated a Manhattan car-theft ring and had traced its operations from New York to Miami. He flew south to complete the case. Working out of the Miami field office, Welch became acquainted with agents there, including Timothy O'Malley, who, he quickly realized, was a special special agent indeed.

In an office with acute caseload pressures, O'Malley had no assigned cases. His investigative ability was above average, but his horse handicapping expertise was exceptional. He always worked alone and mostly at night, cruising Miami's hotel strip and mixing with the racetrack crowd and gamblers. Other agents admired O'Malley's performance without knowing precisely what he did, but once each year they were grateful for it; Hoover's regular winter visit to Florida, which always featured time at the tracks, generally posed only minimal problems, provided that Special Agent O'Malley was available for duty.

One evening shortly after Welch's arrival, O'Malley sensed that he was under surveillance. Quickly doubling back down a one-way street, he captured his shadow, a distinguished looking man in his sixties. His identification cards were quickly established to be false, and the man refused to talk. O'Malley took him, under arrest, to the field office. There, confidently resisting the efforts of expert interrogators, the suspect said nothing. Working with his false name, however, agents found his hotel. Searching the man's room, they discovered evidence that he had been stalking O'Malley for days. Telephone records added more detail: During each day of his stay, the man had placed repeated calls to an unlisted Washington number.

Fearing that O'Malley had unwittingly stumbled onto some underworld plot and been marked for death, Miami agents wired an urgent request for the Washington field office to trace the Washington number.

Fear proved well founded.

It was the confidential number of an assistant director, Hoover's top subordinate.

Moving instinctively to get clear of Miami's problem, the Washington field office immediately reported the incident to Bureau headquarters. Moments later Hoover's personal assistant was on the phone, barking rigid orders to the Miami SAC. Release the suspect instantly. Quarantine O'Malley. Identify all agents with knowledge of the incident and restrict them to the office, segregated from the others. No agent telephone calls out of the office—not one.

Hoover's chief inspector would arrive on the next plane.

Apprehensive and bewildered, Miami agents reacted reflexively. They could not imagine what catastrophe they had precipitated, but if headquarters was frantic to conceal it, the field would probably benefit by exposing it. And fortunately, without risking direct insubordination, they had one link to the outside world—Neil Welch.

Welch agreed to collect all information concerning the suspect and fly immediately back to New York. On his return, all records of his temporary duty in Miami would be expunged—there would be no record that he had witnessed the O'Malley incident.

Slipping past the incoming Bureau inspector at the airport, Welch escaped to New York. There he carefully briefed two trusted superiors. They suggested a strategy. Slipping back into the office late in the evening, Welch spent the next few nights poring over FBI intelligence files. He studied photographs. Piecing together clues, he made discreet telephone calls to agent friends around the country. Finally he had the answer.

The man arrested by O'Malley, Welch concluded, was a former labor spy who, according to FBI intelligence records, was also Bureau informant XX-1, operated exclusively by Hoover's office—outside normal Bureau channels.

Suddenly the pieces fell into place. Field agents had been mystified by a series of "agent-killings"—incidents in which headquarters, without warning, had discharged highly regarded field agents, giving no hint as to any basis for its action. In every instance, dismissal had coincided with XX-1's appearance in that office on some mission from headquarters.

It flashed through the field: Welch had identified the agent-killer.

Pictures followed. XX-1's photograph was surreptitiously passed from field office to field office, coast to coast. He would remain on Hoover's personal informant payroll for years, but XX-1's cover was gone, and he never operated effectively again.

Welch's triumph percolated through the field organization, building his stature among field agents. In exposing Hoover's personal informant, Welch had coolly risked direct confrontation with the Director himself, displaying a gambler's confidence which awed other agents. He had solved one of the FBI's biggest cases, his superiors confided, but there would never be any record of it—except their glowing performance evaluations, which accelerated his already rapid advancement.

The solution came too late for Timothy O'Malley, who resigned a short while later. Agents speculated that he had uncovered something relating to Hoover's personal life which had made him dangerous, though perhaps, some thought, the master handicapper had simply lost his touch.

At Bureau headquarters, where Welch reported for duty in December 1956, officials agreed that his personnel records were completely in order.

5

Acolyte

They should have called it the Federal Bureau of
Administration. Headquarters seemed to think investigations interfered with its work—I always
thought Hoover should have engaged some outside
outfit to do investigations on a contract basis, so the
Bureau would be free to concentrate on what it
really cared about, which was public relations and
cross-indexing files.

-FBI Special Agent
Clint Graham[1]

The Justice Department Building is a squat, seven-story
structure which sits securely between Pennsylvania and
Constitution avenues, between Ninth and Tenth. A healthy
stone's throw to the north there is a generally seedy commercial strip, its retail mix of liquor, pornography, and cut-rate
tourist trinkets, sprinkled with a constant flux of "Going Out
of Business" and "Lost Lease" signs, proof that the propri-
etors understand human weakness better than business. Beyond a slight rise to the south, the Smithsonian's unlikely red-
brick gingerbread buildings decorate the skyline, structures
so oddly unique that it seems surprising that they share a
common owner with the gracefully elegant White House,
which, from Justice, is an easy ten minute walk west. Looking
in the opposite direction, the Capitol dome is a visible re-

minder that the legislative branch may be watching the executive, although from a distance which suggests that it is unlikely to see much.

Completed in 1934,[2] the Justice Department Building is a
carbon copy of adjacent federal buildings, all serious gray
granite assembled in ponderously high-ceilinged style, structures which could be transported to any country in the world
and still, by some undefinable aura, be instantly recognizable
as government buildings. Even from the outside, it seems
safe to assume that these buildings contain forms and procedures and people who apply them methodically, an assump-
tion which Neil Welch found to be wholly valid in 1956 when
he reported for duty at FBI headquarters in the Justice Department Building. And like long-married husbands and
wives who grow to resemble each other, Hoover's FBI and its
building each seemed to mirror the impervious durability of
the other, and neither seemed at all threatened by two faraway and apparently unrelated events of the mid 1950s.

On May 8, 1954, a hopelessly besieged garrison of troops,
forced finally to choose between starvation and surrender,
laid down their arms and gave up. The gaunt, grim men who
staggered out single file, hands on heads, were French. The
hellhole they were surrendering was Dien Bien Phu, a mis-
leadingly euphonious name which Americans, at the time,
found easier to remember than the name of the country
where it was located, which was Vietnam.[3]

A world away and nineteen months later, a black woman
named Rosa Parks refused to surrender her seat on a Montgomery, Alabama, bus to a white rider. She was fined fourteen dollars. It was a sign of the times that the ensuing protest
did not challenge the relegation of blacks to the back of the
bus but simply sought first-come-first-served seating, blacks
starting in the back and whites in the front. The bus company
refused, insisting that the first ten rows be reserved for
whites, even if blacks had to stand beside empty white seats.
But times were apparently changing, because instead of
blowing over, the protest blossomed into a boycott led by a
black preacher named Martin Luther King, Jr. When the

boycott finally ended, Montgomery's buses were desegregated.[4]

Back in Washington, however, Eisenhower-era tranquility prevailed, and the men in that sturdy gray building never varied their methodical routines. The bulletproof limousine carrying J. Edgar Hoover and Clyde Tolson arrived punctually at the Pennsylvania Avenue entrance at nine o'clock each morning and departed at five o'clock, and tourists could set their watches by the Director's regular eleven forty-five appearance at the Mayflower Hotel for lunch.[5] (Only the rear compartment of Hoover's car rated bulletproof protection, a clear indication that the Director's driver, like the decoy hat he carefully placed on the rear window shelf opposite his seat, was expendable.)[6]

Communism remained Hoover's priority concern. In September 1956 he sent a secret memorandum titled "Communist Party USA—Counterintelligence Program" to FBI field offices, announcing "an all-out disruptive attack against the Party on a broader scale than heretofore attempted by the Bureau."[7] Despite its announced ambitions, however, the new program (soon shortened to "COINTELPRO CPUSA" to reduce Teletype costs)[8] seemed an unremarkable escalation of Hoover's permanent war on Communism. Nothing in its beginnings augured danger, or even change, for Bureau headquarters. There, Neil Welch and approximately four hundred other agents assiduously ploughed through the paperwork regimen set by Hoover years before, acolytes administering the rituals of the Bureau faith, the same yesterday, today, forever.

But it was not the same. The forces spawned by events in Vietnam and Alabama were already moving, invisibly and glacier slow, and would eventually impose on the FBI unwanted—and sometimes impossible—enforcement priorities. No one at Ninth and Constitution would be able to pinpoint precisely when it happened, but the civil rights and antiwar movements, in combination, would for the first time limit J. Edgar Hoover's freedom to select his own targets, thereby fracturing the rock on which he had built his citadel —and his faith.

There was a third, and more imminent, threat to Hoover's empire in the mid fifties, the size and shape of which could have been accurately pieced together from fragments of criminal intelligence scattered throughout the Bureau's own files. It was a threat Hoover had already discounted, however, based on what he knew about it, which was substantially less than he would have known if FBI criminal intelligence had been evaluated as systematically as subversive intelligence. Even so, it is doubtful whether anyone could have changed the Director's mind about the threat in a page and a quarter, and based on his first headquarters assignment, Neil Welch thought it improbable that Hoover ever read anything longer.

Day and night, complex Teletype messages updating criminal investigations clattered into headquarters from the field. Welch's task was to locate the headquarters file on each case, review the Teletype against the file, and summarize both in a short-as-possible "Memorandum for the Director" *(never* to exceed one and a quarter pages). It was an endless exercise involving scores of headquarters agents, whose combined output of crisp memoranda implied firm headquarters control over every major case in the field. It was, of course, illusory. The incoming Teletypes were at least hours behind events, the summary memos days behind, and if Hoover had questions, headquarters was nearly certain not to have answers (since the full facts of each case were available only in the originating field office). Recognizing that crimes were not solved in the Bureau's Criminal Division, agents there concentrated instead on evading Hoover's critical scrutiny, and Welch quickly mastered the blandly authoritative FBI style which seemed to minimize marginal comments by the Director.

The other way to minimize marginal comments was simply to minimize margins, a traditional agent precaution which provoked a classic Hoover anecdote. Confronted with a memo containing virtually no margin space, an exasperated Hoover scribbled "Watch the borders" and routed the memo back. His puzzled subordinates concluded, characteristically, that the only safe interpretation was the literal one, and they promptly dispatched teams of equally perplexed agents to the Canadian and Mexican borders to be on the lookout for whatever menace the Director had perceived.[9] In later years, Hoover would note his questions on a small yellow paper clipped to the memo, and "yellow tag" became the agent signal for dreaded Hoover comments.[10]

The Director, however, was not the only person at headquarters who scrutinized agent paperwork, as Welch discovered shortly after his arrival.

"Dear Mr. Welch," the letter read, "on November 25 and November 26 it was necessary to return two items of outgoing correspondence which had been prepared by you because mistakes were discovered in the mail. These errors indicate a lack of sufficient care on your part in the preparation of official correspondence. Accordingly," it concluded, "you should demonstrate greater thoroughness and accuracy in this phase of your responsibilities so there will be no further reason to criticize you in this manner."[11]

The letter was signed by J. Edgar Hoover, but it had been prepared by the ladies in the reading room. Located adjacent to Hoover's fifth-floor office, the reading room was the final clearance point for all correspondence leaving the Bureau. Agents with shaky literary skills grumbled that the room's rigorous occupants were all "frustrated old maids." In fact, they were not all old, though they were universally female, and whatever their own frustration level, it was undoubtedly less than that which they created by their unrelenting demand for grammatical perfection. Moreover, Hoover had armed his grammarians with censure power, and Welch was astonished to learn that a letter of censure for bad spelling was as damaging as one for letting the suspect escape out the back door.

Ironically, investigative careers could also be cut short by standout literary skills. Agents who displayed these skills risked permanent assignment to the Crime Records Division, a euphemism which seemed preferable to Public Relations and Publishing Department, which was what it was. The mission of agents in Crime Records was to write crime-fighting books, articles, and speeches by J. Edgar Hoover, which only seemed to intensify the insatiable national curiosity about Hoover, to which Records obligingly responded by churning out the Director's favorite song, book, or recipe on request. Every man, woman, or schoolchild who wrote the FBI received a personal letter back signed "J. Edgar Hoover," innocent forgeries courtesy of Crime Records. There was no indication that the Presbyterian minister who wrote in 1956 would not treasure his official response like everyone else.

Indeed, his letter looked fairly standard. The minister praised the Director's numerous good works and strong beliefs, his vigorous commitment to strengthening the moral fiber of the nation. But the cleric had a question: How could fellow Presbyterian Hoover possibly reconcile his deep religious convictions with his frequent attendance at the track and his notorious gambling on race horses?

It was not a new question, and Records had a ready response. Great leaders throughout history, the Bureau reply patiently explained, have had a strong affinity for horses; Genghis Khan and Louis XIV and George Washington all loved their horses, and Hoover's enjoyment of horses was virtually his only escape from the relentless rigors of his position. He always returned to his awesome responsibilities refreshed and renewed after watching magnificent horses race. Certainly, in that context, no one could object.

The minister responded by return mail. "I'm not asking about the horses, I'm asking about the two-dollar bets!"

Somehow the second letter reached Hoover, who promptly pronounced the cleric crazy and ordered that the Bureau have no further communication with him.[12] (The Director would remain a confirmed betting man, and shortly before his death, when the Association of Retired Agents presented him with a bronze stallion paperweight, he joked that the gift horse was "the first I've owned, though I've supported many of them.")[13] Banishing the minister, however, did not erase the suspicion that horse-playing Hoover did not regard gambling as a particularly grave breach of the laws of either God or man. It was an uncharacteristic tolerance, and the Director's inclination to look the other way on gambling partially explained his failure, until November 14, 1957, to see that organized crime was the most immediate threat to his empire.

And by then, it was too late.

They had grown up together, Hoover's FBI and American organized crime, both born in the twenties, maturing during the thirties, modifying their activities during wartime even while anticipating the expanded opportunities of peacetime. Although they were presumptive enemies, during their first four decades they competed primarily for newspaper space, and press accounts of gangland seemed to invariably include the word "slaying." Chicago alone notched more than seven hundred mob murders between 1920 and 1933,[14] and while the 1929 St. Valentine's Day execution of seven men (six gangsters and a luckless visiting optometrist) was the most publicized,[15] the most important was probably the murder of Dion O'Banion in 1924.[16]

O'Banion's significance resulted more from what he was not than from what he was, which was leader of a Chicago criminal gang. He was not, however, allied with either of Chicago's preeminent Prohibition-era gangs, the Camorra (linked to a secret Neapolitan criminal society) or the Mafia (Camorra's Sicilian counterpart). O'Banion's execution, while preparing floral arrangements for a fellow mobster's funeral, eliminated any serious outside competition to the Neapolitan and Sicilian gangs.[17] They continued to feud, but four years later Al Capone presided over the merger of the Camorra and Mafia, and the result was La Cosa Nostra.[18]

Through the 1920s, Mussolini's purge of the Sicilian Mafia generated a continuing influx of exiles,[19] and by 1931, organized crime's modern structure had been hammered into rough shape by New York boss Salvatore Maranzano's bloody victory over rival leaders.[20] Maranzano, a charismatic leader who reportedly could snap a man's neck with his thumbs,[21] ended the relentless factional fighting by slicing the entire country into territorial monopolies and giving each gang a slice. Détente did not mean democracy, however, as Maranzano revealed when he acknowledged his accomplishment by assuming the title Boss of All Bosses.[22]

Maranzano also ordered the families to observe a rigid chain of command, providing discipline for soldiers and insulation for leaders, and imposed a curiously genteel code of conduct—a product, fellow mobster Joe Bonanno thought, of Maranzano's early inclination toward the priesthood.[23] Social indignities, such as disparaging comments about fellow members or less than honorable interest in their female relatives, were strictly prohibited,[24] though the code's central imperative was (and is) more basic: Follow orders and never talk about Our Thing.[25]

On September 10, 1931, only five months after Maranzano had been proclaimed Boss of All Bosses, four men proved he was not. Posing as Internal Revenue Service agents, they shot and stabbed Maranzano to death in his Manhattan office. True to his code, they were following orders and never talked, but their orders had come, most agreed, from rival Charles Luciano, who thereby reearned his nickname, Charlie Lucky.[26] The family heads then formed a seven-member national commission to assign territories and settle disputes, burying the title Boss of All Bosses along with Maranzano.[27]

From the commission's first meeting in 1931, its significance was clear: Internal crime family differences would no longer be permitted to jeopardize external opportunities. Newly harmonious, reorganized crime grew rapidly, an iceberg industry—massive, mostly invisible, and dangerous. It boomed through the Depression, the ultimate countercyclical business. Its enormous Prohibition profits were profitably reinvested, sometimes in legitimate business (trucking was an early natural favorite), but more often in gambling and loansharking, where the economics were more compelling. Illegal sports bettors plus neighborhood numbers players anted up millions annually on odds which kept most of the money in the families. The standard six dollars for five dollars shylock loan wildly outperformed the market and every other indicator, throwing off 312 percent annual interest, generally viewed by its recipients as tax free.[28]

The Internal Revenue Service, however, took a different view. Al Capone was finally convicted for tax evasion,[29] which was, astonishingly, the only one of his manifest sins which seemed to coincide with a federal statutory prohibition. The Bureau's impotence against organized crime was inadvertently advertised in its biggest case—Hoover's personal arrest of New York mobster Louis "Lepke" Buchalter in 1939. Buchalter was later executed for murder, but the only federal charge against him was an antitrust violation (distinguishing him both as the only antitrust suspect ever arrested by the FBI Director personally and the only such arrestee to be executed).[30] The tip which led to his arrest, however, had come not from FBI sources but from those of Hoover's gossip columnist friend, Walter Winchell.[31]

It was not until the investigation of the 1950 Brinks robbery that FBI agents finally made any significant penetration into organized crime, and even then it was accidental. Pressured by Hoover's fierce determination to crack what newspapers had headlined the "Crime of the Century," Neil Welch and scores of other agents had combed the Boston crime-scene area, talking to known criminals and numbers writers, bartenders and bagmen, building a criminal intelligence base. Every fragment of information, even if apparently unrelated to Brinks, was carefully catalogued and cross-referenced. It was a technique new to criminal investigations but not unfamiliar, it being the standard procedure for internal security probes. But while Hoover's intelligence on subversives rarely justified his preoccupation with them, the Brinks criminal intelligence unexpectedly revealed criminal activity bigger than Brinks, disclosing to Welch a startling new world of organized crime.

"We discovered that the Italian mob was trying to take

over the Irish and Jewish mobs in Boston. We found that a
small Italian group in Boston's North End had joined the
Patriarcha organization in Providence, to contest the Irish
domination of the docks. We found families dominating the
unions, and the trucking and shipping industries. For the first
time, we began to piece together an accurate picture of the
day-to-day workings of sophisticated criminal organizations."[32]

That picture, ironically, suggested some striking similari-
ties in the daily routines of FBI agents and the organized
crime figures they pursued. Both worked irregular hours,
often late into the night, and their success was largely attributable to the respect they commanded. Their wives knew
virtually nothing about what they did, except that it could be
dangerous, and the awkward inventions they offered to
neighbors ("he's with, uh, an insurance company") were so
transparent it was immediately clear that further questions
were inadvisable. They both traveled often and unpredict-
ably and had healthy appetites for women, but worked and
socialized almost exclusively with men and attended church
with average regularity.

Indeed, aside from a sharp disparity in compensation, the
most obvious distinction between the working conditions of
organized crime figures and FBI field agents was that the
latter had more to fear from J. Edgar Hoover. He had solemnly assured the Kefauver Committee in 1951 that no national criminal organization existed and warned, with revealing inconsistency, that any federal intervention against
organized crime might lead to a national police force.[33] Some
puzzled observers attributed Hoover's uncharacteristic re-
straint to a fear that his incorruptible G-men might be cor-
rupted by big-money mobsters; others concluded he was simply unwilling to target a massive enemy he was unlikely to
defeat.

Hoover unquestionably knew the enemy, however, because arch rival Harry Anslinger had thoughtfully provided a
five-page list, four columns to a page, of the names and cities
of over three hundred crime family members. Indeed, field

agents speculated that organized crime was invisible to Hoover solely because Anslinger's Federal Bureau of Narcotics had seen it first. The agents surreptitiously circulated the "List of Mafia Members Obtained From Narcotics Bureau,"[34] "burning" shiny grayish reproductions on primitive office copiers and passing the list secretly from agent to agent like some heretical religious creed—which it was.

(In 1970, when Welch took over as SAC in Detroit, a veteran agent on the organized crime squad would route him a faded copy of the old FBN list with a remarkable notation: "In 1952, the Narcotics Bureau had the answer but no one would listen . . . every LCN [La Cosa Nostra] member we have is on this list, without exception.")[35]

Even at headquarters, as early as 1953, FBI intelligence files routinely referred to "the nationwide Italian criminal organization," a phrase agents thought described both what Hoover knew and why he chose not to know it. He was simply too adroit a politician. If discovering organized crime meant risking conflict with the Sons of Italy and other politically potent Italian-American groups, then Mr. Law Enforcement would let someone else make that discovery.

(Even after organized crime was "discovered," official sensitivity to its ethnic implications would remain acute, particularly the presumption of Italian dominance. Thus the 1967 President's Task Force Report on Organized Crime noted, with apparent relief, that in a Chicago lottery game "the workers were Negroes; the bankers . . . were Japanese-Americans, although the game itself was licensed by the 'family.' ")[36]

Hoover's strategy seemed risk free. Even if Kefauver held hearings and Anslinger kept lists, the American public would believe only J. Edgar Hoover unless something extraordinary happened. And just to be certain, Hoover formed a small committee within FBI headquarters in the mid fifties with a mandate to determine and document the nonexistence of organized crime.[37]

Ironically, Neil Welch's duty tour at Bureau headquarters was the only time during his FBI career when he posed no particular threat to criminals, organized or otherwise. His workday routine was indistinguishable from that of any other bored Washington bureaucrat, and noontime was frequently the most memorable part of the day.

"We always took the full hour for lunch. Even in terrible weather, agents sloshed around Washington, window-shopping or plain killing time, anything to avoid returning to that paper mill early. Later, when Bobby Kennedy was in office, sports became the main diversion, and agents would sometimes play handball with the Attorney General—which Hoover regarded as fraternizing with the enemy. Kennedy's casual style constantly offended the Old Man's sense of dignity —Justice Department lawyers tossing a football with the Attorney General in his office was a common occurrence, and it made Hoover incoherent with anger.

"Lecturing at Quantico was the other great escape. Field agents from around the country were regularly ordered back for two weeks in-service training, and I volunteered for every teaching vacancy. I generally drove the forty miles to Quantico at a leisurely pace, gave my lecture, had lunch, sat in on someone else's lecture, then finally meandered back, stretching my half-hour lecture into a full day away from headquarters. It was a break from the paperwork, and a chance to catch up with field agents from all over the country."

It was more than that. In-service training was the only exception to Hoover's general ban against large gatherings of field agents, and it served as an informal information exchange, a forum in which agents traded techniques for circumventing headquarters. One supervisor, whose stolen car recoveries had declined from 425 to 389, confided at Quantico that he had inadvertently transposed the prior year's statistic, thus reporting to headquarters 524 recoveries instead of the actual 389.[38] Within days every FBI office in the country, with the exception of Hoover's headquarters, knew that accidental transposition was one cure for declining statistics.

Quietly attentive, Welch absorbed every lesson at Quantico, reflexively sifting out the inevitable exaggeration in agent anecdotes, mentally cataloguing the capabilities and quirks of field offices and agents. Unconsciously he was shaping his trademark, sharpening the Brinks technique, developing a personal intelligence base—except that it was not a criminal organization he was penetrating, it was Hoover's FBI. In 1962, when Hoover reviewed Welch's personnel file prior to reassignment, the records would reveal that Welch had lectured often at Quantico, but not that he had pieced together an encyclopedic knowledge of the FBI field organization in the process. It was knowledge which would mean power, particularly since, not being on paper, it would never be understood by headquarters.

Back on Pennsylvania Avenue, however, Hoover's omniscience and control remained unquestioned. He seemed to know everything about every agent. Once, he wrote Welch a personal letter to commend him for making it to work during a heavy snowstorm.[39] And the Director's authority was reinforced daily by the shell-shocked agents who emerged from private audiences.

By custom, field agents assigned to in-service training at Quantico were permitted a personal meeting with Hoover, provided that they formally requested it, of course. It was a royal prerogative which created constant turmoil among the Director's lieutenants, since the unpredictable Hoover might, in a personal meeting, grant a favor requested by an agent in disfavor. Later he would blame his aides for letting it happen, a hazard which they attempted to minimize by denying Washington training assignments to agents under any sort of bureaucratic cloud, exiling some for years at a time.[40]

Even those who came to Washington, however, sometimes declined the opportunity. Like monotheists everywhere, agents were ambivalent about whether a personal encounter with the Ultimate Authority was more likely to lead to salvation or damnation, and many were content to pass their careers pondering the question rather than risking an answer. But many more requested audiences, sometimes solely for the chance to be in the presence of a historic figure, and they cast an instructive daily drama which Welch studied with a critic's detachment.

One agent, determined to use his audience to obtain a new duty assignment, engaged in a careful, months-long preparation. In the course of it, he studied every available photograph of previous Hoover meetings and discovered that the Director often posed with one hand on the shoulder of any boy in the group. Knowing that, the agent patiently persuaded his own rambunctious ten year old that if the Director put a hand on his shoulder, he should not try to knock it off.

Hoover did, the boy did not, the picture was perfect; but while the agent was congratulating himself on his foresight, the audience abruptly ended—before there was any chance to request new orders. (His family would never let him forget it, and years later, when the children were grown and married, family gatherings always included someone who would recall, "That was great, Dad, how you asked Hoover for a transfer out of Chicago.")[41]

More successfully, a hopelessly overweight agent purchased a new shirt two sizes too large in preparation for his Hoover meeting. At the appointed hour, he charged vigorously into the Director's office, grabbed Hoover's hand, and shook it enthusiastically, thanking the Director profusely for saving his life. For once, Hoover was too startled for words. The agent, tugging at his loose collar, explained that his chest pains and breathlessness had all disappeared thanks to the Director's mandatory weight-reduction program. In moments, Hoover recovered, commending the agent's accomplishment and his impressive physical fitness. The blubbery agent finally departed, still happily pulling on his loose collar, knowing that no FBI inspector—or scale—would ever pronounce unfit that which the Director had deemed fit.[42]

Others tried presents. No one ever actually proved that Hoover could be influenced by gifts, though the regularity with which agents proffered them suggested that possibility, and headquarters Hoover-watchers debated endlessly the link between agent presents and prospects. The conventional gift choices, pastries (especially green cakes) and ice cream (in round cartons, not square) seemed to generate goodwill with Hoover, but not necessarily good orders. In contrast, rapid advancement followed an enterprising young agent's report that he had arranged for Hoover's latest book (written by the Crime Records Division) to be selected as required reading in a big-city parochial school district.[43]

On balance, though, Welch finally concluded that gifts gave no guarantees, and Hoover's unpredictability was his most predictable quality. It was a key element in maintaining the Director's control over FBI men and missions, a control which was widely assumed to be absolute and eternal—until 1957.

They came in through Joe Barbara's front door, donning silk suits and limousines. The lucky ones made it out through the woods, balding, puffing, alligator-shoed city dwellers scrambling across the unfamiliar rolling countryside of Apalachin, New York. Sixty others left in state police cars, thwarting photographers with heads tucked behind outstretched lapels, like bashful birds. It was the biggest roundup of organized crime bosses in national history, and it was an accident.

But it was an accident certain to happen. Three weeks earlier, a barrage of shotgun blasts had liquidated Albert Anastasia's interest in Murder, Inc.—a bloody, professional hit which Albert himself, in other circumstances, would have appreciated.[44] Anastasia's grisly death splashed all over *Life*, his partially covered corpse sprawled lazily beside the barber chair in perfect counterpoint to the methodical men in suits and fedoras collecting evidence at the scene.[45] The murder primed the public interest in organized crime and gave the crime families a compelling reason for a national convention, since it was rumored that Vito Genovese had ordered Anas-

tasia killed to resurrect the Boss of All Bosses title for himself.[46]

Buffalo Godfather Stefano Magaddino had chosen the
Apalachin site, presuming that Barbara's fifty-eight-acre estate assured privacy.[47] It was a rare lapse. With a population
of less than a thousand,[48] Apalachin showcased strangers, and
on November 14, 1957, an astounding one in ten of the souls
within its boundaries was not only a stranger, but a national
crime family leader.

A police officer noticed the suspicious traffic and made a
few quick checks. Roadblocks were thrown up everywhere;
chaos was instant. Gangsters galloped across the countryside
frantically seeking holes in the dragnet, equally frantic police
called in reinforcements to help land their incredible catch,
and some of the country's top criminal lawyers feverishly
tried to figure out where Apalachin was and who they knew
there.

When the frenzy ended, approximately fifty gangsters had
escaped, more than sixty others had been detained for interrogation,[49] and the sensational national news coverage of the
roundup had abruptly changed the public mind. Semantical
purists might still debate whether the spectacle at Apalachin
was organized, but there could no longer be any doubt that
crime family organizations existed, and on an awesome national scale.

Within the FBI, Apalachin instantly triggered emergency
precautions. At headquarters, Welch and other prudent
agents rearranged their schedules to avoid any chance encounter with Hoover, who boiled through the building in a
furious rage. In the Albany field office, the veteran agent in
charge quietly informed Bureau headquarters that
Apalachin was located in Buffalo's jurisdiction; targeted for
blame, Buffalo insisted that the tiny town was in the Albany
district. Before the Bureau's map readers could establish that
he had lost the geographic tug-of-war, however, the crafty
Albany SAC neatly finessed the point. Apalachin was in fact
in his district, he conceded, and the reason that mobsters

from Buffalo and New York and Pennsylvania had convened there was because he had successfully eliminated all organized crime, making it a neutral meeting ground. Hoover, surprisingly, seemed to accept that argument, with the result that headquarters heat about Apalachin was directed everywhere except there.[50]

Outside observers, however, placed the blame not in Albany or Buffalo, but in Washington. The New York *Herald Tribune* wondered editorially what Hoover's FBI had been doing while organized crime was growing up in America, and the Director was incensed by the implication.[51] There had been early complaints about his experience and later isolated criticism of his methods, but no responsible observer had ever previously asserted that J. Edgar Hoover had fallen down on the job fighting crime.

Stung, Hoover deftly regrouped. He quietly let it be known that Bureau intelligence about organized crime had for years been regularly passed to local police, who, after all, had the primary responsibility for dealing with it. He modified the mandate of the headquarters committee on which Welch served, ordering it to determine and document the *existence* of organized crime. FBI field offices, at his direction, converted the previously invisible crime families into an enforcement priority.

At the same time, however, Hoover systematically undermined Justice Department efforts to build criminal prosecutions against the mobsters netted at Apalachin. It was whispered at headquarters that Hoover had deliberately impeded the Justice Department investigation, and in any event agents clearly understood that any failures experienced on that assignment would not jeopardize career prospects.[52] Nevertheless, in spite of Hoover's resistance federal prosecutors eventually convicted a number of crime figures of conspiracy to obstruct justice, based on their accounts or their refusal to give accounts of the Apalachin meeting. Hoover finally had his way, though, when a 1960 Court of Appeals decision reversed the convictions.[53]

In the end, the uniqueness of Hoover's national stature was

confirmed by the absence of any serious demand for his resignation, and his consummate public relations skill salvaged
what could be saved in the situation. But Apalachin had
made clear for the first time that the FBI Director did not
necessarily know what major criminals were up to in America, and his omniscience would never again be universally
assumed.

While Hoover's reluctant discovery of organized crime
changed what he said about it, what his agents did about it
remained essentially unchanged until 1961, when Robert F.
Kennedy was named Attorney General. Savvy and tough,
Kennedy was the first Attorney General whose relationship
with the President was immune to Hoover's backdoor access,
and he quickly made clear his commitment to an all-out FBI
war on organized crime. Field agents, generally skeptical
about Kennedy's appointment (too young, too political, likely
too liberal) and his ability to impose priorities on Hoover,
dropped both doubts in short order. Kennedy ordered a massive offensive against the mob and personally monitored the
progress of major FBI probes. In addition, he enlisted some
of the nation's top legal talent in the campaign, attracting,
among others, Byron "Whizzer" White, Herbert J. Miller, Jr.,
and G. Robert Blakey to Justice Department service.

Indifferent to Hoover's rigid chain of command, RFK chatted easily with field agents he encountered in the Justice
Department Building, communicating his own enthusiasm
and inspiring agent respect and Hoover animosity of roughly
comparable intensity. Even on the few occasions when Hoover made a grudging effort to accommodate the Kennedy
style, the attempt always failed. Learning that Kennedy regularly exercised in a makeshift gym created by agents in a
neglected corner of the Justice Department, Hoover made a
surprise inspection. Trying casual conversation with the startled agents, he observed that the medicine ball seemed to
need more air. Then, taking command, he asked if any other
equipment was needed to make the facility fit for the Attorney General's use. The agents present were so dumbstruck
by his sudden interest—and wary of his motive—that no one

suggested anything, until finally one man broke the uneasy silence and mumbled, "Maybe more wastebaskets."

Of all the Kennedy sacrileges against hallowed Hoover procedures, however, none angered the Director more than Bobby's habit of appearing at headquarters on weekends and requesting the duty agent to supply specific case files for his review. The Attorney General had never had direct access to FBI files; any request for files should be made to Hoover, who would unilaterally determine what was and was not appropriate for AG review. But since a lowly duty agent could not be expected to refuse the Attorney General, Kennedy's unpredictable weekend appearances required the Director himself to spend Saturdays at the office, an unprecedented interference with his ironclad routine. (And of course there was a ripple effect across the country. "Agents were working Saturdays from New York to Los Angeles," Welch recalled, "because Hoover was working in Washington and might call any field office without warning.")[54]

When Kennedy stepped down as Attorney General, Hoover moved immediately to undo all that he had done and perhaps never realized that one Kennedy accomplishment was indelible: When the FBI finally penetrated organized crime, agents gave the credit not to J. Edgar Hoover, but to his nemesis, Robert F. Kennedy.

"In 1961, I was promoted to the inspection staff. Instead of routinely reviewing files, I decided to actually get out on the street with the agents, to get a feel for their cases—and for them.

"In New York, the supervisor took me to President Street, on the waterfront, where the Gallo family was barricaded inside a series of buildings, at war with the Profaci family. Crazy Joe Gallo welcomed us into the compound—the mob respects authority, and it enhanced his status to be visited by an FBI official from Washington.

"Inside, eight or ten men were sitting around a long table, relaxing, and in one corner a couple of others were stewing huge pots of food. Long ladders and ropes were next to the main windows—if the Profaci gang attacked or the police raided, they simply escaped on the ladder to the adjoining building.

"After inspecting the Gallo compound, the supervisor took me to the nearby shrine church. He explained that the Profaci family had sponsored construction of the church, pushing ahead even after the local church hierarchy had refused to sanction the project. On completion, priests and nuns were imported from Sicily to staff it, and the numerous Profaci family members and associates were regular worshipers there. It was a beautiful church, with a number of statues on columns inside; as I was admiring them, the supervisor asked if I recognized any.

" 'Aren't they the twelve apostles?'

" 'Nah,' he said, doubling up with laughter, 'they're the capos of the family—the old man had to get someone to pose for the apostles when he built this place!' "[55]

6

Missionary

Shortly after midnight on September 17, 1962, a light blue sedan eased to a halt on a dirt road near Dawson, Georgia. In the car were three men, aged twenty-one to fifty-five, and a sixteen-year-old youth. One of the men held a jar of kerosene. Flames of race hatred were soon to leap from this jar and destroy the I Hope Baptist Church, a landmark of Negro worship in Terrell County, Georgia.

Due to the hour and the isolation of the area, there were no witnesses to this crime. Nevertheless, by midmorning FBI Agents had determined the identities of the four arsonists involved. Their confessions, obtained the same day, were turned over to Georgia authorities, together with physical evidence we had gathered concerning their guilt.

> John Edgar Hoover, "The FBI's
> Role in the Field of Civil
> Rights," *Yale Political,*
> August 1963.[1]

Circulation figures for the *Yale Political* magazine in Neshoba County, Mississippi, were not available, but it was doubtful, in any case, that the men planning murder there in 1964 would have been deterred by the Director's article. The FBI was not a factor. Racial violence in Mississippi was certain that summer, as was federal intervention, but there was widespread expectation that the federal presence would be troops, not FBI agents. Perhaps because civil rights activists did not regard Hoover's Bureau with particular hope, Mississippi Klansmen did not contemplate it with particular fear. And no one reading in the *Yale Political* magazine that the FBI had solved a Georgia racial crime without witnesses in twelve hours flat seemed inspired to ask how.

Nor did it seem significant, in Mississippi, that President Lyndon Baines Johnson had lived across a Washington street from the FBI Director for nineteen years, trading gifts and gossip in a relationship approximating, as closely as either of these extraordinary men would ever know it, genuine friendship. Their unusual camaraderie was captured in an anecdote which Hoover delighted in telling, which had occurred during one of the Director's evening strolls with the President on the White House grounds. Without warning, Johnson had suddenly shouted, "Edgar, where are you?" Startled, Hoover had replied, "Right here, Mr. President," to which LBJ had responded, "I'm not talking to you, I'm talking to my dog"—a gift beagle which Hoover had previously presented to the President.[2]

And neither the Southerners who admired Hoover's early successes nor the Northern critics who accused him of anachronistically reliving them remembered that his triumphs had included the dramatic infiltration of the Louisiana Ku Klux Klan in 1922, with resulting murder charges against state officials.[3] In any event, however, it seemed a success unlikely to be replicated, since the FBI did not even have a field office in the state of Mississippi.

In retrospect, it was unsurprising that these circumstances were overlooked, because the civil rights clashes in the South had to that point been primarily tests of executive will—Presidents against governors. Their weapons had been competing court orders, federal and state, enforced, respectively, by marshals or sheriffs. When the marshals were outgunned, as three hundred of them had been in 1962 during James Meredith's enrollment at the University of Mississippi,[4] federal troops had come to the rescue. When the violence came without warning, as it had when a Sunday morning firebomb killed four black children in a Birmingham church in 1963, no one did.[5] Certainly Hoover had not declined any missions, but his jurisdiction and manpower were limited, as he frequently reminded. Prior to 1964, he seemed convinced that civil rights had been contested in battles too big, or skirmishes too small, to justify any massive new FBI effort in the South.

The men who would change Hoover's mind, however, were already at work in Mississippi, stalking a young New York civil rights activist named Michael Henry Schwerner. On June 21, they caught up with him near Longdale, Mississippi, where he had gone to help after a black church had been torched to the ground. Schwerner was accompanied by a Queens College student named Andrew Goodman, and the men who followed them were not surprised to find that the third man in Schwerner's car was black, a twenty-year-old Mississippian named James Chaney. Their car, which would be stopped for speeding later that night, was a 1963 Ford station wagon.[6]

The FBI agents who would be handpicked by Hoover for Mississippi were, until the order came, scattered throughout the country, although a majority were either stationed in the South or were Southern by background, a circumstance which would itself provoke controversy. Neil Welch was in Tampa, his first *official* Florida duty station, having been assigned in 1962.

He had arrived at the height of the Cuban missile crisis. The prospect of actual combat with Communists had inspired Bureau headquarters to a feverish state of readiness, and Tampa was the nerve center for emergency message traffic. Virtually all of the messages were standby instructions, to be implemented only if hostilities did in fact commence. But shortly after midnight a few days after his arrival, Welch received one which was different. Summoned to the office from a sound sleep, Welch had begun decoding, and the first word in the message had jolted him wide awake. It was EXECUTE, the action command, the code signal which meant that everything which followed would be implemented at once. Even in the quiet solitude of the code vault, Welch sensed instant tension; the world was on the brink of war, and he had in his hand the FBI action orders.

Certain that he held the blueprint for a dangerous FBI mission, Welch carefully decoded the rest, his mind racing ahead, imagining what dramatic action he would be required to EXECUTE.

ASCERTAIN THAT ALL CARS HAVE FULL GAS TANKS.
CHECK FIRST AID KITS.
LOCATE GAS MASKS . . .
He went home to bed.[7]

After the missile crisis ended, Welch's duties in Tampa turned more routine and centered around the circuses. P. T. Barnum may have exaggerated about how often, but suckers were born with sufficient regularity, Welch discovered, to occupy the Tampa field office. Both Ringling Brothers, Barnum & Bailey Circus and the Royal American Circus wintered there, a habit which generated dependable criminal business, particularly confidence games and the fencing of stolen goods.[8]

His work there was less satisfying than previous assignments, in part because Welch was a newly promoted assistant special agent in charge (ASAC). Under Hoover's peculiar hierarchy, advancement to ASAC presaged promotion to SAC. But in the meantime, because it was invariably sandwiched between two tours as a headquarters inspector, ASAC was a curious limbo position, characterized by professional and personal frustration. SACs systematically excluded ASACs from field office operations, fearful that deficiencies noted would be reported to headquarters during the ASAC's subsequent inspection tour. ASACs were Hoover's missionaries in the field, and their inspection assignments were his precaution to make certain field offices followed the true headquarters faith.

For ASACs with families, the personal pressures were even

greater. For fifteen months prior to his assignment to Tampa, Welch had been an inspector, detailed to field offices around the country and frequently away from Washington for weeks at a time. His promotion to ASAC, Geri knew, would mean more time at home with their two young sons, Chip and Brien. It also meant, however, moving the family from Virginia to Florida and then, almost certainly, back to the Washington area eighteen months later. There was no evidence that Hoover, who never had moved or had family, understood the impact of one on the other. Hard-pressed agent families were routinely forced to forfeit security deposits; children broke up school years; and harried FBI wives almost always presided over moving day alone.

Following Neil's departure from Washington in October, Geri Welch remained behind to make moving arrangements, assisted by their three and six year olds. They all finally joined Welch in temporary quarters in Tampa in time for Thanksgiving dinner—at Howard Johnson's.

Within a few months, it was clear that Welch would indeed spend substantially more time at home during his Tampa assignment, though for reasons other than anyone had anticipated. He was suddenly hospitalized with a combination of infectious hepatitis and severe exhaustion, the second caused by trying to work in spite of the first, and the doctors ordered an extended convalescence. J. Edgar Hoover concurred, writing with almost maternal solicitude:

> Dear Mr. Welch:
>   I have been advised that it is necessary for you to be away from the office for a while due to the condition of your health, and hope this note finds you resting comfortably.
>   Let me urge you to follow the doctor's instructions, making certain you are feeling perfectly well again before trying to return to work.
>   With best wishes.[9]

The Director's concern for the health of his agents was matched by his continuing vigilance over the health of the

Republic. Communists (which he pronounced "commonists")[10] remained his top priority, and Welch, like all other agents, received a drumfire of reminders, titled "Message from the Director," intended to make certain that FBI agents knew the enemy. If the menace was Red, Hoover's prose was generally purple, typified by a statement circulated to agents in 1961.

"The atheistic communist dictatorship now controls one fourth of the earth's surface and more than one third of her peoples," Hoover asserted. "The communist threat from without must not blind us to the communist threat from within. The latter is reaching into the very heart of America through its espionage agents and a cunning, defiant, and lawless Communist Party, which is fanatically dedicated to the Marxist cause of world enslavement and destruction of the foundations of our Republic . . .

"America's emblem is the soaring eagle—not the blind and timid mole. Fear, apologies, defeatism, and cowardice are alien to the thinking of true Americans! As for me," the Director concluded with a rhetorical flourish, "I would rather be DEAD than RED!"[11]

His final phrase would inspire both debate and ridicule, but no one at the time suspected that Hoover's FBI regularly paid other Americans to make the opposite choice. During Welch's recuperation in Tampa, he received a tip that a new Communist cell was active in the area, and after a quick check he traced the activity to two longtime Bureau informants from Chicago. Retired and Florida-bored, they had recruited several fellow senior citizens and formed a Communist organization in the hope that headquarters would pay for their intelligence reports from Tampa, as it had for decades from Chicago.

"I told them to cut out the crap, and get back to shuffleboard!"[12]

Welch could not help wondering, though, how cunning and defiant the fanatically dedicated atheistic Communist threat would be in America in the absence of FBI funding.

Even reduced to acronyms, activist alphabet organizations had proliferated into confusion. The most diligently informed citizen had difficulty remembering that SNCC (Student Non-Violent Coordinating Committee) and CORE (Congress of Racial Equality) were working together in COFO (Council of Federated Organizations). Every Mississippian knew, however, that the COFO-sponsored Freedom Summer meant that more than one thousand Northern college students would spend their 1964 vacation spearheading registration of the state's nine hundred thousand black voters, a project which would, before it was three days old, produce an FBI investigative file code named MIBURN (Mississippi Burning).[13]

By June 23, it appeared that the FBI's verb "burning" was right, though its tense, with respect to the 1963 Ford station wagon agents discovered near the Bogue Chitto swamp, was wrong. The car had been burned, in a white-hot, metal-melting fire, but its remains—and any clues they might hold regarding the whereabouts of Schwerner, Goodman, and Chaney—were already swamp-water cold.[14]

The disappearance of the rights workers had seemed inescapably ominous from the moment, a day before, when it had first been flashed through the Freedom Summer communications network. It was a sense which was heightened, rather than diminished, by the fact that the two men who had last seen the activists alive were both lawmen. Neshoba County Deputy Sheriff Cecil Price, who had released the civil rights workers into Klan country shortly before midnight after arresting them for speeding, reckoned that the three might be involved somehow "with that burned-out nigger church over there at Longdale."[15] Price's boss, Red Man–chomping Sheriff Lawrence A. Rainey, joked that their disappearance was most likely a fund-raising stunt for COFO.[16]

Lyndon Johnson knew the South and knew better. With an eye on November, he dispatched Republican and retired CIA Director Allen Dulles to investigate law enforcement in Mississippi and at the same time ordered his old neighbor to supply some. Hoover acted at once. The missing civil rights workers were presumed dead by the FBI, and J. Edgar Hoover knew precisely what he would need to solve a racial crime without witnesses. By the time Dulles returned with his recommendations, the President had already given the Director a blank check to buy it.

But before he could prove his investigative prowess in Mississippi, Hoover knew he would need a credible FBI presence there. Endorsing a Dulles suggestion, the Director decreed that there would be a field office in Jackson and ordered his assistants to comb Bureau personnel files to find the right men to staff it. Hoover's commitment to the cause of civil rights might be suspect, but his appetite for national recognition was not, and those who doubted his enthusiasm for the Mississippi assignment misunderstood what motivated him. A horrendous crime had been committed, the President had asked him to solve it, the nation was watching, and his FBI would succeed. The exercise was familiar, Dillinger-Lindbergh-Brinks, and its acknowledged master was still J. Edgar Hoover.

After carefully reviewing personnel files, Hoover selected Little Rock SAC Roy K. Moore to head the new Jackson office and named Neil J. Welch to serve as ASAC.

Geri Welch completed the charge card application and handed it to the Jackson furniture store clerk, unaware that her unmistakable New England accent spoke louder than her credit references. He looked at it, frowning doubtfully.

"Where does your husband work?" he finally asked sharply.

"United States Department of Justice," she replied automatically, the standard FBI wives' answer.

"I'm sorry, we can't process this."

At that moment a supervisor appeared, having overheard the conversation.

"Now, Bill, the application's going to be perfectly all right," the supervisor drawled. "I read about Mr. Welch in the newspaper, and he's not in the Justice Department, he's with the FBI."[17]

It was a distinction which, from the beginning, made a large difference. The federal government was the enemy, but the Justice Department Civil Rights Division was actually leading the assault on Mississippi and attracted the most bitter resentment. Even in vacant buildings, the General Services Administration had been unable to locate any office space in Jackson available for rent to the Justice Department. It was only after the FBI was identified as the prospective tenant that two floors in the First Federal Savings and Loan were discovered to be vacant. And then the enthusiastic landlord had insisted on a handshake deal, no need for a written lease—and the absence of paperwork had created almost as much bureaucratic difficulty as the absence of space.[18]

Neil Welch arrived in early July, and his first impressions of Jackson vividly defined the challenges he would face. The air was electric and deadly still, charged with heat and supercharged with racial tension. Fresh blood smears splotched the sidewalk. Welch knew without knowing that the bloody trail would lead to his new office. There, amid frantic construction activity, three black COFO leaders, battered and bleeding from a savage axe-handle attack on Jackson's main street, haltingly described their beating to an FBI agent (while another agent crawled around the floor, trying to cover the new carpet with newspapers before it was stained with blood).

The Mississippi field office had cases before it had files to keep them in, a metaphysical impossibility in Hoover's FBI, and it would be months before the paperwork would catch up with the action.

By the time J. Edgar Hoover arrived, risking a rare venture out of Washington to personally inaugurate the new office, there was no evidence of its recent creation. His men had worked a five-day miracle—ceilings dropped, carpets laid, furniture borrowed, air-conditioned, attention-to-detail round-the-clock, just the sort of D-day exercise at which his organization excelled. There was every indication, when the Director walked briskly through the handsomely stained doors and past an attractive receptionist whose desk was adorned with fresh-cut flowers, that the office had been busily operational for years.

Striding into a conference room jammed with reporters from all over the world, Hoover mounted a newly constructed stage, waiting a few seconds while their chatter faded into expectant silence. Then, crisp and confident, he outlined his plans. There would be a cooperative effort, he promised, with Mississippi law enforcement officials; the FBI would not supplant local police. He was certain that the FBI would be a positive force. He was pleased to have the governor's support in a joint effort to restore law and order to Mississippi, and his men were already in the field at work.[19]

Later, agents would attribute their success in Mississippi to Hoover's own personal popularity there and to the careful tone which he set that day. His law and order speech was a dual message masterpiece: The press was impressed by what Hoover said he would do, and Mississippians heard and liked what Hoover said he certainly would not do, which was to give FBI protection to civil rights workers.

"In the first place," he said, "the FBI is not a police organization—it's purely an investigative organization, and the protection of individual citizens, either natives of this state or coming into this state, is a matter for the local authorities." Eliminating any doubt, he concluded, "The FBI will not participate in such protection."[20]

What Hoover really planned, however, was never stated and had already started. He would do to the Ku Klux Klan what he had done to the Communist Party—penetrate it so thoroughly that he would eventually know more about who was under Klan sheets, and what they were planning, than all of the imperial wizards and grand cyclopses combined. It was not a task which agents could accomplish in business suits, and the Director did not explain publicly how it might be done. But he made it clear from the beginning that he could do it.

In a private meeting with Governor Paul ("Stand Tall with Paul") Johnson prior to his press conference, Hoover had stated that there would be a price for FBI cooperation with local police authorities: Klansmen must first be dismissed from the Mississippi Highway Patrol and State Police. The governor did not argue. He would be more than willing, he replied, indeed would have done it himself—if only he knew who they were.

J. Edgar Hoover had handed him a list.[21]

Hoover's FBI had declared war, but, unlike the Justice Department, he had carefully avoided making Mississippi the enemy.

Walter F. Dunn was born and raised in Sullivan's Hollow, a hamlet in the heart of Smith's Canyon, Mississippi. As far back as anyone could recall, it had always been Klan country, and old-timers could remember when a Main Street sign warned "Nigger Be Out of Town by Sundown."[22] In 1951, after an undergraduate degree at the University of Southern Mississippi and a law degree from the University of Mississippi School of Law, Dunn joined the FBI,[23] entering the class ahead of Welch.

For the next thirteen years he worked Mississippi from the New Orleans field office, becoming acquainted with Roy K. Moore in the process. When Moore opened the Jackson office in 1964, Walter Dunn came with him. Dunn had some early misgivings about Neil Welch ("he's so quiet until you get to know him real good you get the impression he's an introverted type individual"),[24] but watching Welch handle the pressure-packed Jackson office while Moore traveled the state, he quickly became an admirer.

Misgivings about Dunn and the background he typified, however, were not as readily resolved, and civil rights leaders charged repeatedly that the FBI's work in Mississippi was undermined by overreliance on Southern agents. The agents on the scene strongly disagreed. On one occasion, on his way from Gulfport to Jackson, Dunn stopped in a small town where the FBI agents assigned, all Northerners, had proved impotent at curbing Klan violence. The town's leading citizens welcomed Dunn warmly, but their leisurely chat had a

concrete objective: What do we have to do, they finally asked
Dunn, to get these damn Yankees out of here?

Dunn had the answer.

Stop night riding. Stop violence. And identify the Klan
leadership.

Dunn's conditions were instantly accepted and readily implemented since the chief of police was also head of the Klan.
Dunn phoned Roy Moore, who transferred the Northern
agents immediately and ordered an agent from Texas and
one from Louisiana to take charge of the office. Klan violence
ceased at once, and the open cases were soon solved.[25]

Dunn was indispensable. He taught agents to shake a stick
inside their cars before entering, a precaution which would
expose any concealed rattlesnakes. When snakes were in fact
discovered in agent cars, Dunn arranged "a little fatherly
talk" with the men who had put them there. And when an
FBI informant was accidentally exposed penetrating the
Klan, it was Walter Dunn who let the Klansmen know that
retribution was inadvisable.[26]

Anonymous callers threatened to burn down his house,
and Dunn frequently found himself at odds with old acquain-
tances, inconveniences he shrugged away, explaining simply,
"I'm from a law enforcement family."[27]

Critics would continue to question Hoover's personal commitment of conscience to the civil rights probes in the South,
but his commitment of men and resources was by midsum-
mer 1964 unarguable. More than four hundred agents were
detailed into Mississippi, and their selection reflected Hoover's acute awareness that his own reputation was at risk.
Eyebrows had been raised by his choice of Welch, who had
no particular sponsor among the powerful headquarters lieutenants and who, at thirty-eight, was young for a major ASAC
assignment, but the Director's instincts proved infallible.

"Neil was the perfect balance for Roy," one agent concluded, recalling the combination. "They broke the mold
after they made Roy Moore—dynamic, tough, unpredictable, he made the organization. But two Roy Moores would

break any organization, and Welch supplied the rest, the solid, dependable leadership that made it all work."[28]

And it was all work. Hoover had zealously preserved the FBI's immunity from civil service overtime limitations (as well as from its hiring requirements), and agents in Mississippi routinely worked seven days a week, from dawn past dark. FBI wives endured marriage to missing persons, as breaking cases frequently kept their husbands up and away overnight without advance warning. Geri Welch countered by bringing the boys into the FBI office every Sunday and extracting Neil for dinner in a Jackson restaurant, the only regular family gathering of the week. Hoover's success, however, had always had an inverse relationship to the arrival of his agents at home for dinner, and the Director was determined to succeed in Mississippi—as he regularly assured another notorious nonrespecter of dinnertime, Lyndon B. Johnson.

In the beginning, breaks came slowly, slowly enough to totally exhaust the infinitesimal presidential patience. Johnson wanted instant law and order in Mississippi, and if the Bureau could not supply it, the 82nd Airborne could. The Jackson FBI office received an urgent telegram from headquarters asking for an on-the-scene assessment of a proposed military occupation of the state. (Johnson was not the only one contemplating a military offensive. Mississippi Highway Patrol Chief T. B. Birdsong had received a message from a self-commissioned Mississippi colonel, volunteering fifteen thousand men with full field equipment and combat weapons to run the Yankees out. Birdsong had diplomatically replied that the "colonel" should maintain his men in bivouac at their present location, awaiting further orders.)[29]

After carefully considering the Bureau telegram, SAC Roy Moore said no. Military force was not required. The FBI and state authorities together could control Klan violence and assure voter registration, he wired Washington, provided they were given time to establish their operations.

Washington officials remained skeptical, doubting especially the likelihood of federal-state cooperation, which was

understandable since they were unaware of the two factors
which would make it happen—Special Agent Tomlinson and
the bootleg tax. Nominally dry, Mississippi winked at boot-
leggers, who could buy unofficial official sanction by payment
of a special "tax." Local sheriffs collected the tax, kept detailed payment records, and theoretically forwarded all monies collected to the state treasurer in Jackson. It was a system
which Homer Tomlinson understood intimately, having previously been a sheriff, and one which he had customarily
monitored for his good friend, Governor Johnson. But as the
FBI pressed for results in Mississippi, ol' Homer's visits with
local sheriffs seemed to become more regular, and his scrutiny of their records often resulted in a precipitous reduction
of the sheriff's annual income. The sheriffs were bewildered
until they realized that Homer's visits tended to follow
closely after local Klan violence.

"We could settle a county down in no time," Welch recalled, "because of that tax. Most of the sheriffs disagreed
with the federal position on civil rights, but *all* of them
wanted to keep collecting that bootleg tax, without interference from Homer or anyone else."[30]

Facing increased pressure, the Klan retreated and regrouped, concentrating its strength in fierce pockets of guerilla resistance. In a rural county near Natchez, two prominent Klansmen announced that they would kill the next FBI
agent who came to town. That was sufficient invitation for
Special Agent Paul Cummings, who organized a squad of
G-men and headed for the Klansmen's favorite bar. Standing
in the middle of the dusty main street, Cummings dared the
Klansmen to come out and deliver on their threat. No one
appeared. Cummings then pulled his gun, shot out the windows of the saloon, and departed; there were no subsequent
threats from that county.[31]

But there were other threats. A Klan Bureau of Investigation ("KBI") was created to counter the FBI, and its members
placed the wives and children of agents under surveillance,
harassing them with taunts and anonymous phone calls. It
was a serious miscalculation. The most dangerous members

of the KBI were systematically identified and assigned to agents selected solely because they were comparably dangerous. The agents had full discretion. During the next few months, a number of men previously involved in Klan violence around the state seemed, by remarkable coincidence, to experience misfortune. Some disappeared from the area. Some were forced to leave Mississippi for health reasons. A few took unplanned trips to places like Mexico and seemed to lose all interest in the Klan upon their return.[32]

It did not take long for Mississippi Klansmen to realize that the FBI was capable of restoring law and order in inverse sequence, and, faced with the prospect of being victims of violence themselves, the Klan quietly declared a moratorium on it.

"We were at war," Paul Cummings said, "and we used some muscle. It was either that or the 82nd Airborne."[33]

It was a war in which the momentum had already shifted. The FBI field organization was taking shape in Mississippi, aided by men in bib overalls and pickup trucks, who did not look at all like agents. They patiently pieced together the bits of intelligence which would enable the FBI to penetrate the Klan. Of necessity, much of what they did was invisible, and as a consequence civil rights workers insisted that the FBI was not doing enough. Feeling the impact, however, Mississippians argued the opposite; Roy Moore and Neil Welch won the respect of their agents by listening to neither.

"Dozens of police brutality complaints followed every public demonstration. Eyewitness accounts were so contradictory that we started filming every major demonstration—and the arrests which usually followed—so we could evaluate the cases independently. Review of the films confirmed our suspicion that a few Civil Rights Division attorneys were actually manufacturing police brutality complaints.

"One of our informants was arrested, and as soon as he was released a Justice Department lawyer interviewed him. The lawyer advised him how to file a formal complaint about the beating and mistreatment he had received—without ever asking whether there had been any.

"Another time, a woman who had filed numerous brutality complaints came to our office to identify the Jackson policeman who had beaten her. Previously, as the Civil Rights Division attorneys knew, the photographs had always been arranged starting with the chief, then captains, lieutenants, in order down through the ranks. This time, we masked the names and shuffled the order.

"She never really looked at the pictures, just started counting. When she reached number seven she announced that he was the one—by chance, she had picked an officer who had been out of the state on vacation at the time of the alleged incident.

"We suggested that she might want to look more closely at the pictures, and she promptly counted to seven and identified the same man again. By this time, the Justice Department lawyers were protesting vigorously, accusing us of intimidating the witness—I finally grabbed two of the lawyers and threw them physically out of our office.

"The lawyers immediately complained to Washington, and the Civil Rights Division came after my scalp, charging me with brutality, but Hoover backed me 100 percent and the issue died."[34]

Somehow the heat of the sun seemed moderate compared to the shimmering waves of blast-furnace fury reflected back up from the red clay, but the men watching the bulldozer cut into the earthen dam were indifferent to both. Through the morning and into the sweltering afternoon, they patiently watched and waited, knowing they would find what they were looking for in the dam on Old Jolly Farm in Neshoba County.

At 3 P.M., they found Michael Schwerner, face down in the clay; two hours later, Andrew Goodman; then James Chaney. Each had been shot to death.[35]

It was never explained how they had known where to look, and the horror of their discovery obscured any curiosity at the fact that Hoover had—again, as in Georgia—solved a racial crime without witnesses. And no one thought it particularly significant that the search warrant authorizing the excavation, which would be upheld in repeated federal court challenges, had been prepared and signed by a Mississippian from a law enforcement family—Special Agent Walter F. Dunn.[36]

Seven men, including Deputy Sheriff Price, would be imprisoned for the crime, the first time in history that a white Mississippi jury would send white Mississippians to jail for a federal civil rights violation.

Later, looking back on the feverish activity of 1964, agents realized the intensity of the investigative effort had simply overwhelmed them, obliterating the ordinary details of everyday life, triggering bizarre reactions.

Walter Dunn recalled the day his wife called, excitedly reporting that a violent tropical storm was roaring in from the Gulf with plummeting barometric pressure already collapsing the doors on their home. She frantically asked what to do. He calmly replied, "Call the weather bureau." Then he hung up the phone and went back to the investigation.[37]

And on November 18, 1964, when a group of journalists asked J. Edgar Hoover about Martin Luther King's charge that Southern agents had undermined the Bureau's effectiveness on civil rights, the Director responded that King was "the most notorious liar in the country,"[38] an observation which instantly spawned its own violent storm of reaction.

The FBI's accomplishments in Mississippi would be regarded by many as the capstone of Hoover's career, but his attack on King would permanently tarnish his undeniable Mississippi achievements; chief among them, ironically, was the FBI's successful protection, in the face of repeated secret death threats, of Dr. Martin Luther King.

7

Memorandum for Mr. Tolson

On April 22, 1966, I saw Inspector Neil J. Welch of the Inspection Division, who is under orders of transfer to Buffalo as Special Agent in Charge. Mr. Welch makes a substantial personal appearance, and I would rate him average.

I outlined to him the general duties of a Special Agent in Charge and the imperative need for running a field office with a firm but fair administration.

J. Edgar Hoover, *Memorandum for Mr. Tolson*, April 29, 1966[1]

It was, at once, reassuring and disquieting. There had been thousands of previous—and would be hundreds of subsequent—memoranda from the Director to Mr. Tolson, and their numbers alone implied comforting continuity and suggested that Hoover's FBI might be magically immune from the torrents of change convulsing every other American institution in the 1960s. Also, in a decade in which Miss-Mrs.-Ms. would provoke bitter debate, it was comforting that Hoover's closest associate would always be, with courtly formality, Mister Tolson—unless that somehow suggested that Hoover was out of touch with the time, perhaps unaware that "firm but fair" was code for keeping urban Negroes under control, perhaps even unwilling to acknowledge that Negroes had become Afro-Americans and then blacks.

Still, Hoover had endured world war and peace, Depression and prosperity, systematically assimilating the idiom of every era, and his clinical differentiation of beatniks ("long hair and beards, unkempt clothes and sandals") from hippies ("drug users, enamored with esoteric rituals such as 'love-ins,' 'be-ins,' and 'happenings' ") in a mid-sixties article[2] suggested that this decade might be no different. The Director, it seemed, would define and punish "Public Enemies" as effectively as ever, which is why FBI headquarters did not give particular credence to the Berkeley observer who, after watching Mario Savio and Sproul Hall make each other household words in 1964 (the former occupying the latter in support of something called the "Free Speech Movement"), warned, "All the old labels are out; if there were any orthodox Communists here, they would be a moderating influence."[3]

> I also called his [Welch's] attention to the fact that the Agents in the Buffalo Field Division had closed only 12 cases per Agent in March, 1966, and I felt this was low and should be between 13 and 14 cases per Agent . . .
> I discussed with him also the fact that the Agents in his office had spent 12.6 percent of their time in the office in March and I thought this was excessive and should not exceed 10 percent of their time.[4]

There was another number worthy of discussion, although Hoover could be excused for not supposing it would have any relevance to Neil Welch's assignment in Buffalo, since of the two people it had affected most directly, one was awaiting execution and the other was dead. Even so, the number thirty-eight seemed to have a lingering primal significance of its own, it being the number of solid, middle class citizens who had watched for more than half an hour while Winston Mosely methodically stabbed Catherine Genovese to death

on a Queens street in front of her home on March 13, 1964—
without ever calling the police.[5]

The New York *Times* had initially judged the crime worth a
three-inch filler, buried among the Lenten religious notices;
the Marble Collegiate Church's bold-type announcement
that Dr. Daniel A. Poling and Dr. Norman Vincent Peale
would speak, respectively, on the topics "You May Conquer
Your Circumstances" and "It's Good to be Alive" overshadowed the brief story, immediately below, that Kitty Genovese couldn't and wasn't.[6] It was two more weeks before the
Times pieced together the details which moved the Genovese murder to the front page of every paper in the country,
documenting a new variety of nightmare. Her screams had
made real sounds ("Oh my God, he stabbed me! Please help
me! Please help me!" and, nearly thirty-five minutes later,
"I'm dying! I'm dying!"), but the thirty-eight neighbors who
heard them were frozen in a tacit conspiracy of silence, inhu-
man indifference chilled even more by their eventual expla-
nations.

"I was tired. I went back to bed."

"We thought it was a lover's quarrel."

"Frankly, we were afraid."

"I didn't want to get involved."

"I didn't want to get involved."[7] Swiftly, a sentence and a
sentiment—or antisentiment—that engraved itself indelibly
in tens of millions of memories.

On trial, Mosely confessed to the Genovese murder and
two others, leaving it to sociologists to debate whether the
horror of his crimes or the terrifying silence of thirty-eight
witnesses was more threatening to society. The sentencing
judge, less analytical, disposed of all questions in a brief statement.

"I don't believe in capital punishment, but I must say I feel
this may be improper when I see this monster. I wouldn't
hesitate to pull the switch on him myself."[8]

Courtroom spectators applauded.

The switch was never pulled, however, and Mosely's death

sentence was ultimately commuted to life, to be served in Attica State prison, just east of Buffalo.[9]

> I discussed with him the general racial problem and while there is no specific indication of this problem at the present time in the Buffalo Field Division, he should be certain to have adequate informant coverage to be alert if it should develop.[10]

The admonition was not surprising, given that informants were most useful in the context of organized conspiracies, such as the Communist Party, which Hoover likely viewed as both analogue to and instigator of the general racial problem. Unfortunately, the effectiveness of informants assumed the predictability, or at least the rationality, of events, assumptions which had been buried with the smoldering rubble of Watts the previous summer. By the end of 1966, forty-three more race riots[11] had proved Martin Luther King and J. Edgar Hoover as impotent as everyone else in controlling the movement, which had veered from civil rights to blacks-only "Black Power," consuming its leaders with a frequency reminiscent of the French Revolution.

Nevertheless, the Director's warning to Welch would be a matter of record, and Bureau headquarters held comparable warnings in similar memos for every SAC in the country, all carefully preserved by Mr. Tolson. Whatever happened, it would be clear that the Director had seen it coming and had warned against it, so that racial violence could never escalate into something Hoover found even more intolerable, which was embarrassment to his Bureau—or himself.

> I discussed with him [Welch] the imperative necessity for intensifying the coverage of the Cosa Nostra "family," the head of which is Steve Magaddino, who is a member of the nine-man "commission."[12]

Born in the tiny Sicilian village of Castellammare in 1891, Stefano Magaddino had emigrated to the United States in 1903 and was, as the Niagara Falls *Gazette* put it gingerly, "associated with a string of beverage distributorships here, beginning in 1927."[13] Prohibition had made his market, and while more than five hundred thousand persons were arrested for violating the Volstead Act,[14] Magaddino was not among them, emerging instead as one of a handful of Castellammarese who converted the nation's thirst for illicit liquor into national power.

Once established, Magaddino had branched into other businesses as well. His company distributed a nonalcoholic concoction called Home Juice door-to-door in Buffalo, and newly arrived immigrants understood by word of mouth that while Home Juice did not necessarily improve one's health, failure to buy it could have the opposite effect. Business boomed. And for those for whom Home Juice was an insufficient tonic, there was the Magaddino Funeral Home (which, it was rumored, occasionally used twofers, dispatching a paying customer in the upper portion of a casket along with a Magaddino enemy beneath, the two being separated for eternity by a false bottom).[15]

Despite Hoover's expressed interest in him, however, Magaddino had peacefully coexisted with the FBI for more than three decades. Indeed, once he became a major mob power by designating Maranzano as commander in chief in the Castellammarese war,[16] a move which ultimately determined the outcome, Magaddino regularly had more difficulty evading his friends in crime than his enemies in law enforcement. A 1936 bomb intended for him killed his sister next door (a mishap attributable, Joe Valachi later told a Senate committee, to the killer's confusion on addresses),[17] and in 1958 a hand grenade crashed through his kitchen window but failed to explode.[18] His onetime protégé and cousin from Castellammare del Golfo, Joe Bonanno, marked Don Stefano for death in the early 1960s, but by then the boss of Buffalo had become a national LCN power, and he neatly turned the tables.[19] Magaddino's men grabbed Bonanno as he walked with his attorney on a New York sidewalk in broad daylight, and sometime during his subsequent two-year "disappearance" Joe Bananas finally decided that retirement in Arizona was required for his health.[20]

In contrast, the attention Magaddino received from the FBI was almost comforting. The only serious threat had occurred in the early 1960s, when agents had, without benefit of court order or warrant, surreptitiously installed dozens of listening devices in organized crime haunts across the country, including the Magaddino family funeral home in Niagara Falls. (The eventual revelation of the taps sparked a debate over whether they had been authorized by Hoover or by Attorney General Robert Kennedy or by both; based on the enthusiasm with which he listened to them when he visited the New York office, agents generally concluded that it was Kennedy, and they admired him for it. Kennedy himself later told close associates that he had understood the taps to have been made by New York City Police.[21] In any event, Ramsey Clark, who became Attorney General in 1967, ended the debate by killing the bugs.)[22]

LCN leaders had quickly sensed the suddenly expanded agent awareness of their activities, but Magaddino boldly countered by putting the FBI under surveillance, ordering his men to record agent names and license numbers and carefully monitoring FBI comings and goings at the Buffalo office. Hoover's insistence on agent punctuality made the task easier than it might have been, and agents' regulation haircuts, shoeshines, and white shirts eliminated any mystery about their identity. In a short time, Magaddino's soldiers made them all and knew who would be working bank robberies and who should be following them.

(Despite the extensive wiretaps, agents were regularly frustrated by the seemingly instinctive reflex which prevented LCN leaders from making incriminating statements on tape. One agent explained it sardonically. "When a male Sicilian child is born, his uncle goes to the delivery room with a pin and a tape recorder. He sticks the pin in the baby's behind, and if the recorder picks up the scream, the baby is immediately destroyed. They've been doing this for centuries, and they've developed a whole strain of people who cannot be heard on recording devices.")[23]

It is not recorded whether Magaddino's ears were burning on April 22, 1966, but it is doubtful that he would have had any more acute sensation of foreboding than that, even if he had personally witnessed the Hoover-Welch meeting that date. Any observer would have seen that the man listening to Hoover was Courteous and Obedient and could have guessed, from his solid, earnest features, that he was also likely to be Trustworthy-Loyal-Helpful, Brave-Clean-Reverent, and every other virtue in between. The first impression would have been comforting to Don Stefano, who had never, in seventy-five years, had any difficulty with a Boy Scout.

Magaddino might have noticed, because he had a professional's eye for size and strength, that Welch appeared to have both, though a less practiced observer would have concluded that Welch was about the same size as the six-inches-shorter Hoover (who had placed his desk on an unobtrusive raised platform to encourage precisely such illusions). Even so, Magaddino would have sensed no threat in that either, since the few contacts between the LCN and FBI were historically, by unspoken accord, neither personal nor physical.

(A rare exception to this understanding occurred when Special Agent Pat Foley was badly beaten by LCN enforcers while photographing mourners at Carmello Lombardozzi's funeral in New York. Agents never forgot that Foley was visited in the hospital by Bobby Kennedy; the LCN enforcers were also visited, by a group of brawny agents who administered an unforgettable beating and restored the unspoken truce.)[24]

Indeed, if there was anything threatening about Neil Welch in 1966, it was the simple fact that Hoover had selected him, at thirty-nine, to be the youngest SAC in the entire FBI. The "Memorandum for Mr. Tolson" did not disclose whether that meant that Welch had had spectacular accomplishments in the past or was expected to in the future; if it were the latter, however, it was entirely predictable that they would occur first in Buffalo.

Prior to departing for Buffalo, Welch arranged for his wife and sons to meet the Director, who chatted with them cordially and posed for the ritual picture. As they were leaving, Hoover suddenly asked Geri Welch what she thought about her husband's promotion. Forgetting her carefully prepared remarks, but determined not to offend, Geri replied quickly, "I just want to say thank you, Mr. Hoover, for sending us to Buffalo."[25]

It was not a sentiment normally evoked by orders to Buffalo, as Hoover's startled expression confirmed—but it was one which would, in the next four years, be widely shared by Buffalonians.

8

Skeptic

We always had good, professional, bank robberies. You didn't just go out and stick up banks—you worked up through candy stores, drug stores, liquor stores, check cashing places, finally graduating to banks.

Then one day an elderly woman walked into a bank with a bottle of nitroglycerin, and demanded all the money. She scored again and again, and pretty soon every drunk and creep was hitting banks. It took all the class out of bank robberies, and for the first time, other agents began teasing our bank squad:

> Little old lady, dressed in brown,
> Knocking off all the banks in town.
> -Special Agent Clint Graham[1]

The 1965 budget of the United States seemed to invite variety, requiring only that the five hundred and one vehicles to be purchased by the FBI be suitable "for police-type use."[2] By unvarying habit, however, Hoover ordered Plymouths or Fords, always look-alike four-door sedans with conspicuously distinctive radio antennas—somber, unmarked vehicles, unmistakably police. It was a pattern which made undercover work virtually impossible, and field agents had for years badgered headquarters—without effect—for less readily recognizable cars.

Hoover's inflexibility in choosing official vehicles, however, was in marked contrast to the relative freedom allowed in their use. Headquarters cared about what agents weighed and drank, how often they paid bills late and slept with women not their wives, but not, apparently, about their minor accidents and traffic tickets. Because high-speed chases had been, since Dillinger days, the cliché prelude to G-man capture of dangerous desperadoes, the Bureau accepted without question the consequent rumpled fenders and blown engines, and it rarely recognized, thanks to the professional courtesy of local police, that agents sometimes damaged their cars in less heroic circumstances.

Accordingly, the rash of automobile repairs approved by the Buffalo office in the late 1960s did not stir any official curiosity in Washington and seemed to imply only that a disproportionate number of Buffalo agents were bad drivers. Headquarters would have readily accepted that, since Buffalo's frigid winters produced both treacherous driving conditions and a natural destination for FBI disciplinary transfers, and bad agents might be expected to be bad drivers as well. Certainly no one imagined that the proliferation of Buffalo car repairs had any connection to Neil Welch's assignment as special agent in charge.

Although the Buffalo *Evening News, Courier-Express,* and Niagara Falls *Gazette* had all reported Welch's April 1966 arrival as news, each article accompanied by the same solemn file photo, the event seemed, objectively, closer to "dog bites man." Certainly the transfer of a single SAC was not news—Hoover kept all fifty-nine of them in perpetual motion. He had once reassigned an SAC three times so rapidly that his family, left behind to sell the house, moved directly from the first to third assignment, missing the second city altogether. The practice would have been newsworthy only if it ceased.[3] Nor did Welch's sole comment ("I've been to Buffalo a number of times and I'm sure I'll like it here") seem to justify headlines, though a careful reader, noting his role in solving the Brinks robbery, Weinberger kidnapping, and civil rights murders, might have concluded that his accomplishments did.

To the vast majority of Buffalonians, however, Welch's arrival was a matter of indifference. Law enforcement in Buffalo, as elsewhere, was personified by the chief of police. The only FBI chief anyone knew was named Hoover, and the identity of his local special agent in charge had not, in the past, seemed to have any obvious impact on FBI performance. There were, of course, occasional citizens, including Stefano Magaddino and Buffalo's bankers, who had a distinct business interest in the Bureau, but they would have scanned the news articles only to confirm that Welch did not, in fact, plan anything new. Even diaper-service salesmen and realtors, professionally curious about newcomers, would have been discouraged, respectively, by Welch's age (thirty-nine) and salary (eighteen thousand dollars). And if insurance agents thought newspaper descriptions of Welch described a prospect, it was only because their insight into his life expectancy was actuarial rather than actual.

Indeed, just as Agriculture Department employees had recently come to outnumber the nation's farmers, an aging bureaucracy more potent to itself than others, it was probable that those most directly affected by Buffalo's new SAC would be neither career criminals nor ordinary law-abiding citizens, but rather the eighty-five FBI agents assigned to the Buffalo office. Certainly they evidenced the most acute interest in his coming, combing the agent grapevine for Welch quirks and qualms. Hoover's state-of-the-art communications system flashed Bureau rumors and gossip across the country as efficiently as fugitive descriptions, and sometimes nearly as often.

Unaccountably, though, the grapevine carried no hint of what Welch might do as SAC, or even how he had happened to become one. The Buffalo assignment itself proved he was not a Hoover favorite, and he seemed to have no sponsor among the headquarters lieutenants (who were already grappling for position on the chance the seventy-one-year-old

Hoover might prove, after all, mortal). Welch's promotion to SAC made clear, though, that headquarters viewed him as neither threat nor innovator, essentially synonymous defects, which meant Bureau officials had probably forgotten the only encounter, nearly ten years before, which should have warned them he might be both.

"In the late 1950s, Hoover returned from his winter vacation—he called it a Miami office inspection trip—extremely agitated about jewel thieves. One of his wealthy friends had lost a valuable jewelry collection in a resort hotel robbery, and Hoover was determined to develop a new FBI program to stop professional jewel thieves.

"I was unit chief for interstate crimes, and we created a working group to develop a plan. An old jewel thief named Sticks Reilly—who actually hid jewels in his wooden leg— had given me an education on the subject back in Boston, and I knew jewel thieves were often expert and discriminating criminals. Because of that, however, it was generally possible to identify the best ones operating around the country at any given time.

"Working from that premise, our group proposed that the FBI identify the fifty top jewel thieves in the country, then subject them to a continuous intelligence effort. We would know where they were at all times, and when they moved into resort areas following the high-society crowd, we would be able to keep them under constant surveillance.

"We submitted the proposal through the chain of command, persuading everyone it was realistic and likely to be effective—until it reached the assistant directors. At that point, without explanation, the project was suddenly taken away from us. We were told we had fulfilled our mission, and our plan was turned over to a committee of savvy old FBI bureaucrats for revision, which was, of course, the end of it.

"I was angry and demanded an audience with my assistant director. After hearing me out, he asked a totally unexpected question. 'How long has Mr. Hoover been Director?'

"Puzzled, I did the arithmetic mentally and told him

thirty-four years. He said, 'That's right, and that's your answer.'

"I told him respectfully that I did not understand the answer. At that, he became impatient and snapped, 'Neil, the Old Man has been Director thirty-four years, and it's too late for anything new—just too late for anything new!' "[4]

Although not among the highest waterfalls in the world, or even in the United States,[5] Niagara Falls is sufficiently awesome that the Indians residing nearby thought it prudent to appease the gods who had presumably created it by annually dispatching their most beautiful maiden over its edge in a canoe.[6] Later, with divine indifference, the same gods accepted the less attractive but more willing victims who took the 182-foot plunge in boats and barrels, entertaining the hordes of honeymooners who were one of two industries spawned by the falls. Hydroelectric power was the other, and high-tension lines carrying current from the surging Niagara crisscrossed the skyline everywhere, strung between towering shrugging standards which marked the land almost as distinctively as the falls themselves.

Like all tourist towns, residential Niagara Falls was a more exciting place to visit than live, and the plain white houses which lined its quiet streets would have been equally at home in dozens of declining Northeastern neighborhoods. Its population was an ethnic mix but mostly Italian-American, judging from the restaurants sprinkled among car repair shops and laundromats along Pine Avenue. And while the prominence of the nearby Bowl-O-Drome presumed bowling the primary pastime, it was baseball which had distinguished Niagara Falls's most famous son, Sal "The Barber" Maglie.[7] And it was neither baseball nor bowling which held Neil Welch's attention as he lunched in Niagara Falls one bright June day in 1966, but instead the other game in town, not advertised in honeymoon brochures—illegal gambling.

Luigi's Restaurant featured red drapes and velveteen wall coverings, plastic flowers, and excellent Italian food. And Stefano Magaddino's regular patronage was equivalent to a four-star Michelin rating. The agent briefing Welch, Paul Browne, did not speculate whether Magaddino was big because of gambling or vice versa, but he was certain both were permanently entrenched, a fact of life partially explained by the Canadian currency exchange rates posted by the cash register. Niagara Falls was a border town, traditionally tolerant of activities permissible on either side, and it was Prohibition-proof liquor from Canada which had originally made the Magaddino crime family's power.

Welch did not seem impressed. He asked quiet questions about the family, chewing on the answers with his lunch, noncommittal features masking any reaction. Buffalo agents had warned Browne that Welch was inquisitive, a quality which veterans were prepared to tolerate in a new SAC— especially one as young as Welch—knowing that experience would normally kill curiosity. Welch's first few questions had seemed appropriately naive, and Browne had responded patiently. He had not realized exactly when casual conversation had turned into careful interrogation, though by the time coffee came he was uncomfortably aware that Welch's deliberate Midwestern cadence carried a hard edge.

"Paul, we know who runs the Magaddino family," Welch concluded, waiting for the check, "and we know the family bookmakers are doing a multimillion dollar business here in Niagara Falls. Now why is it we have no informants, and no cases?"

Browne fidgeted with his napkin.

"Boss, they own everything and everybody," he finally replied. "We can't conduct any surveillance on them, because they're constantly watching us. Once I went into a store for a routine purchase, and when I got back from the office I had a call from the owner. He said he wanted to help the FBI, but could I please stay out of his store—right after I left, he said, two men in business suits came in and asked, 'What did Paul want?'

"The people who aren't on the family payroll are indebted to them somehow," Browne finished, "and everyone in town wants to be in the good graces of the Godfather."[8]

It was, as Browne explained, an understandable desire. Several years before, a small-time mobster assigned to monitor a construction project had been summarily ordered to report to Magaddino. Picked up by two brawny enforcers, the mobster was driven to Magaddino's home and escorted into the back yard, where he found the don sitting alone, enjoying the sunshine, an oddly formal figure in a cobra-backed chair. The enforcers melted into the background, leaving the perspiring mobster standing awkwardly in front of the frail old man.

Finally Magaddino spoke. Courtly, polite, he recounted how he had believed his *soldato* to be an honorable man and had placed him in a position of trust, only to be disappointed. The man's only responsibility, the don continued, had been to count the cement trucks at the site and to be certain that the family received the agreed-upon payment per truck, but the man's numbers had not been truthful. Perhaps there was an explanation?

Feverishly, the mobster insisted that he had made an honest count and that he could prove it, but he had passed his numbers along to Tony. If there was any mistake, it must be Tony's mistake. He himself had never broken the trust.

Expressionless, Magaddino weighed the defense. Suddenly he commanded, "Look at the sun!"

Bewildered, the man glanced quickly skyward and then back at Magaddino.

"No. *Look* at the sun!"

The terrified hoodlum stared into the sun.

Long moments passed.

"Today, you see the sun," Magaddino finally intoned, passing judgment. "Tomorrow . . . Tony . . . he no see the sun."[9]

For four decades, Browne concluded, FBI agents had come and gone, while Magaddino had reigned in the shadows and in the sunlight, untouchable and untouched. Since the enforcement of federal law had never seriously interfered with Magaddino's ruthless enforcement of his own, the good citizens of Niagara Falls had never been required to make a choice, though if it came to that, their prudent option would be to cooperate with the organization more likely to prevail.

That organization, in 1966, was directed not by J. Edgar Hoover, but by Don Stefano Magaddino.

The 1967 news photo happened to be Neil Welch with Bernadine Kush in Buffalo, but it could have been any agent, anywhere, because it was the most timeless FBI tableau of all: wide-eyed bank teller describing just-completed bank robbery to grimly efficient FBI agent.[10] From the beginning, Hoover's FBI specially safeguarded banks for essentially the same reason Willie Sutton robbed them—they were presumptively where the money was—and in every field office, the bank squad was the "heavy squad," the "cigar squad" (after the large ones bank squad agents typically smoked), the elite. It would be another decade before someone asked the heretical question, Why should the FBI assume jurisdiction over a fifteen-hundred-dollar bank robbery but not a fifty-thousand-dollar payroll theft next door? But any careful observer of Buffalo news photos in the late 1960s would have surmised that Neil Welch had already concluded that banks were no longer where the big criminal money was.

Front-page pictures of Welch with furs, Welch with jewels, and Welch with hijacked merchandise soon outnumbered pictures of Welch with tellers. When Welch was pictured with stacks of money, it had come more often from gamblers than from banks. (Even so, Welch would continue, always, to find bank robberies *in progress* irresistible, regularly racing with his agents to the crime scene.) Most of the photos were never seen outside the Buffalo area, however, so that even after Welch was pictured with increasing regularity arresting suspects with several names each, headquarters did not immediately realize that he had de facto demoted bank robbers and subversives into second-rate threats, behind organized crime.

FBI headquarters did, of course, receive certain photographs from the Buffalo field office, most notably the routine updates of individual agent file photos, but these were glanced at only to determine whether they had arrived by the prescribed tickler date. There was no particular headquarters interest in what the Buffalo agents actually looked like, certainly no reason for their file photos to be examined by the FBI laboratory, and absolutely no suspicion that such scrutiny might show traces of beards retouched away or hair airbrushed back to regulation length. Indeed, the file photos generated precisely the same official curiosity as the numerous car repairs which had coincided with Welch's arrival in Buffalo, which was none.[11]

When a picture from Buffalo finally did command the attention of Bureau headquarters, on March 21, 1968, it was a photo of Welch with a slim black man firmly in custody. As a technical law enforcement matter, it had more to do with Hoover's old priorities than Welch's new ones. The capture, however, like the crime which preceded it, transcended law enforcement priorities, and for a national audience of millions the picture crystallized cold courage. Welch himself would remember the case as a routine apprehension, except for some difficulty with his new bifocals, but Attorney General Ramsey Clark and J. Edgar Hoover, in rare agreement, wrote to tell him otherwise, commending Welch for heroism "in the highest tradition of the FBI."[12]

Matthew Kulaga was severely beaten, bound, and robbed, his wife tied to a bed and raped, and they considered themselves lucky.[13]

The cold butchery of Kitty Genovese had receded into the public subconscious, a vague horror which still could be instantly resurrected by a scream in the night—always sharpened by the unforgettable self-indictment "I didn't want to get involved"—but its terrifying details had become progressively blurred by time . . . until March 18, 1968.

On that date, Winston Mosely escaped from Buffalo's Meyer Memorial Hospital, where he had been taken from Attica State Prison for the removal of a concentrated-juice can he had forced into his rectum.[14] Following the operation, he had suddenly attacked his guard and in seconds he was gone, and with his escape the grisly details of the Genovese killing flooded back into focus.

Once outside the dreary yellow hospital, Mosley limped-ran across a busy street, desperately searching for sanctuary, which he managed to find a few blocks further in the run-down, unoccupied frame house owned by the Kulagas, at 278 Dewey Avenue.

There, for three days, he was a passive spectator at his own manhunt, watching the massive police effort on the Kulagas's television, living on oranges and preserves, regaining his strength.[15] On Thursday morning, when the Kulagas stopped by to check on the house, he was ready. And after a leisurely two-hour assault he finally departed, taking with him a loaded .32 caliber revolver, assorted jewels, cash, two of Matthew's cigars, and their 1962 Comet sedan.[16]

Mosely headed west on the New York State Thruway.

Trinity Church sat serenely in an open field, well back from the narrow road in front, a calendar-scene church with a clean, white, frame steeple, as tranquil, nearly, as the adjacent cemetery. Located on Grand Island in the Niagara River, Trinity Church presumably offered refuge from both cares of the world and the mainland, and the only apparent reason for worry, as the children arrived for nursery school on March 21, was that the recent rain would produce muddy little shoes. Otherwise, the arrival ritual was routine, a brief occasion for parents to socialize, which Gladys Costanzo extended by stopping across the street for coffee with Mary Patmos after dropping both of their children at the church.

At home with her six month old, Mary Patmos appreciated company. Although Gladys Costanzo did not know it, Darlene Wirtz planned to stop by a little later in the morning as well, ostensibly to adjust a nursery school bill, but really to visit.[17] Grand Islanders were mostly good neighbors, in part because there had been, historically, so few of them. Even after the bridges built to the mainland in the 1930s jumped the population from 626 to 16,000,[18] it remained a pleasant, close-knit, bedroom community, and the Patmos garden

apartment in Williamsburg Court was typical of the comfortable suburban housing which attracted residents. Almost everyone worked somewhere else, but Niagara Falls and Buffalo were both close commutes, an easy ride east on the New
York State Thruway.

Three hours later, Gladys Costanzo returned to the
church, right on schedule to pick up the children, although
she must have thought she was running late because she was
running.

Running frantically.

Mosely.

Mosely. Gun.

Mosely. Mary and the baby.

If she did not return with a car in twenty-five minutes, he
would kill Mary and the baby.

Precious seconds ticking, Gladys Costanzo phoned her
husband from the church, desperate to know what to do. Jim
Costanzo knew: He called the Buffalo FBI and asked for Neil
Welch.[19]

"I started with what I knew. I knew where Mosely was,
knew he would kill his hostages instantly if he saw a police
car, knew I couldn't get there in twenty-five minutes.

"I radioed my ace, Frank Ryan, an agent who could handle
anything. He was about fifteen minutes from the church—I
told him to get to the church and take command there.

"Then I telephoned the church. The line was busy, but for
once I was able to do what I had often tried unsuccessfully—
persuade the operator to break into the call for an emergency.

"The pastor was highly emotional, so I ordered him to sing
hymns or say prayers or do whatever he needed to get control of himself and to follow Special Agent Ryan's orders to
the letter.

"Then I called Buffalo Chief of Detectives Ralph Degen-
hart, a close friend. I asked him to come to my office immediately, not telling him why. We jumped in the only car we had,
a broken-down old Plymouth, and raced for Grand Island."[20]

Gladys Costanzo called Mary and said she had been delayed by a party at the nursery school.

A few minutes later Mary called the church.

She asked Gladys to come back.[21]

"I got on the car radio with Ryan at the church, trying to line up a story for this woman. We had two hostages at risk—we weren't going to let her go back in the apartment and have three.

"We finally decided she would drive a car to the building, park in front of the Patmos window where Mosely would see her, get out, and place the car keys in plain view on the roof, then turn around and walk slowly back to the church.

"We thought Mosely might bite on it—and we hoped if he came out, he would come alone."[22]

If the driver had been looking for adventure, his career choice would have been an over-the-road rig instead of a diaper-service truck. He was singularly unprepared for the two carloads of men with guns who confronted him just down the road from Williamsburg Court.

Welch had spotted the truck and ordered agents to bring it to the command post he had set in a shopping center, a half mile from the apartment. There, the terrified diaper man was received by a swelling swarm of police—New York State policemen, Buffalo policemen, Erie County sheriff's deputies, and FBI agents—bristling with submachine guns, shotguns, and every hand gun imaginable.

There was no time to explain.

They stripped off his uniform and put it on a detective, while a handful of police and agents scrambled into the back of his truck. In seconds, the truck was heading back down the road to the total bewilderment of its dazed driver, who watched its disappearance—while in his underwear.

The critical reconnoitering of the area, precluded by Welch's order to keep police vehicles out of sight, would be accomplished by the diaper-service truck, now driving sedately into Williamsburg Court.[23]

"Now we knew exactly what Mosely could see from the apartment.

"About fifty of us made our way by foot to the rear of the apartment complex. Immediately behind us was a crowd of reporters and television crews, who had materialized from nowhere.

"I took the forward position at the corner of the Mosely building. The woman drove up in front—she could see us but he couldn't—got out where Mosely could see her clearly, waved the car keys, and put them on the roof.

"But before she could walk away, Mosely put his gun to the baby's head and motioned her to come inside. The woman started to break down and headed for the front door. Another agent and I eased around the corner, creeping through a muddy flower bed, and grabbed her off to the side before she could go back in.

"We weren't sure if Mosely had seen us, but Plan A had come up a cropper, and I realized we needed Plan B in a hurry."[24]

Robert Hunter left his apartment with his briefcase, walked a few yards, and stumbled into a scene from a movie.

A silent movie.

Dozens of law enforcement officials were crawling into position around the building, automatic weapons everywhere, and dozens of other people with cameras and notepads were fanned out behind them.

Even if he might have believed his eyes, his ears made it impossible, because they heard nothing, no sound at all. It was not real.

A rangy man with glasses signaled to him. He wanted to borrow a telephone.

Mrs. Hunter made Neil Welch take off his muddy shoes. Welch looked up the Patmos number in the phone book and to the woman who answered, he said, "May I talk with your guest?"[25]

"I had not planned any particular conversation with Mosely, but he and I were on the telephone together, so I told him I was the FBI chief in the area, and state, county, city, and local police under my supervision had his apartment surrounded. There was no possibility of escape.

"He mostly listened.

"I told him he should not do anything stupid or harm his hostages, and I would be over to speak to him so we could resolve the matter without further difficulty.

"By then, I had a hunch—that I could talk to him."[26]

Surrounded. He had been surrounded before, alone with Kitty Genovese surrounded by thirty-eight people, invisible people just like the ones the man said were out there now. They had not interfered.

"I could run much faster than she could, and I jumped on her back and stabbed her several times. She fell to the ground and I kneeled over her."[27]

One of the invisible people had yelled at him then, the only time—"Leave that girl alone!"[28]—just like the man on the telephone now, someone he couldn't see, telling him what to do.

He had interrupted the murder to move his car.

"I realized the car was parked where people could see it and me, so I moved it some distance away. . . ."[29]

"I had a feeling this man would close his window and go back to sleep and sure enough he did. . . ."[30]

"I came back because I knew I'd not finished what I set out to do."[31]

She was gone. He had glanced around furiously, tried one door—locked—next one she screamed, shrieked, cold knife cut, scream, gargling bubbles, blood.

He had walked away leisurely then, still surrounded, still in control, what he set out to do finished.[32]

Here, now, it would be the same.

Men moved outside, and he jerked his gun up at Mary and the baby.

Three men.

He held up one finger.

"I rapped on the door. He opened it just enough for me to edge through, then he jammed his automatic pistol in my stomach and I was off balance and it pushed me backward into a chair.

"Simultaneously, he slammed the door and chain-locked it while I made hand motions to the woman with the baby, who scooted into a back bedroom and slammed the door.

"He pointed the gun at me, and we maneuvered around without much conversation, totally involved with each other.

"Then we heard glass breaking in the rear of the apartment, and we both knew the woman and baby were out.

"We were about five or six feet apart, standing, tense.

"I finally sat down. I tried to project calm and confidence, like it was a poker game, and started talking again. I talked about his mistakes, his life in prison, FBI shows on television, the impossibility of any escape, whatever seemed to catch his interest.

"He ran the gamut of emotions. Sometimes he was highly agitated, nervous, like a cat with its hair standing up, then he would seem calm, then suddenly he would be anxious and excitable again.

"He kept cocking and recocking his gun, holding it dead center on my chest. He didn't realize it, but I had a small snub-nosed revolver pointed at him too, although it was in my weak left hand, in my overcoat pocket.

"The apartment was too hot. It was a cool March day, and I was warm as soon as I got inside—I couldn't take off my overcoat, because of my gun, and my glasses started steaming over.

"Worst of all, it was my first day with new bifocals. I was trying to judge sight angles, the angle of his fire and mine, and no matter where I moved he seemed to be in that fuzzy breaking point between far distance and close distance on my new bifocals.

"It was a helluva way to get ready for a gun battle. I finally decided to take off my glasses until the steam cleared off, but then I laid them down and couldn't find them. It forced me to take my eyes off him—I was groping around and he asked what I was doing and I said looking for my glasses, had he seen them?

"It was not what they teach at the FBI Academy, but it turned out to be a welcome diversion for both of us.

"I shifted the conversation to prison life. I told him we could make sure his rights were respected, and he could contact me afterward if he had any problem there.

"We were at a delicate point in the conversation when the phone rang. It kept ringing.

"I told Mosely it would be best if I answered it—we couldn't get anything accomplished with that phone ringing. We maneuvered around each other, neither of us taking our eyes off the other or giving up our sight patterns. I picked it up.

"It was a television news reporter, who wondered what was going on. I told him Mosely and I were discussing things calmly and thanked him for his interest—he told me he had deadline pressures, and his editor wondered how long the crew would have to stay out there. I apologized for the delay and told him I was certain Mosely would understand his problem.

"It was like the bifocals—it broke the tension.

"I hung up the phone, walked over to him, stuck out my hand, and said, 'Give me that gun, Winston. Now's the time.'

"He looked at me and handed over the gun."[33]

"Mr. Welch! Mr. Welch! You've just spent exactly fifty-eight minutes at gunpoint facing a demented three-time killer, a lifer with nothing to lose—how do you talk to a man like that?"

Pause. Deliberation.

"Very . . . politely."[34]

No one could ever say that J. Edgar Hoover was the oldest man in the FBI, simply because, with characteristic attention to detail, he always kept a few agents even older on the duty roster. They did not necessarily appear for work, and whether their duty was active was arguable. It was beyond debate, however, that the Director was seventy-three when Welch met with him following the Mosely capture, and his appearance of ruddy good health could not obscure the fact that he had been debilitated by age—politically. Agents saw, perhaps more clearly than Hoover himself, that the Director's annual presidential exemption from mandatory retirement, initiated by Lyndon Johnson in 1965, operated to strip the Bureau, year by year, of the political independence Hoover had spent four decades building.

Other coming changes, essentially generational, would have been invisible to Hoover simply because his insight was more acute as to past, rather than to future, generations. He was undoubtedly reassured, for example, to note that the Bureau employee publication which reported Welch's visit also pictured the agents attaining twenty-five years of service, and they were still all male and white (and the publication's centerfold, "Miss Print—May, 1968," was fully and chastely clothed). But he could not have imagined the metamorphosis which would occur over the next quarter century, particularly since the students who infuriated him by chanting "One, two, three, four, we don't want your fucking war" were eligible to avoid it—by joining Hoover's FBI, by then a draft deferment.[35]

Law enforcement had been simpler in the 1930s, and the big cases of that era increasingly dominated the Director's conversation, which may explain why he was unusually attentive to Welch's account of the Mosely capture. It was his own encounter with Kreepy Karpis in 1936, good man against bad man (though Hoover, unlike Welch, had been completely covered by a few dozen other good men with guns), conducted with courage and success. The memory must have been warm and agreeable, the confirmation that at least one agent could still handle cases like Hoover himself even more satisfying. He commented and questioned, fatherly proud that Buffalo groups had named his agent "Man of the Year" and "Hero of the Year." Hoover would have even enjoyed Welch's new nickname, "the Cardinal," bestowed by Buffalo agents certain he was destined to become a prince of the church, Hoover's Church.

The Director never imagined, as the meeting ended, that the Cardinal already was presiding over a schism, having secretly created a splinter sect in Hoover's FBI.

The one-story complex of drab yellow-brick buildings on North Forest Avenue looked sufficiently noncombatant to fit comfortably into the residential neighborhood, its cyclone fence probably just a bureaucratic requirement, its barbed wire topping some weekend warrior's wishful thinking. The sign in front, "U.S. Army Reserve Center—Amherst," was fully accurate as far as the army reservists knew, and even the officers who had authorized the FBI to move a dozen agents into an unused corner of the facility in the late 1960s were not precisely certain what Neil Welch planned to do from there which could not be done in the Buffalo FBI office downtown. There was no particular concern, however, because everyone knew that FBI agents had as much discretion as army privates; the activity, whatever it was, would certainly have been approved, through channels, by J. Edgar Hoover himself.

Once the FBI moved in, it was mildly surprising that they did not install the standard "Federal Bureau of Investigation" sign on the building, and the maintenance personnel who went inside periodically never saw an FBI seal or Hoover's picture on the wall. Eventually, however, it became clear that there was an explanation for that. Most of the men who worked at the site were apparently not FBI agents at all (a conclusion later supported by the fact that the several FBI listings in the Buffalo telephone directory never included the North Forest Avenue location). Indeed, the only agent regularly present at the Reserve Center seemed to be the man in charge, Francis Ryan, a husky six-footer with a cop's confident bearing and an agent's regulation haircut. The others, flaunting beards and sideburns, gaudy rings and gold chains, were the walking antithesis of Hoover's twin commandments, "Never embarrass the Bureau" and "Look like an agent."

But Welch thought they were the right men. Ryan could be trusted—Welch's closest friend in the FBI had assured him of that—and Welch had personally evaluated the motivation and abilities of the others. He had deliberately assigned several disciplinary problems to Ryan, knowing that minor infractions often reflected an agent's impatience with the Bureau status quo, and he had tried to measure men who could cope with abrupt isolation from family and friends. It was an inexact science, however, and Welch could not afford a single miscalculation.

Back in the Buffalo field office, the men who did look like FBI agents also looked angry, knowing only that twelve agents had disappeared from the office but that their cases had not, instead being reassigned by Welch throughout the office. They did not know where the twelve had gone, but there was a general suspicion that they could not be doing any useful work, wherever they were—because they had no cases. Despite the widespread resentment, however, no one ventured to ask the SAC directly where he had sent the men, and so it was several months before they finally pieced together the answer: Neil Welch had created the first full-time undercover surveillance squad in the history of the FBI.

The technique was not new. Fifteen years earlier, Welch had successfully impersonated a laborer at a New Hampshire nursing home, wearing the prescribed gray work clothes as he tended the grounds, the perfect vantage point from which to cover an extortion in progress at the residence next door.[36] Later, in Mississippi, Welch helped to refine surveillance techniques against the Ku Klux Klan and had become convinced by the FBI successes there that undercover criminal intelligence was a valuable investigative tool.

It was also, by the mid-1960s, a necessity. Ramsey Clark's Justice Department ordered the FBI to shut down all warrantless wiretaps,[37] an edict which Hoover effectively lampooned by total compliance. He had FBI wiretap equipment collected nationwide and ceremoniously buried in the ground at Quantico. Complaints poured in. Local law enforcement agencies had come to rely on FBI wiretap intelligence—as had a number of important federal officials—and the Director helpfully explained to every caller that the Attorney General had ordered the shutdown. It was not long before President Johnson was drawn into the furor, which was of course what Hoover had intended, and the Bureau ultimately restored a select few of the wiretaps which the Attorney General had pulled—restored at the request of the President.[38]

Nevertheless, Clark's shutdown order caused a drastic reduction in FBI intelligence about organized crime, which had been drawn largely from illegal taps in crime family homes and haunts around the country. (Pre–air-conditioning, the quality of intelligence was subject to seasonal fluctuation, typically being best in cold weather, when family members were inside near the microphones, and marginal in the summer, when they relaxed on the front stoop.) The setback seemed irreversible, since even the most imaginative agent could rarely get close enough to any major crime figure to obtain probable cause for a court-approved wiretap; the difficulty had been inadvertently explained by Hoover himself in an interview.

"You won't find long hair or sideburns à la Namath here," the Director stated, with firm satisfaction. "There are no hippies. The public has an image of what an FBI agent should look like."[39]

It was a disability not shared by Ryan's men who worked

out of the North Forest Avenue reserve center. They dressed like mobsters and mixed easily with mobsters, lounging in wide-open night spots and driving flashy customized cars (which had been standard FBI cars until Welch sent them in for what he innocently, but accurately, described to head-quarters as "body work").[40] They were not FBI agents, the Magaddino family was certain, any more than the two el-derly ladies who frequently lunched near Stefano Magaddino at his favorite Italian restaurant, chattering in old-country Sicilian, were FBI agents.[41]

And indeed, in a sense, the men Welch had assigned to his surveillance squad were not FBI agents at all. As one of them commented, "I had the feeling that, on paper, we didn't exist."[42]

In Hoover's FBI, what did not exist on paper did not exist at all.

Neil Welch calling for Mr. Hoover.

A Bureau supervisor took the call. Or tried to—Welch re-fused to talk to him.

Neil Welch demanding to talk to Mr. Hoover.

It was not done. SAC's did not simply pick up the phone and dial the Director, so the call was bucked to an assistant director, who curtly insisted on knowing what Welch wanted.

Welch wanted to talk with Mr. Hoover.

Seething headquarters officials finally transferred the call to Miss Gandy, Hoover's longtime personal secretary, and Welch agreed to leave his message with her.

"Please tell Mr. Hoover," he requested politely, "that I got Magaddino for him."[43]

It was a sensational announcement, and stunned head-quarters officials immediately demanded to know why they had not been informed of the indictment. Welch's answer was unthinkable: There was no indictment. Not bothering with a grand jury, he had arrested Stefano Magaddino, the most powerful member of La Cosa Nostra's elite national commission, along with nine other major organized crime figures, the same way a reckless driver would be arrested—on a simple complaint. It was, headquarters grudgingly conceded, legal—but simply not done.

Welch's critics in Washington did not, however, include J. Edgar Hoover. A Senate committee had identified Magaddino as the "irrefutable lord paramount" of Buffalo-area organized crime five years earlier,[44] which made the arrest certain to be valuable at appropriation time, and the $530,000 Welch had seized from Magaddino's attic and funeral home ensured the sort of sensational press coverage Hoover loved. Welch did his part there too, in responding to a reporter who asked about the defense claim that Magaddino was too ill to be fingerprinted. "It won't hurt. We just want to hold his hand."[45]

The seventy-seven-year-old Magaddino apparently found the entire procedure to be painful. On receipt of his arrest warrant, he went promptly to bed, claiming illness, which agents derisively diagnosed as Sicilian flu. Welch accommodated the infirmity by scheduling a bedside arraignment, which turned somewhat indecorous when agents bounced the don's mattress up and down. While sucking on an oxygen tube, the don gasped in between bounces, "Take-a the gun! Take-a the gun and shoot me, that's what you want!"[46] When the arraignment was over, Welch escorted the judge into a sealed-off room behind the don's parlor and asked him what he was reminded of by the ten chairs formally arranged in two rows in front of a larger armchair. The judge studied the room for an instant, then replied, "Why, it's a goddamn courtroom!"[47]

Most of all, though, the Director liked Welch's statement, in every news account, that J. Edgar Hoover had personally coordinated the investigation and arrests. And even as nominal coordinator,[48] he was not at all curious about how Welch had managed to slip his agents into the clandestine restaurant meetings at which Magaddino's lieutenants accounted for gambling proceeds and passed the money under the table. It was just as well. The Director might have had difficulty comprehending that Welch's probable cause had come from

a Sicilian-speaking, gray-haired old lady, who had been recruited by the surveillance squad and who, after eavesdrop-
ping on lunchtime conversation for several months, began
switching the napkin holders at Magaddino's favorite table so
that he could speak into the one containing the tiny micro-
phone authorized by the court.[49]

Eventually, after several years of pretrial wrangling, the
court ordered that the Magaddino informants be identified
or the charges dropped, and the government, observing
ironclad FBI procedure, protected its informants and with-
drew the case. By then, however, fallout from the arrests had
disintegrated the crime family, splintering it into feuding
factions. The Magaddino leadership had been broken by the
FBI's revelation that he had $530,000—and that in a year in
which he claimed profits too meager to permit normal cash
distributions to family members. Indeed, the embarrassment
of riches had been evident even as the arrests were occur-
ring, most eloquently articulated by Magaddino's daughter-
in-law, who said of her husband, Peter, "That dirty son of a
bitch. Until today I never thought there was a Mafia—I asked
him to take me to Florida this winter and he told me we were
broke!"[50]

No one recognized it at the time, but the Magaddino case
was also a watershed event for the FBI, defining battle lines
in the conflict between headquarters and field which would
flare in Hoover's final years and rage after his death. Neil
Welch would be a principal combatant in that struggle, and
undercover criminal surveillance—pioneered in the Magaddino case, later to be refined in Detroit and perfected in
Philadelphia—would be his primary weapon.

The notion of assigning agents to full-time criminal surveillance work was, on several grounds, a heretical innovation.
Hoover had decreed that all cases had equal value, a fallacy
required to infuse significance into the statistics he regularly
rained on Congress, and he required that all field agents
carry comparable caseloads.

Welch's surveillance squad had no assigned cases at all.
Their cases would be those developed by their penetration of

organized crime—which was itself a forbidden activity. Accordingly, any success or failure by Ryan's unit had equal potential for disaster—if discovered by Hoover. The Director's opposition to undercover criminal work was historic and well known, apparently reflecting his fear that criminality, like scarlet fever, could be contagious. Agents exposed close up to criminals might become criminals.

It does not seem to have occurred to Hoover—perhaps because he never had the opportunity to become acquainted with Mario—that the major organized crime families and their myriad illegal enterprises would remain permanently impenetrable unless FBI agents learned to work undercover with criminals.

Indeed, while Hoover lived, the notion that it might be possible to cripple the LCN underworld undercover would never even be seriously debated at his Bureau, because of a single overriding institutional concern. Headquarters could not control agents who worked undercover. There would be no record of where they went and what they did, no files for inspectors to inspect, no statistics to justify punishment or reward. That was the heart of the heresy. It would gradually become clear, as Welch's skirmishes with Hoover's lieutenants escalated, that they were fighting about control, struggling to determine whether officials at Bureau headquarters or SACs in the field would inherit control of Hoover's FBI.

Mario was indifferent.

A ranking New York City organized crime figure, he had decided to assist Welch's undercover agents for reasons of his own. He was only vaguely aware that J. Edgar Hoover even existed and had open contempt for most FBI field agents. Nevertheless, from the time he first approached Welch in the late 1950s until his death from heart failure in 1982, Mario was a uniquely productive informant—a nationally known crime family figure who worked for the FBI. His information would prove as useful in Detroit and Philadelphia as it had in New York, generating dozens of mob convictions, and his insights from a career of crime became the unorthodox basic training for Welch's undercover agents.

Welch's alliance with Mario—like the existence of his off-premises surveillance squads—would remain secret from Bureau headquarters until after Hoover's death in 1972, but by the late 1960s a barrage of front-page Buffalo headlines confided that he was obviously doing something different.

RAID YIELDS FORTUNE IN LOOT[51]
POLICE ARREST 4 HERE, FIND $150,000 GEMS[52]
5 HELD IN $1.7 MILLION ART THEFTS[53]
FEDERAL AGENTS SMASH GAMBLING RING HERE[54]
FBI ACCUSES 5 OF MILKING VEGAS FLIGHTS[55]

Case after case, Welch matched and surpassed his previous accomplishments, backed by an enthusiastic team of agents who would follow him anywhere, as they proved in July 1969. For three days, Welch led thirty heavily armed agents on a house-to-house search for a kidnapper, coordinating the massive dragnet by helicopter. By then, Buffalonians had become so accustomed to Welch at the scene of the crime that no one (except a few disgruntled members of the Canadian Parliament) thought it particularly remarkable that the resulting headline revealed the crime scene to be forty miles inside a foreign country.

KIDNAPPED GIRL IS FOUND IN ONTARIO—PATRICIA ANN MARTIN IS "ALIVE AND WELL," FBI CHIEF REPORTS[56]

Celebrated by agents as "Welch's invasion of Canada," the case also proved memorable for other reasons. Welch had gone alone into the small bedroom where the emotionally distraught kidnapper, a large woman named Ann Ikeda, had barricaded herself; as he tried to persuade her to surrender, she nervously stroked a large stuffed animal on the bed. Suddenly it moved, and proved to be a very much alive ocelot, "one size smaller than a damn leopard!"

Then, after making the arrest, Welch was confronted by a bewildered State Department official, who wondered why the FBI was arresting a Canadian citizen in Canada. After Welch talked his way past that objection, the official informed him that Lindbergh-law kidnapping was not extraditable un-

der the existing treaty with Canada—a defect which Welch
cured by magically producing a New York State kidnapping
warrant seconds before Canadian officials moved to throw
out the case.[57]

Success followed success. Congratulatory letters from Hoover, a prized rarity for most agents, cascaded into Welch's
Buffalo office in numbers which made them routine, a phenomenon which simultaneously infuriated and neutralized
the jealous headquarters hierarchy. They had, however, a
reliable remedy for problem field offices—inspection.

Inspectors from Bureau headquarters were universally
dreaded visitors in the field, in part because of their reputation for arbitrary unfairness—but in larger part because the
price of their approval was often quite tangible. Inspectors in
the field expected and received free meals and entertainment, gifts and trips, and the agents under inspection knew
that "samples" of local industry and commerce, preferably
wine and liquor, were always welcome tokens. Predictably,
inspection reports showed a clear correlation between a field
office's generosity and its performance rating. The inspectors
often returned to Washington with bulging suitcases, and
their careful inventory of booty received was one of the most
closely studied statistics at headquarters—a benchmark to be
surpassed in the next inspection of that office.

But inspection was generally believed to be effective in its
primary objective, which was to assure headquarters control
over the field. As one agent explained, "Although the rule
said each agent had to run one hundred miles a day, headquarters knew that no one ever ran more than two or three
miles. But if Hoover was angry, then the inspectors swooped
in, and you were disciplined for not running one hundred
miles a day."[58]

The difficulty was that Hoover was not angry at Welch, and
so the inspectors who swooped into Buffalo fluttered back to
Washington, reporting as always what the Director wanted to
hear: Welch's office was running smoothly, by the book.
Welch had taken a calculated risk and won—for the time.
The inspectors had not seen the North Forest Avenue site, of

course, nor Frank Ryan's agents who worked there, and they did not realize that a simple head count of Welch's agents would have showed him twelve men short. The inspection report changed no minds among Hoover's lieutenants but did dictate a change in timing: The threat which Welch represented could not be addressed until Hoover perceived it, which would not happen until October 1971.

But even before that, the Director could be induced to strip Welch of his Buffalo power base. On May 10, 1970, the day the Welches went to settlement on a new home they had purchased in Buffalo, Hoover wired him orders to report, as agent in charge, to Detroit.[59]

At his farewell party, Buffalo agents presented Welch with a plaque on which two highly polished bronze spheres were mounted, oversized ball bearings. It was a memento which did not, for anyone in that room, require explanation. Opinions differed as to whether the plaque commemorated Welch's defiance of Mosely, Magaddino, or Bureau headquarters, but everyone agreed that the Cardinal had fully earned his brass balls.

Mario, for reasons of his own, concurred.

9

Mario

"What I liked about you, Welch, you were a go-getter.

"What you did for me, I couldn't believe.

"But no amount of money could have made me work with you guys. I was no fucking paid informant. It was what you did. I couldn't live with myself if I took money. I wouldn't even let them pick up my hotel bill.

"After I started with you, I worked with an agent in Miami, and I wound up supporting the Bureau. My agent needed sixteen hundred dollars, he couldn't get it from Washington —so I gave it to him. The Bureau doesn't seem to understand that when you're out there knocking around, you need a roll of cash. When they're buying drinks, you have to grab the bill, and it's all cash.

"Can you imagine blowing a whole deal because someone caught you with a queer credit card?

"Next time I saw the agent's boss after giving him sixteen hundred dollars, I said 'Hey, this is reverse shylocking—I oughta charge you vig.'

"He didn't even know what vig was. I had to explain, on loan-shark money, I'm supposed to charge you interest every week.

"That's the trouble. Most agents have no idea what goes on out there, and when you help them, it puts you in jeopardy along with them. Most agents don't even understand that undercover is the only way. I asked an FBI supervisor how he was planning to get inside the mob and I couldn't believe what he told me.

" 'Legwork.'

"One time I was helping the FBI on a guy who was heavy into queer money. I went to the guy, told him who I was, and gave him five names, family members, that he could call to check on me. I told him I would come back in twenty minutes. When I came back, he was ready to do business. He gave me fifty thousand dollars in queer money to show my buyer.

"I called my agent and told him we had scored. He said he was tied up on something, he'd come see the money tomorrow. I said 'Fuck you. I could have a traffic accident or anything and I'm holding this guy's money. Fuck you and the white horse you came in on.'

"After you went to New York, Welch, they had a female agent on a jewelry case. She and her partner were supposed to make a million-dollar buy in a hotel room at 3 A.M. The agent tells her to put on her nightgown—she says, 'Oh no, I can't do that.' He says 'OK, then get outta here, I'll get a hundred-dollar hooker and she'll do a better job.' That's how agents are going to get killed—if I come in there at 3 A.M. and the broad is all dressed, I know something's wrong.

"How do you expect to penetrate the mob? Irish guys can't. You should have a school in Washington and take a guy like me and teach agents what moves to make. If you're supposed to be from Brooklyn and you don't know Carmen, you're dead. That simple. Carmen, that's all, they won't even give you a last name—and if you try a bluff, you're still dead, because they'll check.

"To me, it became a game, a challenge—but I had to feel comfortable with the agent. Sometimes it's impossible. You can't make every college kid into a wise guy—they don't know how to dress, how to talk, how the hell do you take them anywhere?

"I took one agent, gave him a list of names, members from all over the country, and made him memorize them. Then I gave him a test. After that, he was OK. When someone asked

'Do you know Joey in Tucson?' he would say 'Sure, I know Joey and Frank through Mario.'

"He could go anywhere. I made unbelievable cases with him, and he kept getting promotions and awards, plus once in a while he'd get a seven-hundred-and-fifty-dollar raise, which was funny, since we were breaking up millions of dollars' worth of action.

"Finally they gave him a five-man squad, and he called me up and said 'Mario, you've got to break these guys in.' So I did. I worked with all of them, taught them how to walk, how to talk, the moves, everything. And they were good.

"If the Bureau really wanted to break the mob, all they need is about ten agents, trained like that. Give them funds, whatever the job calls for, and let them operate.

"They could break any syndicate wide open.

"But those idiots who sit in Washington with all those fucking flags behind their desks, Welch, they don't want to."

10

Heretic

The first person Bureau headquarters ordered Welch to find in Detroit was the whiskey man.

Not that he had ever been lost. For as long as anyone could remember, the Detroit office had supplied untaxed Canadian whiskey for shipment to top Bureau officials, one of countless small accommodations to mollify headquarters and one made possible by the whiskey man. But when a new SAC arrived, it was necessary for him to renew the contact, with the appropriate introductions, of course, to make certain there was no interruption of the flow.

After several weeks of ominous silence from Welch, a headquarters official finally made a gingerly inquiry.

"Yes, I located him," Welch replied, to Washington's palpable relief. "As a matter of fact, he died rather suddenly, and I was just on my way to his funeral. Perhaps you would want to send a contribution, in view of his long years of service?"

"Oh, shit!"

The Bureau phone slammed down.[1]

Daily at dawn, Detroit Edison blew its stacks, setting the mood in the FBI office across the street with fine black soot. It layered every surface, every day, reminding agents with each smudge that they were in the bastard office of the Bureau, where the most reliable law was Murphy's.

A bullet accidentally discharged in the Detroit squad room

did not simply bury itself in the wall, as in other field offices. Instead, it crashed through a glass-paneled door, ricocheted crazily down the marble-walled hall, whined through the steno pool, and finally came to rest in the startled U.S. marshal's office, a mishap matched only when a confiscated shotgun somehow blasted a shell through the closed trunk of a Detroit agent's speeding car, wounding a woman on the street.[2] The wrong man, arrested occasionally by agents everywhere, seemed to be invariably in the company of prominent citizens when agents blundered in the Motor City, and mistakes quietly made right elsewhere regularly made headlines in Detroit.[3]

"If it happens anywhere, it'll happen in Detroit" was the agent axiom about trouble, which happened there often enough that the city on the Detroit River was nicknamed River City, a career graveyard which consumed a record nine SACs in less than seven years.[4] The office was renowned for its bunker mentality, exemplified by its report to headquarters, when the office was faced with a shortage of cars, that it had somehow developed a surplus of agents; giving back agents seemed more prudent than asking for additional automobiles.[5] Any remaining flicker of agent morale had been extinguished along with the bloody 1967 riot, which blazed twelve days, killed forty persons, and suggested that Detroit after dark was more hospitable to crime than to punishment. Taking no chances, the office ordered all post-riot arrests completed prior to 6 P.M., a curfew aimed at preventing headquarters recriminations rather than Detroit crime.[6]

Avoiding Washington's attention carried risks of its own, however, because the Bureau's neglect was never benign. Hoover had not bothered to visit Detroit in decades, and his absence assured the office's permanent presence in the dreary and dilapidated federal courthouse.[7] All efforts to move to a new location were rebuffed—gloom ballooned. Leaving for the streets, agents often tossed a handful of paper clips into the small fans churning the stale air.[8] It was a trademark farewell gesture, which sprayed the room with metal and accurately reflected the disposition—and discipline—of the men Neil Welch found when he arrived in Detroit in May 1970.

But Welch also discovered in Michigan the only indispensable ingredient for success in the business of crime fighting—an abundance of quality crime. The Purple Gang had organized crime in Detroit early, qualifying for charter membership in La Cosa Nostra, and the family business was generously flavored with labor racketeering and spiced by political corruption and pervasive street crime. After his first survey of the state, which revealed the annual total of FBI gambling cases in Michigan to be roughly half the number he had produced in Buffalo monthly, Welch pronounced the state a "virgin forest" of organized crime and left no doubt that lumberjacking was on his mind.[9]

He encountered some initial resistance from his agents. At a conference of resident agents from the local FBI offices in Grand Rapids, Flint, Saginaw, Kalamazoo, and other small cities, a veteran agent advised Welch, paternally, that organized crime did not really exist in the outlying regions; it had always been limited to Detroit. In that case, Welch replied evenly, since organized crime was to be his top priority, he would simply close the local offices and move all agents back to Detroit. In agitated whispering among themselves, the agents immediately reconsidered, and a few minutes later they reported that organized crime was, indeed, alive and flourishing throughout the state of Michigan.[10]

The ghosts which Bureau headquarters saw in Michigan dictated different priorities. To the extent that Washington's preoccupation with internal security required the actual existence of at least one hotbed of radicalism somewhere, the place which had spawned the Black Panthers, White Panthers, Students for a Democratic Society, Republic of New Africa, and Nation of Islam held obvious potential as a national showcase.[11] And with Welch's arrival, the Bureau's battle against subversion finally had an assured payoff—either the New Left would be crippled by his success in implementing COINTELPRO, or Welch's career would be ruined by his failure.

In the end, the conflict in Detroit over FBI priorities and techniques—internal security versus organized crime, COINTELPRO versus Welch's covert criminal surveillance —would escalate into a battle over the future direction of the FBI itself. And ironically, Welch's summary execution of the whiskey man would forecast the outcome, demonstrating that headquarters was impotent to force Welch to do anything which the aging Hoover had not personally approved.

There was no public announcement when the survey company moved its operations into the basement of the warehouse at Fourth and Fort streets, although business moving back into downtown Detroit was, in late 1970, something of a rarity. From appearances, though, it was not much of a business. Office furniture and files were moved in without any prior renovations to the run-down space (which, it would be remembered later, did not even include toilet facilities), and potential customers were greeted by a locked front door. The rent was probably minimal, but it was still difficult to imagine that the men who occasionally came and went, always carrying large rolls of blueprints, were doing enough to cover it.

From the Anchor Bar next door, it was not clear at first whether the surveyors were good neighbors or bad. They never patronized the Anchor (which distinguished them from most other nearby workers, especially those at the Detroit *News* across the street, who found the Anchor so inviting so often that newspaper management had plans to turn it into a parking lot).[12] But neither did they pound on their common wall when the bar crowd became too raucous. Perhaps they knew that any protest would have been futile. A Detroit institution, the Anchor operated by its own rules. When an emergency decree closed every bar in town during the 1967 riot, the Anchor's green doors stayed open,[13] understandably, since the city's mayor and a sprinkling of its councilmen, judges, and police were regularly present behind them.

The most dependable patron of all, however, was Charles

Sherman. He arrived punctually every morning at seven-thirty, seated himself on his personal bar stool at the end, and ordered bacon and eggs. A rumpled man in his mid sixties, Sherman was a somewhat improbable barfly since he did not drink. But he remained rooted to his stool until ten-thirty daily, within easy reach of the pay phone on the wall, which he answered every time it rang. His conversations were invariably brief, but he had dozens of them every morning. He departed, on schedule, just before the lunch crowd arrived.[14]

Sherman's attraction to telephones, the surveyors next door knew, was well established. On one of the most recent of the sixty-five occasions on which he had been arrested, he had been found at home amid a clutter of *Daily Racing Forms*, methodically working two phones and six extensions. He was also known as Chickie, and for years he had been known, as well, to be the central figure in a massive gambling network which cobwebbed the entire state of Michigan.[15]

The garbage yielded evidence that he had "feasted on Florida citrus fruit from trusted friends"; the lady across the street reported that vandals had ripped down his Christmas lights; someone else thought he had been seeing a psychiatrist about his nightmares. But the real bombshell was that anyone would dare to rummage through J. Edgar Hoover's trash and question his neighbors, and the news in Jack Anderson's New Year's Eve column was that the seventy-five year old Hoover could be criticized with apparent impunity.[16]

1970 had been a very bad year.

The Kent State tragedy had been followed by a leaked report that the FBI considered the shooting unjustified, which Hoover angrily rebutted by claiming that "extenuating circumstances" had caused the guardsmen to fire.[17] The leak and the rebuttal, together, managed to inflame both sides of the political spectrum, right and left, an acrobatic feat which a younger Hoover could never have accomplished. More protests came when Special Agent John Shaw was forced out of the FBI for writing a paper, in a college night-school class, mildly critical of Hoover's policies. Hoover's harshness was then tragically counterpointed when Shaw's wife was found to be dying of cancer, leaving him unemployed with four small children. (Hoover nevertheless refused to reconsider his "with prejudice" termination, which effectively barred Shaw from all law-enforcement positions.)[18] The Director was attacked on the floor of Congress for his undocumented charge that the Berrigans planned to kidnap Henry Kissinger.[19] And Hoover seemed to confirm Ramsey Clark's charge that he was "petty" by calling Clark a "jellyfish" in response.[20] But the strangest exchange of the year was saved for last, a hot little firefight triggered by Hoover's mid-December observation on presidential security.

"You never have to bother about a President being shot by Puerto Ricans or Mexicans. They don't shoot very straight. But if they come at you with a knife, beware."[21]

New Mexico Senator Joseph Montoya led the outcry on behalf of the nation's Hispanics (which required some acrobatics of his own, since to avoid saying that they could so shoot the President, Montoya had to cast Hoover's remarks as an aspersion on Hispanic character, rather than marksmanship),[22] and the Director was forced to acknowledge by return mail that he "readily understood the concern which prompted you to write," though he carefully avoided any apology and attributed the problem to undefined "misinterpretation."[23]

While Hoover faux pax made headlines, however, Neil Welch found the most troubling news of 1970 in a hardly noticed Hoover success—his veto of the Huston Plan. Sidestepping an urgent presidential demand for intensified domestic intelligence, Hoover declined to participate in the proposed burglaries, mail intercepts, and electronic surveillance, making it clear that the Huston Plan was not his plan.[24] (Later, critics would contend that Hoover's objections reflected a more acute appreciation of bureaucratic turf— which the plan would have split between the FBI, CIA, DIA, and NSA—than of constitutional principle and that he eventually permitted partial implementation of the plan anyway.

By then, though, his answers, if any, had been buried with him.)[25]

But Welch was convinced the Huston Plan was not Huston's either. FBI Intelligence Division head William C. Sullivan had chaired the committee which fathered it, and while it would have taken a paternity suit to be sure, Welch strongly suspected that the Huston Plan was really the Sullivan Plan with a White House imprimatur. Even those who called him "Crazy Billy"[26] never questioned Sullivan's mental capacity, and Welch had tangled with Sullivan over internal security tactics enough to understand the origins of both the nickname and the plan. (Welch's surmise was accurate. After Hoover rejected the plan, young Tom Huston advised H. R. Haldeman that the FBI officials responsible for domestic intelligence operations "privately disagree with Mr. Hoover and believe that it is imperative that changes in operating procedure be initiated at once.")[27] Sullivan was not crazy enough to challenge Hoover directly, yet, but through his close relationship with Assistant Attorney General Robert Mardian he could arrange for proposals rejected by the Director in-house to be made again by the White House, a bold end run which measured Hoover's age more accurately than a calendar.

The import of the Huston Plan, then, was not in Hoover's rejection of it, but rather in the fact that a Hoover subordinate had staked his FBI future on pleasing the White House rather than the Director. It meant that Assistant Director Sullivan had a strategy for expunging the first word from his title, betting that White House enthusiasm for his domestic intelligence initiatives would insure their success and his succession. It was a tactic which jeopardized field agents more than Hoover (who, after all, could and soon would fire Sullivan), leaving them uncertain whether bag jobs and wiretaps urged by Bureau headquarters had been approved by Hoover or the White House or by no one. And for Neil Welch in Detroit, Sullivan's new dominance sharply raised the stakes in the controversy over internal security which had smoldered between the two men since 1968.

DATE: 5/10/68

TO   : All SACs
FROM   : Director, FBI
SUBJECT: COUNTERINTELLIGENCE PROGRAM
         INTERNAL SECURITY
         DISRUPTION OF THE NEW LEFT

Effective immediately, the Bureau is instituting a Counterintelligence Program directed against the New Left Movement and its Key Activists . . .

The purpose of this program is to expose, disrupt, and otherwise neutralize the activities of the various New Left organizations, their leadership and adherents . . .

Law and order is mandatory for any civilized society to survive. Therefore, you must approach this new endeavor with a forward look, enthusiasm, and interest in order to accomplish our responsibilities. The importance of this new endeavor cannot and will not be overlooked.

DATE: 5/23/68

Remylet to all offices dated 5/10/68, advising of the institution of captioned program. In addition to the analysis requested therein, due at the Bureau by 6/1/68, you are instructed to prepare a separate communication to reach the Bureau on or before 6/14/68, to include the following detailed information:

1. *False Allegations of Police Brutality.* Detailed information is desired to counter the widespread charges of police brutality that invariably arise following student-police encounters . . . It is anticipated this data can be used through friendly news media to vividly portray the revolutionary-type actions and militant nature of the New Left movement.

2. *Immorality.* Specific data should be furnished depicting the scurrilous and depraved nature of

many of the characters, activities, habits, and living conditions representative of New Left adherents.

3. *Action by College Administrators.* Set forth information to show the value of college administrators and school officials taking a firm stand in resisting militant minority elements attempting to disrupt or take over college campuses. Specific examples should be given to show the results of being firm, as opposed to a vacillating attitude in considering student demands . . .

DATE: 5/29/68

In connection with your review of college campus newspapers, you should commence submitting articles which might be utilized for appropriate dissemination. Items submitted should be extremely radical on their face, use profanity or be repulsive in nature. It is anticipated that these articles, editorials, et cetera, can be effectively utilized through dissemination to responsible individuals, such as state legislators, friendly news media, and the like . . .

DATE: 7/5/68

. . . As an economy measure the caption "COINTELPRO-NEW LEFT" should be used on all communications concerning this Program.

DATE: 10/9/68

ReBulets 5/10/68 and 5/23/68.

The above communications advised of the necessity of taking immediate action to expose, disrupt, and otherwise neutralize the activities of the New Left . . .

Despite these instructions and in the face of mounting evidence of their moral depravity, little evidence has reached the Bureau to indicate field offices are using this information to best advantage.

To make this program more effective in this re-

gard, each office is instructed to be particularly alert
for this type of data. Where a student is arrested
during a demonstration or his participation in a
demonstration is accompanied by the use of or en-
gagement in an obscene display, this information is
to be promptly incorporated into an anonymous letter which can be directed to his parents . . .

COINTELPRO-NEW LEFT was a natural extension of the
Bureau's counterintelligence efforts against the Communist
Party, which had relied heavily on crank calls and fraternity
pranks such as ordering pizzas for fifty to be delivered, collect, to a cell meeting of fifteen Communists.[28] The indis-
criminate use of such tactics against the New Left would,
when discovered, make COINTELPRO an instant bad word,
obscuring the legitimate value of counterintelligence and in
the process crippling the FBI's ability to penetrate organized
crime. But that was not yet clear in 1968. It was obvious from
the beginning, however, that if the Bureau messages creating COINTELPRO were an accurate barometer of Weatherman pressure, the storm center was confined largely to Washington. Neil Welch—and most other SACs in the field—did
not believe that the FBI mission included reporting obscene
gestures to parents, and COINTELPRO planners at headquarters were frustrated from the start by Welch's refusal to
participate in the program.

Welch's defiance, however, was not as risky as it seemed,
because there was considerable uncertainty about the participation of another FBI official, namely J. Edgar Hoover.
COINTELPRO directives always came under Hoover's signature, but the specific follow-up orders frequently came via
the "B System," a whisper-down-the-lane network which by-
passed official headquarters channels.[29] Baltimore told Boston, which told Buffalo, and it was generally surmised that no
one told Hoover.

Certainly no one told him about the demand for anonymous letters which triggered Welch's first COINTELPRO
clash with Sullivan in late 1968. The directive had been for

agents to flood the local media with letters from "A Concerned Citizen" and "An Angry Taxpayer," attacking the tolerance for radicalism at an area university. Welch had viewed the plan as silly and dangerous (since FBI prose was perhaps the most recognizable institutional idiom in the country) and ordered his agents to ignore the request.

A few weeks later, Sullivan called, his celebrated temper at full boil, and furiously berated Welch on a trivial, unrelated issue. Finally Welch interrupted.

"What's your *real* problem, Bill?"

"It's the letters, goddamn it!" Sullivan roared. "When we order letters, you're going to produce letters!"

"Whoever dreamed up that plan is an idiot!" Welch shouted back. "I'll write those letters when I see Hoover's signature on a piece of paper ordering it."

"Neil, you know damn well Hoover won't approve these things," Sullivan had replied, adding that his Intelligence Division had to work around the Director on many of its priority projects, a disclosure which confirmed Welch's suspicion and reinforced his refusal.[30]

By 1970, however, it was apparent to Welch that Hoover was equally unwilling—or unable—to stop COINTELPRO excesses, perhaps because the amount of paperwork filed at headquarters varied inversely with the propriety of the project. Often, Bureau records simply did not exist. Field agents received COINTELPRO indoctrination—orally—when they went to Washington for in-service training, and they returned to Detroit with bizarre counterintelligence schemes so regularly that Welch initiated a formal debriefing program.[31] Those hopelessly poisoned by their Bureau instruction were summarily reassigned to the bank robbery squad, where they could do no harm.

Even that precaution was not totally effective, as Welch discovered on October 23, 1970, when he received a letter from Bureau headquarters asking for evidence that the proposed counterintelligence step against the Black Panther Party for which he had requested "a quart of foul-smelling liquid and dispenser" could be accomplished with proper security.[32]

Welch went wild.

He ravaged the correspondence files while bellowing at his supervisors, promising violence on everyone involved. It took only a few minutes to find the letter request, which had been prepared, predictably, by an agent fresh from in-service training.

> The Bureau is requested to prepare and furnish to Detroit in liquid form a solution capable of duplicating a scent of the most foul-smelling feces available. In this case, it might be appropriate to duplicate the feces of the specie sus scrofa.
>
> A quart supply, along with a dispenser capable of squirting a narrow stream for a distance of approximately three feet, would satisfy the needs of this proposed technique.[33]

Welch instantly killed it three ways in Washington, notifying the Bureau that the project did not have his approval, that it was not contemplated, and that the request should be destroyed.[34] In Detroit, he moved to starve the COINTELPRO projects which did require paperwork, ordering top supervisor Norm Rand to lock every double-zero (internal security) file in his safe and to refuse all requests for access.[35] (The internal security files would cause Welch one final problem, though, when Bureau headquarters finally insisted on opening Rand's safe five years later and discovered that all of the files had mysteriously vanished.)[36]

Welch succeeded and failed. The distilled feces of pig (which, its Bureau inventors proudly claimed, had a permanent potency which belittled the best efforts of the biggest skunk and would dictate the demolition of any room in which it was sprayed) never reached Detroit, but the COINTELPRO program which had produced it continued to proliferate crazily. Assistant Director Sullivan could not prevent Welch from canceling the order, but he would find an opportunity to make him pay the price.

Although they would have mutually resented the comparison, it was an irony of history that the declining authority of two great twentieth-century bureaucrats was simultaneously chronicled by pictures on walls. This irony was sharpened by the fact that, of the two, the pictures signaling the disintegration of J. Edgar Hoover's empire were considerably more inscrutable than those foreshadowing the decline of Mao Tse-tung.

Indeed, an observer viewing the amateur landscapes which graced Welch's Nine Squad area would have had difficulty imagining that they were revolutionary, even given Hoover's firmly established artistic preferences. In the early years, field offices had been limited to hanging pictures of Hoover himself (a universal selection), photos of FBI training scenes (a time-lapse shot of multicolored tracer bullets searing a shadowy landscape was the favorite), or framed copies of the Director's favorite credo, "Loyalty" ("If you work for a man, in heaven's name work for him; speak well of him and stand by the institution he represents . . ."). All were available from headquarters in numbered copies, suitable for framing.[37] After the war, agents who had seen the world wanted to see more variety on their walls. While Hoover stopped safely short of letting a hundred flowers bloom, he did tacitly approve field office display of historical scenes, such as the *Battle of Lexington,* and railroad prints, usually *Horseshoe Curve.*[38]

The Director might even have tolerated the Nine Squad landscapes, but for one radical feature—the walls on which they hung were not in the Detroit FBI office, but rather in the basement of a Dearborn commercial complex, where Welch's criminal surveillance squad operated without Hoover's knowledge or control.

While the Nine Squad site remained covert, Welch's disregard for headquarters priorities was no secret to anyone at the Detroit field office. In September 1970, in a dramatic all-agents meeting in a large federal courtroom, he had announced the reassignment of every agent in the office, deploying an unprecedented 60 percent against organized crime and downgrading internal security from top to bottom in importance.³⁹ It was a dangerous reversal. No FBI agent had ever been disciplined for lack of success against organized crime, while Bureau censure for failure to meet internal security quotas was automatic, which meant that Detroit agents would be forced to run the gauntlet he was throwing down to headquarters.

He had more. With rhetorical irreverence ("If they can't run a better shop and keep their personnel, why should the FBI be the collectors of their stragglers?"),⁴⁰ Welch abruptly warehoused the previously priority military-deserter cases and Selective Service violations, assigning a single agent to go through the paperwork motions for headquarters without any actual investigative effort. (Later, Welch discovered that by simply writing to draft dodgers and deserters, suggesting that they surrender, he surpassed the previous results of massive investigations).⁴¹ Still, Welch was expected to announce a bold initiative against the Bureau's "Private Enemy Number One," the Weatherman group, because he had sent agents to Ann Arbor to explore the feasibility of enrolling, undercover, at the University of Michigan. Instead, he reported his conclusion that such a project would succeed but that the Weatherman threat did not justify the resources, and he ordered his agents to stay off the campuses.⁴²

And privately, after the meeting, Welch ordered Nine Squad agents to stay out of the Detroit FBI office, apparently confirming the report which was by then being whispered incredulously over the field agent grapevine.

"We had all heard wild things about Buffalo," Special Agent Jim Sandler recalled. "It was rumored that some of their agents never went to the office, didn't keep street cards or time cards, and went flying around the country without the Bureau knowing about it. But knowing how headquarters operated, no one thought much of that could be true."⁴³

Having been named to head Nine Squad, Sandler was the first to learn otherwise. Welch manufactured an excuse for him to go to Buffalo, where Frank Ryan briefed him on off-premises criminal-surveillance techniques.[44] Seeing Ryan's Buffalo operation, Sandler understood immediately that compliance with the orders of SAC Welch was likely to place him in jeopardy with FBI Director Hoover. But Welch had, again, accurately sized up his chosen agent, and Sandler had no difficulty making a choice. He would boss Nine Squad for Neil Welch.

Back in Detroit, Sandler went to work. He knew a vice president at the Bank of Dearborn (where most agents banked) who put him in touch with the Dearborn office-complex owner, who was happy to supply any space the FBI needed, no questions asked.[45] During the next month, the nineteen men in Nine Squad traded dark suits for work clothes, laying down carpet and throwing up dry wall, running the wires and phone lines required by the state-of-the-art electronic equipment which they moved into their basement office. As it gradually became apparent that they would spend more hours at the surveillance site than at home, they added kitchen and sleeping facilities, finally completing the project with a small gymnasium area.

"The man is here!"[46]

Without warning, Welch came to inspect. Agents followed expectantly as Sandler escorted him through the site, waiting to see if their work would have his approval. Welch said nothing until he had seen it all, then turned to face the squad.

"Men, I would be proud to have the Director here today to see what you've done," Welch said (a statement which conveyed more approval than truth). Then he launched into an enthusiastic pep talk, predicting that Nine Squad would spearhead a dramatic breakthrough against crime. It was a forceful, animated performance, which excited even the cynical veterans, and Welch concluded with a promise which they all would have laughed at two months earlier.

"Our program is going into high gear, and I can assure you of one thing: We are going to bring organized crime in the state of Michigan to its knees."[47]

No one laughed.

No one doubted it.

And everyone was pleased when Welch paused on the way out to compliment them on their art work, landscapes painted by one of the Nine Squad agents.[48]

Fresh from her honeymoon, it was understandable that the new Mrs. Hartman was somewhat unnerved, since she had expected to spend her first night in Detroit with one FBI agent, not three.

Unfortunately, the Hartman apartment happened to be in the precise location agents needed to monitor a court-approved wiretap, and Special Agent Hartman's FBI colleagues did not think he would mind if they installed their equipment in his second bedroom. It was regrettable that most of their monitoring had to be done at night, but the two agents did move out promptly once the project was completed, four weeks later. It was, in retrospect, only one of a number of small inconveniences associated with the Anchor Bar investigation.[49]

Neil Welch had recognized, sooner and more clearly than others, that the court-supervised wiretaps authorized by Title III of the 1968 Omnibus Crime and Safe Streets Act[50] was a potent new weapon against organized crime. Probable cause for Title III surveillance of the Anchor had been obtained without difficulty, but the probe had nearly died at birth. One of the first conversations overheard by the FBI revealed that the Detroit *News*, having purchased the Anchor to demolish it, was likely to bust the bar before the FBI could.[51] Welch intervened. He managed to persuade publisher Peter Clark to defer demolition while agents installed the sham survey company in the space next door, but that accommodation created a new complication. The *News* would keep Welch's secrets only if it knew them, which meant giving a reporter access to the Detroit FBI office while the undercover investigation continued. Flabbergasted agents, knowing that press contacts could be fatal in Hoover's FBI, navigated around the "newsy" in their squad room in wide, careful circles, with the approximate respect they might have extended to a man-eater.[52]

Man-eating was a more concrete concern at the survey
company site adjacent to the Anchor, where the undercover
agents were certain the huge sewer rats they heard—but
could not see—were capable of it. From January until May
1971, agents worked through the night in their dank, un-
heated space, meticulously compiling evidence of the gambling empire operating in the bar next door. It was miserable, monotonous work, aggravated by the absence of toilet
facilities, an inconvenience which agents remedied by opening a T joint in the pipe which ran through their space. There
was another difficulty—Welch's Anchor Bar investigation
had mushroomed across Michigan so dramatically that
agents, having begged and borrowed all they could, were
running short of electronic surveillance equipment.[53]

"Some guy yelled something about the FBI and I looked
and Chickie and this other guy named Black Joe were gone,"
an astonished bar patron reported. "I thought they had got
away."[54]

They had not.

On May 6, 1971, promptly after he finished his bacon and
eggs at the Anchor, Chickie Sherman was arrested by FBI
agents on gambling charges, a misfortune which had occurred as regularly as his birthday, but which was, this time,
different: The FBI dragnet which snared Chickie also caught
Black Joe and 149 other citizens, including 16 Detroit police
officers. Directed by Neil Welch, 400 agents struck simultaneously in 37 Michigan cities, a precision blitzkrieg which was
the largest gambling raid in FBI history. When it was complete, organized crime was not quite on its knees, but its
pockets had been vigorously picked. Welch announced that
the gambling network had grossed nearly $1 million daily.[55]

He was in a position to know, it developed, because the
FBI had the entire case on film. The Detroit *News*, which
seemed to have exceptionally detailed coverage of the investigation, reported that undercover agents had, with court
approval, mounted an ultrasensitive television camera flush
against a hole in the survey company wall and filmed the

Anchor action continuously for two months. The camera, Welch said, was similar to the one used by astronauts on the moon, and defendants hoping for a silent movie were disappointed by the disclosure that FBI sound men had snaked microphones along the water pipes into the Bar.[56]

The most significant aspect of the case, however, was the fact that it was announced in Washington by Attorney General John Mitchell[57] (who had been briefed on it by the Strike Force attorneys who had prepared the wiretap applications, documents which would later damage many of the prosecutions because they had been signed by Mitchell's top assistants rather than the Attorney General himself, as the law required). Neil Welch had conducted the largest gambling raid in history, the first videotaped investigation ever, and J. Edgar Hoover read about it in the newspapers.

(Even without the Director claiming personal credit for the case, Welch had competition. Immediately prior to the raids, he was sitting with Detroit *News* editor Martin Hayden when the Justice Department press officer called to leak the story. Hayden said he already had it—the astounded press officer said that was impossible. Hayden handed the phone to Welch, who said, "We beat you, you bastard!")[58]

> ". . . I can spot a Red, always
> Under every bed, always,
> Presidents come and go
> But they get to know
> I will boss the show, always."

The actor, escorted by an elderly companion, hobbled unsteadily off the stage, and the Gridiron Club audience broke into uproarious laughter. It was Saturday, March 20, 1971, and everyone who was anyone in official Washington was laughing at J. Edgar Hoover, which was the most conclusive evidence to date that the last line of the skit was false.[59]

It was already clear that the coming election would be the first one in which a major-party candidate thought attacking Hoover made political sense. Three weeks earlier, Senator

George McGovern had sharply criticized the Director for his dismissal of Special Agent John Shaw, buttressing his blast with an unsigned letter from ten FBI agents who charged that the Shaw case was not an isolated incident and, even more mutinous, that the FBI's statistical accomplishments were "for the most part, phony."[60] (McGovern should have realized, however, that paper would always be the wrong weapon to use against Hoover, even if he was politically debilitated. The Director saw McGovern's ten-agent letter and promptly raised it, releasing a supportive letter from twenty-one Bureau officials.[61] When someone suggested that they had no choice but to concur, Hoover immediately showered McGovern with more than two hundred similar letters from FBI clerks and secretaries.)[62]

Hoover was not the only one sending information on the FBI to McGovern. On March 8, a group calling itself the Citizens Commission to Investigate the FBI burglarized the local FBI office in Media, Pennsylvania, departing with nearly one thousand previously secret documents,[63] the most embarrassing of which arrived in Senator McGovern's mail a few days later. McGovern returned the documents, unread, to the Bureau, but the newspapers which also received copies felt no such compunction, despite Attorney General John Mitchell's plea that disclosure of the documents could "endanger the lives or cause other serious harm to persons engaged in investigative activities on behalf of the United States."[64] The papers published the documents, which detailed COINTELPRO-NEW LEFT strategy, and it was promptly apparent that Mitchell had been half right. No FBI lives seemed to be endangered, but J. Edgar Hoover's reputation was seriously harmed.

Hoover reacted reflexively. He angrily transferred the Media agent in charge to Atlanta and complained, through spokesmen, that the published documents presented a distorted picture of FBI activities. No one argued. College professors and Black Student Unions (along with a Boy Scout leader who had planned a camping trip in Russia) seemed to be the targets of Bureau COINTELPRO efforts, based on the documents, and that certainly was a distortion of FBI priorities. Worse, the intelligence activities which Hoover's critics claimed excessive would prove insufficient to solve the Media burglary; despite a massive effort, Hoover was impotent to crack his own case.

(Hoover was nevertheless determined to lock barn doors, using the Media catastrophe as a pretext for the wholesale closing of FBI resident agencies (local offices), which he had always viewed as dangerously independent since they reported not to headquarters but instead to the area field office. In Michigan, Welch was ordered to close two of his eighteen RAs and to assign agents full-time to guard the others. He refused, pleading inadequate manpower and pointing out that the two proposed for extinction happened to be the hometowns of an important congressman on the appropriations committee and a United States senator. Frustrated, the Bureau inspector ordered Welch to select two others. Welch roared back, *"You* pick two!" The inspector declined, and it was dropped.)[65]

The critical fusillade intensified. Senator Edmund Muskie charged that undercover FBI agents had infiltrated Earth Day;[66] House Democratic Leader Hale Boggs accused Hoover of ordering wiretaps on congressmen;[67] and when there seemed to be a lull in those firefights, the FBI obligingly fired three secretaries for antiwar activity in their off-hours, triggering a new barrage of criticism.[68] Indeed, as 1971 progressed, Hoover himself emerged as the most frequent violator of his longtime dictum "Never embarrass the Bureau," and before the year ended, one Hoover blunder proved worse than embarrassing.

From the earliest airline hijackings, the Director had issued rigid orders that any hijacked craft which landed must not, under any circumstances, be permitted to take off again. Agents were to shoot out the tires and refuse refueling, no exceptions. It was the sort of no-nonsense approach which had been successful against crime in the thirties, and which field agents, who regularly ignored the command, knew would be disastrous in the sixties and seventies. A TWA pilot had confirmed their view in 1969, charging that the FBI's unsuccessful effort to keep his aircraft on the ground at Kennedy Airport was "irresponsible and reckless."[69] (Retaliating immediately, Hoover had prohibited any future travel on TWA by FBI personnel.) The pilot of a small plane hijacked in Jacksonville in late 1971 was less fortunate. His final moments were on tape, and after the Bureau lost a court effort to keep the recording secret, the nation's newspapers printed the chilling transcript.

> PILOT This is 58 November. Uh, this gentleman has about 12.5 pounds of plastic explosives back here and, uh, I got no, uh, yen to join it right now so I would please . . . appreciate it if you would stay away from this plane.
>
> TOWER This is the FBI. There will be no fuel. Repeat. There will be no fuel. There will be no starter. Have you cut your engines?
>
> PILOT Uh, (gasp), I don't think this fellow's kiddin'— I wish you'd get the fuel truck out here.
>
> TOWER 58 November. There will be no fuel. I repeat. There will be no fuel.
>
> PILOT This is 58 November. You are endangering lives by doing this, and uh, we have no other choice but to go along and, uh, for the sake of some lives we request some fuel out here, please.

Moments later, the FBI shot out the plane's tires. A gun battle erupted. When it was over, the hijacker had killed himself, his wife—and the pilot.[70]

Stung by the tragedy, Hoover summoned the SACs from all major FBI field offices to Washington for a conference on hijack procedures, an unprecedented action. (He had historically taken pains to prevent group gatherings of SACs and had instead ordered them to report individually to his office, seeing two each week, for in-depth performance reviews. Agents maneuvered to rig the pairings, seeking to shine by comparison with an SAC in trouble, which had its own risks since Hoover's wrath might spill over. In later years it no longer mattered, because the Director was frequently confused, commending the SAC in for discipline and violently berating the one who had expected praise. He finally dropped the two-a-week ritual altogether in the early 1970s.

The SACs thought the hijack conference was a promising indicator that headquarters was ready to address the critical problems they faced in the field, and early on the first day they extended an invitation for the Director and Mr. Tolson to be their guests at dinner.

The first thing J. Edgar Hoover noticed that morning was the locator sheet, a report which showed where each key FBI official would be that day. Incredibly, it indicated that all of his major office SACs were right there in Washington.

What were they doing?

Who had authorized it?

One of his lieutenants gingerly explained they were discussing hijack procedures, on his instructions, and that they would enjoy entertaining the Director and Mr. Tolson at dinner.

Hoover exploded. If all of his field commanders had time to meet in Washington, they must not have enough to do in the field. And in any event, they should spend their time in Washington working, not having dinner parties.

The SACs were informed that the Director did not have time for dinner and neither did they.

He never appeared at the conference.

The last line of the Gridiron satire echoed through 1971, its mockery steadily amplified by reverberation from Bureau blunder to crisis and back, until finally Hoover could no longer ignore it. It was an irritation which had actually gnawed since the year before, when editorial writers had responded to the resignation of Hoover's energetic assistant director Cartha "Deke" DeLoach by wondering, out loud, who was going to run the FBI now. (On learning of

DeLoach's planned departure, Hoover told him bitterly, "I thought you were the one who would never leave me," revealing, perhaps unintentionally, a self-view of divine dimensions.)[71] Hoover's simmering anger over that question had then been inflamed by the building consensus that its answer was no one. Finally, in June 1971, he decided to prove that he was still boss at the Bureau.

He would do it, as he had over the years, by arbitrarily transferring a handful of SACs around the country, starting with Neil Welch, whose name came readily to mind because he had been obstructing Sullivan on COINTELPRO.

Neil Welch communicated to Hoover by mail, which was futile, and by Miss Gandy, which was not.

His letter explained that personal circumstances precluded acceptance of his transfer to New York City and that since he had been in Michigan only a scant year such a move would be highly disruptive to major investigations.

Then Welch called Miss Gandy, the Director's trusted secretary since 1919, and asked politely if she knew why he was being demoted.

She firmly disagreed. His transfer to head the Organized Crime Division in New York City was an important promotion and certainly did not reflect any dissatisfaction on the Director's part.

Welch persisted. He already had total responsibility for the fifth largest FBI office in the country. New York would be a shared responsibility with two other SACs, so it was a clear demotion, and he wondered why.

By the end of their conversation, Welch had gently steered Miss Gandy to the conclusion that he was ungrateful for a major promotion, and the headquarters message traffic which followed captured Hoover's sputtering fury.

6-29-71
TO: DETROIT
FROM: DIRECTOR
PERSONAL ATTENTION

DISREGARD TRANSFER ORDERS, JUNE TWENTY-EIGHT, ONE NINE SEVEN ONE, PENDING FURTHER NOTIFICATION. END

7-2-71
REBU TELETYPE JUNE TWO NINE . . . THESE ORDERS ARE AGAIN PLACED INTO EFFECT AND RECIPIENTS SHOULD ADVISE BY RETURN COMMUNICATION EARLIEST DEPARTURE AND ARRIVAL DATES. END

7-6-71
YOUR PENDING TRANSFER TO NEW YORK AS SPECIAL AGENT IN CHARGE OF THE ORGANIZED CRIME DIVISION IS HEREBY CANCELED. END[72]

It was a summer storm, brief and violent. Hoover flip-flopped furiously, changing his mind twice about whether Welch's orders to New York City were, in fact, a promotion. He finally decided that the dependable Miss Gandy was right, as she usually was; the transfer orders were an attractive promotion for Welch, which, because of his ingratitude, would be canceled.

J. Edgar Hoover was still boss of the FBI show.

"A respected Detroit businessman came to see me, extremely upset.

"He told me that his fifteen-year-old daughter had recently stopped at the public library on her way home, checked out a few books, and left.

"Immediately afterward, a man wearing a 1940s-style hat had approached the librarian, claiming he was an FBI agent, and demanded to know what books she had checked out, how often she visited the library, whether she ever met people there or tried to influence anyone.

"The librarian happened to be a family friend, promptly alerted him, and after he told his daughter, she remembered seeing the same man following her several other times.

"From his description, I already knew who the agent was. I checked our indices and found a subversive investigative file on the girl. She had written for literature from a group the Bureau was monitoring, and as a result, we now had a Special Agent following this schoolgirl everywhere she went.

"I showed the file to her father—he was as horrified as I was. I told him that these were strange times, that he and his daughter had been the victims of some outdated thinking, and I was sorry.

"Then I tore up the file, every page, right in front of him—and said that if I ever got sued I would deny having seen him!

"After the man left, I grounded that agent—permanently. He had been doing what he thought right, but operating under the old rules. I had to make clear to him that the times had changed, even if Hoover's rules had not."[73]

(The public library also figured in a second clash of Bureau rules, as Welch discovered in Detroit. Old-line intelligence agents believed they should spend their time poring over secret files—but if they did it in the office, their "Time in Office" statistic would skyrocket into the disciplinary zone. It was a dilemma they resolved by surreptitiously taking the intelligence files from the office—in violation of another Bureau rule—to the public library, where they could be reviewed in leisurely tranquility.)[74]

Bureau inspectors flooded into Detroit in September 1971, relishing the certainty that Welch would finally fall. There was never particular suspense about the outcome of FBI inspections, but any possibility for surprise in this one had been eliminated by Hoover's continuing anger over Welch's ingratitude. Detroit would fail, Welch would be disciplined, and the only questions were for what and how much.

Possibilities abounded. His summary termination of the subversive investigation of the girl in the library had been whispered back to headquarters, and of course the Bureau had rigid rules regarding the destruction of files, so there was double potential there. The Intelligence Division had finally recognized that Welch was only going through the motions on draft dodgers and deserters and doing less than that on subversive groups. At a Bureau conference on intensifying subversive coverage, Welch's representative had made no contribution at all except to ask why bother, since no act of violence had been attributed to the group under discussion in over forty years.

(The off-the-record answer, from a senior Bureau supervisor, had been an astonishing acknowledgment that the particular organization in question was no threat and that Bureau coverage of it was a waste of time. The supervisor would even concur in termination of the effort, provided it was deferred for six months, which was how much time he needed for retirement. It was, Welch later said, as rational an explanation as he ever heard for the insanity which the Bureau's bureaucrats had institutionalized in COINTELPRO.)[75]

The inspectors were certain that Welch's files on the League of Revolutionary Black Workers (LRBW) would be a fertile field of misconduct since he had brazenly defied a direct Hoover order to penetrate that group the previous spring, and the crackling correspondence from their unprecedented shoot-out had been bootlegged all over headquarters. Hoover had demanded intensified informant coverage of LRBW, charging that its members were active in DRUM (Dodge Revolutionary Union Movement), CRUM (Chrysler Revolutionary Union Movement), and LRUM (Lincoln Revolutionary Union Movement). Welch had replied that LRBW was a handful of dissidents in the United Automobile Workers union, questioned the probable cause for any penetration, and concluded, innocently, that because of the "great risk of embarrassment to the Bureau, I would suggest that this matter be presented to the Attorney General for his views and approval."

Apoplectic, Hoover had fired back seven single-spaced pages in response, documenting the dire threat of the LRBW from sources as disparate as the Senate Subcommittee on Internal Security and the New York *Times*, the British Security Service and *Newsweek*, and renewing his order that Welch penetrate the group. Addressing Welch's heretical suggestion, Hoover conceded that the Attorney General might be consulted regarding any potential criminal investigation but asserted emphatically that "his authority is not necessary for our intelligence investigations" (a remarkable statement which Welch had "always suspected was what they thought at headquarters" but never imagined Hoover would put in writing).[76]

The fourteen-man inspection team stayed two weeks and turned the Detroit office upside down.

When they were finished, what they had found were three file folders which, instead of being properly filed, had somehow slipped under the bottom drawer of a file cabinet.[77]

They had not found the proof of Welch's dereliction of duty, nor the smoking gun which would shoot his career. The chief inspector came close to discovering Welch's covert surveillance site at Dearborn, having heard enough rumors to ask about it specifically, but Detroit agents all said only the SAC could answer that question and Welch refused. And they did not find it particularly impressive that Welch had retooled the Detroit office to produce major criminal cases with assembly-line regularity, underscored by his arrest, in mid inspection, of the grand dragon of the Michigan Ku Klux Klan within hours after the Klan had firebombed ten school buses.[78]

But three misfiled files were significant and would certainly suffice. (Welch had an answer for that too. He noted in rebuttal that they had *not* been found "on a window sill, in the back seat of a Bureau car, in the trash, or under the water cooler," but were in fact in the filing cabinet, the defects of which he attributed to the General Services Administration. The inspector responded, snappishly and unarguably, that they were *not* where they were supposed to be.)[79]

On October 19, 1971, Hoover advised Welch that while his criminal intelligence and informant programs were excellent, his administrative operations were unsatisfactory.

"Based on these continuing administrative deficiencies," the Director concluded, "you are being censured and placed

on probation. If no immediate corrective action is taken . . .
you will be removed as Agent in Charge."[80]

Three months later, Detroit was reinspected and passed
with excellent ratings in all categories.

Welch had not made a single change in anything.

Several years later, immediately before the wrecking ball
swung to demolish the Anchor Bar, two men in business suits
approached the foreman. There was something in the basement, they said, which had sentimental value to them,[81] and
they had brought an acetylene torch to salvage it.

The foreman shrugged his approval.

Inside, the men neatly severed the T joint from the sewer
pipe, which had been their only relief facility during the
Anchor Bar surveillance, and took it away.

Later, they mounted it on red velvet and presented it to
Neil Welch, who displayed it proudly in the Detroit field
office.[82]

11

Death

Shortly after 9 A.M. on Tuesday, May 2, 1972, a supervisor from FBI headquarters phoned Special Agent Norm Rand in Detroit, requesting routine information on a case. Nearing the end of the call, Rand asked conversationally, "What else is new?"

"Well," the supervisor replied, "Hoover died."

"Hoover died! *Hoover* died?!"

"Yeah. But don't tell anyone I told you."[1]

It was not a secret which would keep. By the time housekeeper Annie Fields discovered his body in bed about 9 A.M. (a casualty, at age seventy-seven, of hypertensive cardiovascular disease, the doctors thought, though no autopsy was conducted to confirm that),[2] it was universal whispered knowledge throughout the Bureau that the Director had not yet arrived for work. The significance of that was uncertain, though, since his legendary punctuality had slipped in recent months.

The next ritual always closely scrutinized was the Bureau nurse's regular visit to Hoover's office to administer an injection (of vitamins, it was said, though agents were never certain),[3] a daily event which headquarters Hoover-watchers carefully timed, believing its duration might reveal something about his health or at least his mood. The nurse did not come at her regular time that Tuesday, and the quiet frenzy of fifth-floor activity which came instead portended that she would not be needed again.

Hoover's death was not formally announced until more than two hours after discovery of his body, a delay which was itself a tribute of sorts, since it resulted from the frantic efforts of official Washington to answer the two questions he had successfully evaded during life: What was in his personal files, and Who in government (if anyone) had authority over him (and would thus be the appropriate person to announce his death).[4] It was finally decided that both questions might have a common answer. The Attorney General clearly had authority over the Federal Bureau of Investigation, a recurring delusion, and so it was Acting Attorney General Richard Kleindienst who announced Hoover's death at 11 A.M.[5] Kleindienst also ordered Assistant Director John P. Mohr to seal Hoover's office, change its locks, and report back to him when that was accomplished.[6]

Kleindienst's order, unfortunately, lacked the required bureaucratic precision. Mohr promptly complied in full, and it did not become apparent until sometime later, too late, that the Attorney General had successfully captured a large bag of air. Hoover had nine offices and only his *personal* office had been ordered sealed, and that office contained only, as the loyal Miss Gandy later testified, "his desk and regular office furniture."

No files.[7]

Field agents were stunned, which, given Hoover's age at death, was itself stunning.

Neil Welch, with hundreds of other agents across the country, groped to understand the sense of loss.

"He was a father figure. It left a void. I guess we thought that body would live forever."[8]

    MS. ABZUG How long were you associated with Mr.
        Hoover and in what capacity?
    MISS GANDY First as confidential clerk in July of 1919,

and in steps from that time to Executive Assistant at the time of his death.

. . .

MISS GANDY We had two sets of files. Mr. Hoover's personal correspondence was one set, and the so-called official confidential files was the second set.

. . .

MS. ABZUG What happened to those files that were marked personal?

MISS GANDY They were, on Mr. Tolson's approval and with Mr. Gray's approval, destroyed as Mr. Hoover wanted done.

. . .

MS. ABZUG What was generally contained in the official and confidential files: What is the nature of those?

MISS GANDY That would be hard for me to describe.

. . .

MS. ABZUG Was everything in the personal file destroyed?

MISS GANDY Everything in the personal file, as I reviewed them before I destroyed them, was destroyed with the exception of a folder on the dogs. I kept the file on the dogs' pedigree for Mr. Tolson's information. There may have been a folder about maintenance of Mr. Hoover's house. I would have kept that. That is the kind of material that was in the personal files, and also his personal correspondence of course.

MS. ABZUG Did you look at every single personal file?

MISS GANDY Every single page and every single personal file.

MS. ABZUG I am going to read you a list of names and subjects, and in each case I would like you to comment, tell me if there was anything in the personal files on any of these people or subjects.

Mail openings?

MISS GANDY No.

MS. ABZUG Informants?

MISS GANDY No.

MS. ABZUG Wiretappings?

MISS GANDY No.

MS. ABZUG Black-bag jobs?

MISS GANDY No, indeed.

MS. ABZUG What about the black-bag job memorandum which indicates that it was a personal file?

MISS GANDY It looks like a mistake on my part; that
is, to put the P.F. on it when it should be O.C.

MS. ABZUG Where did you actually put it? Where did
you put it when you filed it?

MISS GANDY I have no idea at this date. The date of
that memorandum is what?

MS. ABZUG The date of the memorandum is July 19,
1966.

MISS GANDY How in the world could I remember
that?

MS. ABZUG That would be difficult.

MISS GANDY At seventy-eight years old that would
be difficult.

MS. ABZUG You are doing remarkably, Miss Gandy. I
compliment you.

    . . .

MS. ABZUG Were there any letters in there concerning Martin Luther King, Jr.?

MISS GANDY I doubt it very much. There would have
been no reason for it. This was a collection of
almost fifty years.

MS. ABZUG Do you think those letters might have
had some value?

MISS GANDY There were autographs which could
have been of value.

MS. ABZUG And you tore those up?

MISS GANDY Indeed, I did.

MS. ABZUG Knowing that they might be of value to
the estate of Mr. Hoover?

MISS GANDY Mr. Hoover would not have allowed
them to be used if he had been living. I had my
instructions.[9]

The table in the Mayflower Hotel where Hoover and Tolson had lunched on Monday (and almost every other week-
day since the early 1960s) was held empty, the red, white, and
blue ribbons which draped it the only acknowledgment that
the Director might not be coming in again. He had looked
well on Monday, Mayflower employees agreed, one of them
adding that Tolson was "the one who's been looking terrible."[10]

At the Anchor Bar in Detroit, scene of Welch's massive
gambling raid the year before, drinks were priced at one
cent apiece in celebration of Hoover's death.[11]

He would not have minded. The Director himself had for
years enjoyed a Jack Daniels highball or two in the evening
(though he considered martinis "poison"), and off-duty
agents could safely take an occasional drink—but never more
than two.[12]

Any agent who had ever served in the FBI could have
glanced at the letter and immediately identified its sender.

Dear Mr. Welch:

Through you, I am pleased to commend the personnel of your division who worked so effectively in
connection with the investigation of the Illegal
Gambling Business case involving Ray Lee Atkins
and others.

All of these Agents approached their responsibilities with enthusiasm and aggressiveness and
thereby contributed substantially to the results at-
tained. I want to ask that you convey my genuine
appreciation to them for the high caliber of their
efforts.[13]

But when the letter came out of a Bureau typewriter on May 3, its sender was dead, lying in state in the Capitol Rotunda. That was not, however, as lifelong companion Tolson knew, an excuse which Hoover would have accepted for late paperwork. And so, on the day after Hoover's death and the day before his funeral, during the only twenty-four hour period in his life when Tolson himself was top man at the Bureau, he signed the letter.

Sincerely yours,
Clyde A. Tolson
Acting Director

The Bureau continued to function smoothly. Miss Gandy instructed Mr. Mohr to handle the funeral arrangements, as Mr. Tolson had ordered, a command chain which made it comfortingly clear that Hoover himself was, somehow, still in charge. His Bureau family occupied the front-row seats of honor at the service. The only discordant note came, predictably, from field agents, who had, in the flurry of last-minute details, been overlooked in the official seating arrangements. It was finally agreed that the agents in charge would enter National Presbyterian Church through a side door and sit in the pews sometimes occupied by the choir, which positioned them perfectly to glare directly at the headquarters hierarchy throughout the service—over Hoover's dead body, which reposed in a flag-draped casket at the front of the church.[14]

It poured rain, all day.

Eulogies were delivered by President Nixon and Chief Justice Burger, and the service itself was conducted by Rev. Dr. Edward L. R. Elson, Senate chaplain, National Presbyterian pastor, Hoover friend. Elson visited Hoover on his birthday each New Year's Day, but the Director's passing caught him by surprise. "I wrote the Eisenhower funeral three years in advance," the cleric acknowledged, revealing less than intimate insight into the plans of the Almighty, "but this one was a little more sudden."[15]

Facing a church full of law enforcement and political elite,
punctuated by fifteen congressmen who were both (having
previously been special agents), Elson prayed that "we may
be as strong as he was strong, brave as he was brave, loyal as
he was loyal."[16]

Once signed by Tolson, the letter to Welch flowed routinely into the pulsing stream of Bureau paperwork—papers
to be routed, sorted, mailed, and filed, moving papers proving that the institutional heartbeat was steady and strong,
confirmation that Hoover's death had changed nothing at
FBI headquarters.

But by the time the letter reached Neil Welch in Detroit,
the mail itself had become one of countless daily reminders
that nothing would ever again be quite the same. Field offices
had for decades planned their schedules around "Bureau
mail," which arrived once daily in a large box, airmail special
delivery from headquarters. The box was rushed directly to
the SAC, who had a large knife ready for its ceremonial
opening, and agents usually contrived some excuse for loiter-
ing near his office until the mail inside was sorted, knowing it
could include their promotion or demotion, censure or transfer, edicts from Hoover without warning or appeal. Once
each week, moreover, Bureau mail brought a letter from
Hoover to all SACs, which invariably recounted a horror
story of agent misconduct set in a thinly camouflaged location ("In a small Southern field office . . ."), completed by a
dire and personal warning about the consequences of any
repetition ("I want you to know that I am highly displeased
about this, and prepared to take drastic action if such misconduct should ever recur in any office").

By the time Tolson's letter of May 3 was received by Welch,
the institution of Bureau mail was as dead as Hoover himself.
The drama was gone. Airmail special delivery boxes from
headquarters would sit unopened in field offices for days at a
time, and when the mail was finally sorted it would be done
by a clerk.[17]

When agents brought a suspect in for questioning, they sometimes attached a device to his arm which, they solemnly assured the man, would reveal immediately whether his answers were truthful.

After May 2, 1972, that device was a lie detector.

Prior to that date, because of the Director's adamant opposition to lie detectors, the device was usually a standard office dictaphone machine with extra wires and lights added for theatrical effect. Agents had discovered, over the years, that when they snapped "The machine says you're lying!" it did not always matter what the machine was.

"I received a call at 2 A.M. from Josh Doran, our senior resident agent in Flint.

"His office had been working an extortion case, in which the victim had received very precise instructions to place the demanded fifty-thousand-dollar payment on the rear seat of an abandoned car in a run-down section of town.

"With great difficulty, Doran's agents managed to slip into the neighborhood unnoticed, and after the victim placed the money on the seat, they patiently watched the car through a frigid Michigan evening. When no one had picked up the money by midnight, they decided to call it off—they ordered a police wrecker to tow the car away, so that anyone watching would not be alerted to their surveillance.

"Once the car was in the police garage, they were startled to discover that the money was gone!

"A closer inspection of the car revealed a large hole under the rear floor mat, and when they went back to the site, they discovered that the car had been parked with that hole precisely over a manhole in the street!

"It was the kind of disastrous case which could have ended Doran's career and mine, and I was laughing so hard I nearly fell out of bed.

"That was when it really hit me, for the first time, that Hoover was dead."[18]

12

Whirlwind

John Whalen's 1970 conviction for burglary in Lenawee County, Michigan, was not particularly devastating, arrests and convictions being tolerable occupational hazards for a professional—so long as they did not result in imprisonment. He remained free pending appeal, which his lawyer assured him would reverse the conviction. This meant that his seven-to-ten-year prison sentence remained purely hypothetical until the summer of 1972, when the affirmation of the Michigan Court of Appeals proved his lawyer wrong.

As a professional, Whalen did not intend to make the same mistake twice. For his appeal to the Michigan Supreme Court, he would rely not on a lawyer, but instead on a Detroit bail bondsman named Harvey Wish, who assured him that a thirty-thousand-dollar bribe would fix the case in the Supreme Court. And wishing to be certain of his freedom, Whalen thought it advisable to have insurance on his Wish, which he obtained by telling the Detroit FBI that he was going to bribe a Michigan Supreme Court justice and agreeing to wear a concealed recording device while he did it.[1]

The next time Whalen talked about his case with Wish, on August 8, 1972, his body bug recorded their conversation, and while portions of the tape were unintelligible, the name that Wish mentioned was unmistakable.

Swainson.[2]

It was improbable enough to be a Wish fabrication. John B.

Swainson had returned from the war with a chest full of medals and no legs, a genuine hero, and had moved swiftly from state senator to lieutenant governor to the second-youngest governor in Michigan history. Returning to private practice, he had continued to command respect for his public service, working unselfishly with organizations as disparate as the American Legion and the Easter Seal Society, and had been mentioned as a possible candidate for the United States Senate.

The investigation might have ended there, except that John B. Swainson had also, in November 1970, been elected to the position of justice of the supreme court of the state of Michigan.[3]

The two men walked briskly through the lingerie section of Weigelman's Department Store, studiously indifferent to the diaphanous slips and frills which framed their path. The clerk was not fooled. Men who bought lingerie generally approached the task with determined disinterest, sometimes circling the area several times before returning to make a gift selection. These two were likely prospects—until they reached the concealed mirrored doors on the far side of the room, moved quickly through them, and abruptly vanished.

Continuing past a storage area, the men made their way onto a freight elevator, which dropped them with grudging deliberation to the basement of the building. There, they walked down a short hall and disappeared, a second time, behind an unmarked door.

Dry-cleaned.

The elaborate approach was Jim Sandler's Nine Squad invention, a precaution designed to leave would-be followers bewildered in the lingerie department. It was an emergency procedure for the rare occasions when Detroit surveillance-squad agents suspected that they might, themselves, be under surveillance.

No one suspected that on Friday, September 22, 1972.

Nevertheless, Neil Welch could not resist employing the

procedure on that date, because it was his first opportunity ever to dry-clean the Director of the FBI.[4]

Inside the surveillance-squad site, L. Patrick Gray surveyed the operation Welch had kept secret since 1966—and was astounded. Radios crackled updates on a criminal surveillance in progress, while agents operated a formidable array of electronic equipment, monitoring court-approved wiretaps. At least Gray hoped they were agents. If he had not been escorted in by Welch, the director might well have thought he had stumbled into La Cosa Nostra headquarters, a room filled with busy men, some bearded and others mustachioed, all dressed with the gaudy good taste of Mafia enforcers. On one side, an agent was arranging wigs and disguises, and in the garage in back other agents worked on a flashy fleet of automobiles. Gray gaped at the scene.

There were more surprises to come. A master of show-and-tell, Welch had prepared a three-hour presentation, complete with charts detailing the surveillance squad's success against organized crime and a full briefing on current cases. (He omitted his favorite embellishment, a whispered disclosure that the drywall-over-cinder-block was "solid lead—it stops the Russian microwaves.")[5] But before he could begin, Gray, regaining his composure, interrupted.

"Who knows about this at headquarters?" he demanded, surveying the extraordinary activity around them. "Who has seen this beside you and me?"

The room fell suddenly silent as Welch considered the question deliberately.

"That's it," he finally replied. "Just you . . . and me."[6]

It was the same question—and answer—which would in another context soon destroy Pat Gray's career, with profound consequences for the Federal Bureau of Investigation.

The beginnings had augured success. Welch had first met L. Patrick Gray four months earlier at an all-SAC meeting in Washington, a democratic innovation which inspired hope that more than a name had changed at Bureau headquarters. There were other promising indicators. Gray immediately relaxed the rigid dress and hair-length regulations which agents both resented and ignored, and while he wore an American flag pin in his lapel, he conceded to a reporter that he did not "see a Communist in every single bedroom,"[7] a refreshing intimation that either his eyesight or imagination was inferior to Hoover's. But the former navy captain had a strong bulldog profile remarkably reminiscent of his predecessor's[8] (a coincidence which gave unexpected new validity to Martha Mitchell's famous quip, at a dinner honoring Hoover, that "if you've seen one FBI Director, you've seen them all"),[9] and he projected a comparable command presence. When he addressed his field commanders, he faced them with crisp confidence, "his feet spread wide like he was on the bridge of a ship."[10]

Even that instinctive nautical stance, however, would not preserve Gray's balance in the heavy weather coming, and the seeds of a storm had already been in the air at that May meeting. Praising Hoover's abstention from partisan politics, the White House had declared its intention to prevent the choice of his successor from becoming an election issue (a declaration roughly as real as Hoover's abstention) and had named Gray only *Acting* Director, postponing the permanent nomination until after November.[11] It was a deft political stroke, which allowed the nation six months to mull whether Richard Nixon or George McGovern would be more likely to appoint a strong FBI Director. Unfortunately, in the interim, it also stripped Gray of any chance to become one, signaling Hoover's passed-over lieutenants that their ambitions might be revived if the Acting Director was enmeshed in the Bureau's problems before he had time to solve them.

Worse, instead of removing Gray's clouds, the White House salted them with Press Secretary Ronald Ziegler's announcement that Gray would "not necessarily" be considered for the postelection permanent appointment, although he would not be ruled out either.[12] Gray's limbo might turn off partisan debate about his selection, but his tenure would clearly turn on his election-year performance—which the White House would have a perfect opportunity to evaluate, when, the following month, five men were charged with burglarizing the Democratic National Committee in the Watergate Complex.

Despite the torpedoes, Gray ordered all ahead full, and the SACs were impressed with his skill in asserting command without repudiating the prior FBI course. He organized his tasks in precise, handwritten memos, paying careful attention to the details of reconciling past and future, as exemplified by his instruction on official portraits.

> Tell Mr. Felt that Mr. Bishop—or whoever handles this sort of thing—can send out my official photos to the Field Offices for display as the Acting Director. But Mr. Hoover's photos are *not* to be discarded. His are to be placed in a place of honor in Field Offices with a suitable inscription underneath.

And, canny enough not to trust the field's sense of suitability, he concluded his instruction to headquarters with the directive "Commence preparation of suitable inscription."[13]

But if Gray's military experience smoothed his takeover, it was also responsible for the only discordant note which Welch heard at the May SAC meeting. The new Director requested input and ideas from his field agents in charge—but only through the Bureau chain of command.[14] It was a requirement which would have the opposite of its intended effect, confining Gray himself rather than the SACs. The links in the headquarters command chain were all surviving Hoover lieutenants, and Gray's rule would make him their captive. The information he received would be what they decided he needed to know, which would prove to be significantly less than it might have been had they not been already maneuvering to succeed him.

Gray had followed his May meeting in Washington with a whirlwind tour of FBI field offices. That symbolic gesture was appreciated particularly by agents in Detroit, who had last been visited by an FBI Director in 1943.[15] Gray had helicoptered in on June 12 to cut the ribbon opening the new FBI office there and flown out again less than three hours later,[16] an appearance so dramatically effective that some agents rated him a "savior," and even the more cautious counted themselves as believers.[17]

(Detroit's new office, the improbable product of a two-year Welch guerilla campaign against the Bureau bureaucracy, gave agents an additional cause for enthusiasm. Unable to obtain headquarters approval to move his offices from the decrepit federal courthouse, Welch had persuaded sympathetic city of Detroit building inspectors to condemn the FBI quarters, and when that failed to move Washington, he had warned that the United Automobile Workers union was likely to organize the FBI clerks if they remained in the building. Headquarters finally proposed moving the office into a second-class facility, which Welch quickly approved, assuring Washington that his agents would not be tempted by the brothels in the same block. Hoover of course killed that proposal instantly, and in the end the Detroit office moved into brand new, first-class office space, the finest FBI facility in the country.)[18]

Enthusiasm replaced surprise as Welch described his Nine Squad operations to Director Gray. Detroit's covert surveillance capability had deeply penetrated organized crime, as Welch demonstrated by inviting Gray to personally coordinate the spectacular arrest of fifty mobsters, cracking a twenty-million-dollar gambling syndicate, planned to coincide with his September visit. (It would have been, for Hoover, an offer he could not refuse. But Gray demurred, instructing Welch ". . . to conduct these without regard for my presence in Detroit. Do it in the regular way and when you are ready.")[19]

Welch's success against organized crime had been extended inevitably into public corruption, and he briefed Gray on major probes underway, highlighted by the Swainson investigation. It had taken an unexpected turn on September 5, when Justice Swainson voted, with the majority of the Michigan Supreme Court, to deny John Whalen's appeal. On September 16, however, surveillance-squad agents had

covertly followed Harvey Wish from Detroit to the Manchester, Michigan, residence of John B. Swainson. They had
watched Wish carry several large packages inside, remaining
there more than thirty minutes. The conversation monitored
on September 22, while Pat Gray was at the surveillance site,
provided new evidence that the bribery scheme was still in
progress.

> WISH What happens, he's already working on it, he's
> got your case and he's going to look at it and see
> what he can do, you know, to get you a hearing.
> If the case is heard . . . if, then you better
> come up with the money.
> WHALEN By when?
> WISH As soon as you can . . . And the court makes
> the decision to review. I know he'll do it . . .
> This is a deal where the worst that can happen
> is, you go to the can and get your money back!
> WHALEN Right, that's right.
> WISH But see this guy has been 100 percent with me.
> I've been in one deal with him where we had
> this arrangement and he couldn't pull it off and
> that was it.[20]

Other important cases were developing while Gray was at
the surveillance site that day, and not all of them were in
Detroit. Despite Miss Gandy's emphatic "No indeed" response to the question about black-bag jobs, agents had conducted a successful one at the Arab Information Center in
Dallas, obtaining information about Palestinian terrorist activities. Associate Director Mark Felt phoned Director Gray
at the site to report.[21] When their phone conversation was
over, agents in the room did not know what Felt had said to
Gray, but it was obvious that the Acting Director was pleased
by what he had heard.

Gray might have been less pleased had he known that the
wily Hoover had, in 1966, written to Tolson that he would not
approve black-bag techniques, concluding firmly that "this
practice, which includes also surreptitious entrances upon

premises of any kind, will not meet with my approval in the future."[22] The Hoover proscription did not extend to lawful foreign intelligence operations (which the Dallas bag job arguably was) but banned burglaries for domestic intelligence and, more important, reflected Hoover's acute awareness that his subordinates (often trying to please the White House) apparently had difficulty distinguishing the two. When a President requested a special favor, Hoover had learned early to be certain that it was on the President's head and not his, a lesson Pat Gray would learn later—and much more painfully.

Completing his Detroit visit, Gray urged Welch to accept a high-level assignment at Bureau headquarters or alternatively a transfer to another field office in need of reorganization.

Welch declined both offers, saying, simply, "There are only two jobs in the FBI worth having. One is mine—and the other is yours."[23]

With Hoover gone, however, both jobs were being buffeted by treacherous crosscurrents which simultaneously destroyed the political independence of headquarters while freeing the field from any semblance of headquarters control. Gray had been unable to accomplish in Washington what he had ordered Welch to do in Detroit, and by summer 1972 it was apparent that the FBI's investigation of Watergate was not being done "in the regular way." White House counsel John Dean had insisted on being present during FBI interviews of White House aides, a major breach of Bureau procedure, and Gray had acquiesced.[24] Later, he shared raw FBI investigative files with Dean, over agent protests. And when agents sought to interview Martha Mitchell, Gray asked permission from her husband John, who undoubtedly spoke for himself when he asserted that his wife would have nothing to contribute. Gray, as a "courtesy," vetoed the interview.[25]

In retrospect, Welch speculates that Watergate might not have occurred had Hoover still been alive. If the conspirators

had sought his approval, his uncanny political instincts would
have almost certainly dictated a denial, Welch believes—for
reasons much the same as those which led to his rejection of
the Huston Plan. If the burglary and related activities had
been attempted without his blessing, Hoover would have
ordered a massive investigation, simply to eliminate the turf
challenge. ("If anyone was going to wire up anything in
Washington, it was going to be Hoover.") Welch speculates,
however, that the results of any Hoover-ordered investigation might have been retained in the Director's personal files
as protection against any presidential delusion that the Director's retirement might be sound public policy, rather than
as material to be utilized in criminal prosecutions.

In short, Welch suggests that the risks of Watergate, had
Hoover still lived, would have far exceeded any possible benefits—a fact of Washington life which even the conspirators
would have recognized.

Welch also recalls that field agents immediately discounted
Gray's declaration that he was moving aggressively on
Watergate when they learned that the Washington field office
was conducting the probe, Washington having always been
viewed by agents as dead last in both aggressiveness and
investigative initiative.

In the field, while Watergate was unfolding, Welch was less
courteous with his superiors than was Gray. When an assistant director asked in June 1972 for Welch's evaluation of
which of his agents would be most suitable, "both physically
and psychologically," for undercover work against the SDS,
Welch replied that he would not recommend any of them.
Anticipating the next instruction, Welch also added that
there were no targets in his area warranting such assignments. Persisting, the official wrote back in August (a personal note, outside normal Bureau mail channels) with a
more specific request.

> Dear Neil:
>   . . . I am trying to get a rundown on the best men
> we would have for undercover assignments for long-

range planning purposes. As you probably know, just before the Democratic Convention in Miami on very short notice we had to select ten of our Mod Squad boys to go down there and work among the street people to try to develop intelligence. We will be doing the same thing when the Republican National Convention starts in the next ten days. Therefore, I anticipate from time to time in the future we may have to call on our best-qualified men for assignments of this type.

I would appreciate it if in a personal note you would give me your evaluation with regard to your best men so that we will have a reservoir from which to draw.[26]

The request was not new. Since 1964, when Deke DeLoach had coordinated an FBI special squad which wired up the Democratic National Convention in Atlantic City (earning the gratitude of his friend Lyndon Johnson and the admiration of Hoover, who scribbled "DeLoach should receive a meritorious award" on the operation report),[27] the Bureau had covered political conventions as faithfully as the television networks did—but for a highly private audience. It was an activity which created political assets for headquarters and potential liability for the field agents who actually did the work, and Welch was not interested. In a short note to the Bureau official, he replied, "I have your note of August 11, 1972, and I promise to give the whole matter a great deal of thought"—and suggested that they discuss it the next time he was in Washington.[28]

The discussion never took place.

But with Gray's problems pyramiding, bizarre domestic intelligence schemes multiplied at headquarters. Welch finally phoned an old friend in the Bureau hierarchy and demanded to know who was approving the insane requests flooding the field.

His friend professed not to know anything about it.

"Everyone in Washington claimed to be in the men's

room," Welch later charged. "I made certain my office was never involved, but I knew what was going on—and so did every official at headquarters."

By 1972, however, with the Watergate cover-up compromising the Justice Department as well as the White House, there was no one in official Washington to tell.

Despite distractions from Washington, Welch's office maintained its consistently spectacular performance in Michigan. A multimillion dollar jewel theft from the elegant Hotel Pierre in New York appeared to be a perfect crime, for a week—the time it took the thieves to move $750,000 in gems from New York to Detroit, where Welch promptly arrested them and recovered the jewels.[29] Hijacker Martin Joseph McNally parachuted from an American Airlines Boeing 727 with $502,000, landing in Peru, Indiana, where he hitched a ride with an agreeable local police chief. An Indiana farmer found and returned $500,000 of the ransom, and two days later the Detroit FBI found and arrested McNally in Wyandotte, Michigan.[30] Agents grabbed a stolen truck containing a $150,000 whiskey cargo, arrested five men, and Welch announced (with mixed metaphor but unclouded meaning) that "we caught them with the meat in their mouths."[31]

The key to Welch's success was his reorganization of the Detroit office into target squads and case squads. The target squads, contrary to Bureau rules, had no assigned cases, but instead they had an open mandate to penetrate sophisticated criminal activity. The case squads, in contrast, operated in traditional FBI fashion, methodically seeking to transform every criminal complaint into a conviction statistic. ("The FBI had always worked on existing cases, when they should have simply sent ten men into town with orders to find the criminal organizations and clean them up," Welch contended.) The target squads sometimes completed their work more quickly than their criminal targets. In the FBI's first major industrial espionage case, Welch's agents infiltrated an international crime ring and arrested a Ford Motor Company research engineer and two Romanian officials for conspiring to steal a secret Ford glass-making process and sell it overseas—before the crime had been committed.[32]

The Swainson case, however, presented the reverse challenge, since agents were convinced by late 1972 that the crime had been committed—but were having difficulty proving it. Pat Gray had been highly supportive. He had written Welch after his visit that ". . . I want you to push it to the hilt, [and] I will be very happy to see the [Swainson] case readied for presentation to the United States Attorney."[33] But the Justice Department was not, repeatedly denying requested wiretap authorizations. Welch grumbled that "the Justice lawyers did not want to find corruption on the supreme court of Michigan or any other state," but he pushed the probe ahead anyway, encouraged by a recent development.

On October 17, even though Whalen was not on its agenda and had no motion pending (his final appeal having been denied by the full court ten days before), the Michigan Supreme Court had nevertheless reversed itself and voted to permit Whalen's appeal—on the initiative of Justice John B. Swainson.[34]

Inevitably, Welch's appetite for action produced controversy. Making a night deposit at 3:15 A.M., a Detroit citizen named Edward Rye was suddenly confronted by two men with guns. Having been robbed once, he pulled his own weapon and shouted, "Don't come any further, I have a gun!" A gun battle blazed, Rye was wounded three times—not seriously—and the ensuing debate over whether the two FBI agents had adequately identified themselves was overshadowed by Welch's uncompromising defense of his men. He ordered Rye charged with assault on a federal officer (a grand jury did not concur, declining to indict) and observed publicly that "If this son of a bitch wants to shoot at our agents, he should be ready to take the consequences. He's both stupid and lucky, stupid for firing at them and lucky to be alive."[35]

Welch's comments earned him editorial rebukes and the

lasting respect of his agents, all of whom knew, at least after the Balloon Bar fiasco, that things occasionally went wrong on the street.

"We learned that a hijacking gang had sprung an experienced getaway driver from prison in Marquette and was planning to rob a bank in the Detroit suburbs.

"We put them under constant surveillance. They stole a blue van to use in the robbery, and we followed it for days, while they checked out potential targets.

"When they finally moved early one Friday morning, they went in an entirely new direction, eventually parking in the lot of a joint called the Balloon Bar—right across the street from the Southfield branch of the National Bank of Detroit.

"We were ready. We moved fifteen cars into the area quietly, with our surveillance team up close, shotgun squads primed for action. We even slipped two agents into the bank to pose as tellers.

"Gang members wandered in and out of the bar every few minutes, obviously waiting for someone else. The delay made us nervous. It was payday, the bank was crowded, and it would be a major problem to keep customers out of the line of fire.

"Finally, the other gang member arrived, and they all went inside the bar to make their final plans. A few minutes later, they came out and got in the blue van, and drove toward the bank. We radioed our agents to move in, and rushed several men in through the side door.

"But the van reached the bank and kept going. We were certain they had not seen us—it had to be a dry run. I ordered a single agent to keep loose contact on the van, staying close enough to track the signals from a beeper we had surreptitiously put on it, and kept my main force of agents at the bank, ready for their return.

"We waited.

"Suddenly police sirens were everywhere! Red and blue lights flashing, police cars screaming past our location, converging about a half mile down the street.

"I radioed our agent following the van and asked what was happening. He said the police had a report of a kidnapping, and he was trying to get details.

"A few minutes later, he caught up with the blue van—it was abandoned. Inside, there was a body, tied up like a mummy—the proprietor of the Balloon Bar.

"We charged into the Balloon Bar full force and found five people on the floor, all tied up! It turned out they had tied up each new customer as he came into the bar, waiting for the proprietor with the safe combination.

"When he finally arrived, they cleaned out the safe and kidnapped him in the van—in full view of fifty FBI agents and police."

The April 30, 1973, letter to President Nixon was signed "Respectfully," from "All FBI Officials."[36]

It was neither.

Rather, it was a defiant last-ditch challenge to Nixon's right to select the next FBI Director, and it was the work of a handful of remaining Hoover loyalists at headquarters, led by Associate Director Mark Felt.[37]

Three days earlier, all field offices had received a blunt telex from Director Gray.

SERIOUS ALLEGATIONS CONCERNING CERTAIN ACTS OF MY OWN DURING THE ONGOING WATERGATE INVESTIGATION ARE NOW A MATTER OF PUBLIC RECORD. AS A CONSEQUENCE, I HAVE TODAY TENDERED MY RESIGNATION AS ACTING DIRECTOR OF THE FEDERAL BUREAU OF INVESTIGATION, EFFECTIVE IMMEDIATELY.[38]

Gray's resignation, a certainty after his admission that he had destroyed files from E. Howard Hunt's White House safe, did not displease the Bureau hierarchy, but Nixon had immediately named William Ruckelshaus Acting Director, which did.[39] For the second time in less than a year, Hoover's heirs had been denied their inheritance, and this time the slap had a special sting, since the men who had masterminded the surveillance of Earth Day were to be directed by the former administrator of the Environmental Protection Agency.

But not for long. Ruckelshaus had made clear that his acceptance of the position was only on a temporary basis,[40] until a permanent Director could be found. The letter from "All FBI Officials" to Nixon offered some less than subtle advice as to where the President might look for one.

> . . . In the search for a nominee for the FBI Directorship, we urge consideration to the highly qualified professionals with impeccable credentials of integrity within the organization itself . . . At this critical time, it is essential that the FBI not flounder or lose direction in its service to the nation because of lack of law enforcement expertise or other qualities essential to the FBI Directorship.[41]

It was, in the context of the Bureau's historic fawning deference to any White House whim, a wide-open mutiny. Moving quickly to control it, Ruckelshaus asserted his authority, ordering all SACs to Washington for a meeting on May 2.[42]

The field commanders arrived primed for a fight—but not with Ruckelshaus.

The meeting was predictably chaotic, and Ruckelshaus stayed only twenty minutes—long enough, according to news accounts, for Felt to display his open contempt.[43]

After the Acting Director's departure, however, mutiny mushroomed into double mutiny—Felt and the headquarters staff had challenged the White House, but the field was in open rebellion against them.

Felt said he was not going to preside over the dismantling of the FBI.

Someone growled that he should do everyone a favor and retire (which he would, with Ruckelshaus's assistance, several weeks later).

Felt demanded order in the room.

Field agents shouted him down.[44]

Impotent to end the mutiny, Felt afterward attempted to deny its existence. In an extraordinary memorandum to

Ruckelshaus about the meeting, Felt expressed his grave concern "that outsiders, particularly White House officials," might have the "erroneous impression" that "dissension and factionalism may exist within the FBI."

"To remove any doubt on that point that you may have," Felt concluded, "you may desire to interview some of our SACs, selected by you at random."[45]

Fortunately for Felt, Ruckelshaus never accepted the suggestion, as Neil Welch's sentiments were typical among the SACs.

"We didn't really give a damn who ran the outfit—we just wanted some reforms which would make it possible for us to be effective in the field.

"We weren't opposed to Ruckelshaus. We were opposed to Felt and that headquarters crowd. Felt tried to take over and he lost all control—agents in charge ran that conference, and afterward, they ran the FBI."[46]

The next month, President Nixon nominated Kansas City Police Chief Clarence M. Kelley, who was also a twenty-year FBI veteran, to be Director.

The appointment was confirmed by the Senate and generally well received among agents, as Kelley's FBI service had been not at headquarters, but as a street agent and eventually SAC—in the field.[47]

Kelley would continue reforms begun by Gray, who was credited by agents with humanizing the FBI, recognizing for the first time the concerns of wives and families in connection with agent transfer policies. (Gray had also actively recruited to add blacks and women to the ranks of his special agents,[48] and he had explored the possibility of creating a Director's advisory board to permit effective non-FBI oversight of Bureau operations, initiatives all strongly endorsed by Neil Welch.)[49] But most of Kelley's first several years in office would be consumed by firefighting in Washington, responding to charges and countercharges swirling around the Bureau.

The continuing Washington controversy would by 1975 erode the percentage of Americans who had a "highly favorable" view of the FBI from 84 percent (in 1965) to 37 percent.[50] Unquestionably, that falling from popular grace was the product of a number of factors, including the deep undercurrent of distrust in federal government in general, precipitated by the Vietnam War and Watergate. The Bureau's involvement in improper activities notwithstanding, the erosion of public confidence overlooked entirely that the FBI field organization continued to perform as it always had —and better.

In Detroit, Neil Welch finally completed the complex Swainson investigation in 1975, and the Michigan Supreme Court justice, although acquitted on bribery charges, was convicted of five counts of perjury and sentenced to prison.[51] The Swainson case, though it would have been impossible to foresee at the time, was a prelude to Welch's major public corruption cases that would follow in succeeding years.

John Whalen, for his cooperation, remained free.

13

Reassignment

A dog chasing its tail. The dilemma had an element of circularity. Even the inventive J. Edgar Hoover had been unable to destroy embarrassing paperwork without creating more. As a consequence, beginning in 1940, he had written a series of memoranda under the suspiciously innocuous heading "Cutting Down Paperwork," setting forth guidelines for the destruction of memoranda "written merely for informative purposes" which "have no place in the Bureau's files and are of no permanent future value."[1] It was vague only to nonagents. In 1944, Hoover ordered that all such writings be on pink paper (reversing, without explanation, his prior preference for blue, stating only that "the Bureau does not wish to have such confidential memoranda prepared on the blue paper in the future").[2] By the 1950s, potentially embarrassing Bureau papers of many colors were simply stamped "DO NOT FILE" to signal discard.[3]

But in the file-conscious Bureau, agents recognized that any paper potent enough for DO NOT FILE status was important and worth keeping. So memoranda targeted for destruction instead proliferated, leaving plenty for Justice Department probers to find when they started searching, in 1976, for evidence of illegal FBI actions. In the New York City office, investigators discovered files of DO NOT FILE paperwork documenting FBI burglaries and bag jobs against the

Weatherman underground.[4] While shock waves from that
were still reverberating, the Bureau's own inspectors discovered the opposite in Detroit.

Dozens of sensitive files were missing—gone without a
trace.

The inspectors flashed the news back to the Bureau, where
official anxiety dissolved into gleeful anticipation once it was
determined that the files had vanished in 1970. The top Bureau officials all knew who had been Detroit SAC then, and
their mutual malevolence toward him was evident in the
general enthusiasm which greeted an assistant director's
confident prediction: "This time, we're finally going to nail
that sonuvabitch!"

The Director fired an urgent volley of questions at Neil
Welch, to be followed by interrogation under oath once his
explanation was known. The relish with which Bureau officials awaited his answers was spiced by their almost certain
irrelevance: If Welch could not make the missing files materi-
alize, his FBI career was over.

Welch had seen the handwriting a year before, in a letter
from headquarters. Ten minutes prior to boarding his Northwest Orient Airlines flight back to Detroit after a series of
routine meetings at headquarters, Welch had been paged in
Washington's National Airport and instructed to phone FBI
Director Clarence Kelley at once. Associate Director Nicholas Callahan had intercepted Welch's call and passed on Kelley's message: Welch was reassigned from Detroit to Philadelphia, effective immediately.

Welch was stunned.

His Detroit field office was the FBI's runaway leader in
major criminal case production and had recently targeted
two new criminal specialties—narcotics trafficking by organized crime and federal government program fraud—with
eye-opening success. Kelley had admired Welch's work twice
in person and dozens of times by mail and had never intimated that a change of SACs might be good for either Detroit
or Welch.

"I thought the Bureau's new policy was to treat SACs with a little understanding," Welch had finally responded absently, wondering how he would tell his wife and sons that they were moving again, this time leaving the boys' high-school friends and athletics behind. "Why didn't you mention my transfer when I saw you this afternoon, so we could have at least discussed it?"

"There's nothing to talk about," Callahan had replied. "Your transfer letter is already in the mail."[5]

It had landed in Detroit before Welch did.

The Bureau's action was capricious but not arbitrary, given that Callahan had two reasons for transferring Welch—one real and unstated, the other the opposite.

The announced reason was that Director Kelley had suggested, as policy, that SACs should not serve in one office more than five years, which Welch's Detroit tenure had exceeded the month before.

The actual impetus, however, had been Welch's computer plan—a precipitating element in the muddle over missing files. With Kelley's support and the aid of several other SACs, Neil Welch had spearheaded a drive to computerize FBI field operations and had presented headquarters with a professional proposal (similar to one adopted by Scotland Yard and the Royal Canadian Mounted Police) which would have revolutionized investigative capabilities and saved an estimated $100 million in the process. The urgency of the need was unarguable, accentuated by the Patty Hearst kidnapping probe, then more than a year old, in which agents were "drowning in information," the sheer volume of which precluded systematic evaluation. FBI data processing had not advanced significantly since Hoover introduced index cards to catalogue subversives more than fifty years earlier.

But the Bureau brass had viewed Welch's pilot program as doubly dangerous. Saving millions meant losing appropriations, an unwelcome prospect, and his proposal would have linked all field offices into twelve *regional* computer systems, thereby advertising the superfluity of headquarters to FBI investigations. With the sole exception of Harvard-trained

Assistant Director Richard Gallagher, senior Bureau officials had coalesced behind Callahan's outspoken opposition to the plan, countering that any FBI computer should be in Washington. There it would reinforce headquarters control over the field (and make an impressive new exhibit for tourists, its massive shiny units, with lights blinking and tapes whirring, thwarting criminal masterminds).

Kelley had finally found the strident objections of his lieutenants more persuasive than his own previous success in computerizing the Kansas City Police Department, and the Welch proposal had been shelved.

Welch's regional computer system would have cost approximately half as much as a centralized system at headquarters, primarily because it tracked the actual flow of FBI work, which of course originated in the field rather than Washington. The FBI has not moved forward with any major computerization in the years subsequent to Kelley's decision and remains, as of this writing, several generations behind the state of the art.[6]

Welch appeared to have been shelved too, it being assumed that transferring him to Philadelphia, a disparaging lateral move, would have that approximate effect. Transfers had always worked for Hoover, a dependable antidote to threats from the field. And his Bureau followers never considered the possibility that Welch, exposed to hundreds of field agents by scattergun transfers, should have been quarantined rather than circulated. Headquarters had already marked him for elimination, an exercise at which it still excelled, and by ending Welch's influence in Detroit the groundwork was laid—even before the missing files assured it—to end his career in Philadelphia.

14

Philadelphia

"Is this Sid Benjamin?"

"Yeah."

"This is Frankie."

"Oh, jeez, I've been trying to get you . . ."

"Hey look, I'm going to tell you something . . ."

"Yeah."

"I'll break your fucking back for you, you don't bring me my money back."

"I, I want to come out there with Domenic on Monday night, how about that?"

"I don't want no fucking appointments with you. I'll come up to your fucking house."

"Can I come out there with him?"

"You better bring me that fucking money here you cock-sucker and stop all that bullshitting. You understand? I ain't going to tell you no more, I'll come up to your fucking house. I'll pull your eyes right out of your head. I had enough of you. You understand?"

Sid Benjamin understood perfectly, as he demonstrated at the subsequent loan-sharking trial of Frank Sindone, at which he declined to testify as a government witness, citing concerns for his health. (Sindone was acquitted.)[1]

But Sid Benjamin was in the distinct minority, the majority view being that organized crime in Philadelphia was more

benign than malignant, an Old World anachronism as mild
and courtly as the man who headed it. Sicilian-born Angelo
Bruno was "the docile don," a quiet South Philadelphia rowhouse dweller who had shrugged off a botched execution
effort in 1959, ordering retirement rather than reciprocation
for his clumsy rival. After that, Bruno was credited with
keeping the Philadelphia LCN at peace and out of the lucra-
tive narcotics business, policies which earned the respect of
his neighbors and a tacit accommodation with law enforcement authorities.[2]

It was a truce which held until 1976, marred only by a
handful of infractions, generally accidental. In the mid 1960s,
a rookie agent doing a routine background check on a federal
job applicant, interviewing neighbors at random, had unknowingly wandered into the chicken shop on Christian
Street and attempted to question its proprietor. Four brawny
men promptly tossed him unceremoniously into the street,
and when he returned to the office, the bewildered agent
learned that he had inadvertently tried to question Phil
"Chicken Man" Testa, the violent underboss of the Bruno
mob. To even the account, half a dozen veteran agents had
immediately returned with the rookie to Christian Street
and roughed up Testa's enforcers, which had reestablished
mutual respect and restored the truce.[3]

But as a policy, the Philadelphia FBI regarded LCN members as it did subversives, as persons to be counted, followed,
and listed in intelligence files—but not charged with serious
crimes. Loose surveillance was the primary enforcement activity, and even that was easily thwarted. Once, an alert ten
year old, presumably unaware that his neighbor had been
described as a "fucking, cold, heartless motherfucker" in a
wiretapped conversation,[4] warned enforcer Frank Sindone
that "I think those are FBI men in that car across the street."[5]
Still, the FBI and LCN maintained an amicable symbiosis,
exemplified by an agent's secret visit with Angelo Bruno
when he entered Pennsylvania Hospital for minor surgery.
After chatting cordially, the agent had asked whether, despite Bruno's insistence that La Cosa Nostra did not exist, he

and his associates might supply information to the FBI in the event of a particularly heinous crime, such as a kidnapping. Bruno had leaned back in bed, smiled thinly, and replied, "Try me."[6]

Neither Bruno nor the agent had any intimation that Neil Welch, who took over as Philadelphia SAC in August 1975, planned to do literally that.

Timely reports, clean cars with tires regularly rotated, and strict compliance with the statistical demands of headquarters were the ritual imperatives at FBI agent conferences, a formula so universal that Welch's agents were startled by his deviation from it.

"I've been in this outfit twenty years," the hulking figure in front of them said instead, "and most of us don't even know what business we are in.

"Certainly FBI headquarters does not know—those paper shufflers in Washington are the last people who would understand our mission in the field."

Pacing slowly, hands planted deep in his pockets, Welch continued. "I'm a lawyer, and I am going to tell you what business we are in—and I want everyone in this room to remember it."

Abruptly, he stopped and faced his audience squarely, challenging anyone to disagree with what he was about to say.

"We are in the business of justice," he finally said softly, letting the words settle. "And we are the cornerstone of the system, because our FBI work product is the only tool which United States Attorneys and federal judges have to make that system work.

"If we fail to produce," he concluded gravely, "the criminal-justice system will fail."[7]

It was, as Welch knew, a fresh perspective. The Bureau's business had always been statistics, and its dominance of field offices varied inversely with their distance from Washington. Even before Welch had arrived at the office, Tom Crane had confirmed for him that Philadelphia, hardly more than one hundred miles removed, was governed strictly by the Bureau book.

Statistics measured success and also effectively precluded it on any significant scale by requiring each agent to work alone, there being no mechanism to divide the statistic should a multiagent team produce one. Accordingly, Philadelphia agents relied on car thieves and cargo thefts for dependably impressive numbers, while maintaining the required ration of informants. These were mostly small-time hoods who could, for a negotiable price of one hundred dollars or less, solve most amateur bank robberies and not much else. And in the event of any statistical deficit, the agents listening to Welch knew that Pennsylvania's several military reservations offered particularly happy hunting, since the Bureau counted traffic offenses and minor assaults there as full-grown federal crimes.

But Welch did not—and the Bureau book had undergone a modest revision with Clarence Kelley's approval of a "Quality Case Program" on an experimental basis.

Using that license, Welch jolted his audience, announcing that agent performance would be evaluated by the quality, rather than the quantity, of the cases—and that he considered statistical accomplishments an indicator of nonquality. Having casually jettisoned a half century of FBI policy, Welch defined Philadelphia's new FBI priorities to be organized crime and corruption—corruption of the political system, the courts and prosecutors' offices, and the police department. And as an explosive afterthought, he added that since criminals stole vastly more money with briefcases and pens than with guns, the FBI would target white-collar crime and defer to local police on routine bank robbery investigations.[8]

An angry veteran was on his feet. The bank squad was the unchallenged office elite, hard men with favorite weapons in shoulder or ankle holsters, a proud fraternity which would not be disbanded without a bitter fight.

"Are you trying to say," he bit off his words, "that if I'm going to interview a bank officer about an embezzlement and I see a bank robbery in progress, I should just ignore it?"

"What you should do," Welch replied deliberately, "is check your watch." He paused while agents puzzled with that. "If your interview was for ten-thirty and your watch says ten-thirty," he continued, matching his challenging glare with a menacing growl, "then you should dodge the bullets, step over the bodies, and go conduct your interview with that thieving son of a bitch."[9]

More bombshells followed. Minor crimes on military bases would be surrendered to military police, Welch announced, and deserter investigations (actually a refined form of bounty hunting, since the military goodwill generated was always reflected in the Bureau appropriations) were dropped. Cargo theft coverage was cut by 60 percent, sparking indignation among trucking companies and airlines, which had found FBI service more economical than routine security precautions, and causing despair among agents who had planned on postretirement security jobs with the shippers, a time-honored FBI practice.[10]

Finally, having learned from Hoover, Welch revoked "any SAC authority currently existing for the carrying out of internal security investigations" and ordered a written report of all telephone conversations between his agents and the Bureau Domestic Intelligence Division. When grand juries probing COINTELPRO abuses forced agents to name names, Neil Welch's, and those of his agents, would not be among them.[11]

Having defined the tasks, Welch promised the tools—his agents would have whatever manpower, money, and equipment they required for success, an unprecedented commitment. He concluded the conference by announcing the comprehensive reorganization of the office into target squads, each agent handpicked by Welch on the advice of his trusted assistant, Tom Crane. The target squads were backed up by a newly created off-premises surveillance squad (which Welch, never troubled by technicalities, ordered to operate from New Jersey, outside his formal jurisdiction).[12] When he was finished, Welch had stretched Kelley's Quality Case concept beyond recognition, shifting $4 million in FBI resources from nonessential to priority activities and multiplying, by 2,500 percent and 1,000 percent,[13] respectively, the commitment of resources to fight official corruption and organized crime.

And in practice, even those startling figures would prove low, because in attacking those two activities Welch would presume that they were one and the same.

On a pleasant day in April 1976, the Bruno gang learned that its first contact with Welch's reorganized FBI had occurred on a frigid night in February.

Once reminded, it was not difficult to pinpoint which night. There had been some unexplained difficulty with the water main in front of Frank's Cabana Steaks. City of Philadelphia workers had taken nearly all night to repair it, working noisily around a manhole on Moyamensing Avenue, a yellow Water Department truck parked nearby. Neighbors had been curious, and after midnight a police officer had finally stopped to check.

"What are you doing down there?" he shouted into the manhole, where a black worker was hammering on pipes.

"Working on the J branch, man, we've got trouble on the J branch!" the worker had shouted back cheerfully, hammering harder and louder.[14]

The officer had shrugged and walked away, and neither he nor anyone else knew, until April 29, that the man in the manhole—and virtually everyone else on Moyamensing Avenue that night—were FBI agents. The Water Department workers, casual pedestrians, even the young couple kissing in the shadows—all were FBI agents, and all were diverting attention from the Bureau locksmith quietly working the lock on Frank's Cabana Steaks, as authorized by a federal court order. Once inside, agents had installed two microphones, finally departing at dawn with the help of the only person around who was in fact what he seemed—a bread man starting his rounds—who gave the agents' battery-dead Water Department truck a jump start.[15]

For the next seventy days, agents listened to and recorded, compiling hundreds of remarkable reels of evidence, supplemented by telephoto pictures—snapped surreptitiously by agents from an apartment across the street—the mobster comings and goings at Frank's Cabana Steaks. On tape, Bruno family members openly discussed La Cosa Nostra—by name—and carefully warned younger members to wait, when any issue was put to a vote, to see how senior members voted, never raising their hand quite as high as the capo.[16] Like all businessmen, the mobsters frequently discussed politics (confirming Welch's conviction that the LCN was inextricably linked to official corruption), but their primary business was loan-sharking, which yielded, according to the tapes, "5 percent overnight," or a comfortable 1,825 percent annually.[17]

The operation ended in a surprise raid on August 29. Dumbfounded mobsters watched in disbelief as agents meticulously searched the premises. After the search, two agents brought in a large steamer trunk and ordered everyone outside while they disconnected the microphones. Out of sight, they removed the pencil-sized bugs and placed them in the empty trunk, then laboriously lugged it back outside, apparently straining at the weight—and leaving onlookers baffled as to where so much heavy equipment might have been hidden.[18] And before departing, an agent returned to place a specially prepared sign in the window of Frank's Cabana Steaks: "No Gambling on Premises."[19]

The sign had doubtful enforcement value, and the steamer trunk was a prankish deception, but the central message from Welch's agents was unmistakably clear: La Cosa Nostra's truce with the Philadelphia FBI was permanently ended.

Success turned to frustration after agents gave their evidence to Philadelphia Strike Force attorneys to prepare the prosecutions. Welch had long been a critic of Strike Force effectiveness, and the Philadelphia attorneys met his worst expectations, delaying the cases literally for years. Mob justice proved swifter than the federal variety. That was apparent on March 21, 1980, when a shotgun blast blew a gaping hole below Angelo Bruno's right ear as he sat in his car after dinner—confirming that he was indeed too docile to survive the brutal competition for Atlantic City gambling action.[20]

Seven months later, Frank Sindone (who had complained on tape that "This business is gonna make me steal all my life —I'll get out of there one day, you watch, I'll get the fuck out")[21] was found in a garbage bag, bound hands and feet crabbed behind his back, shot three times in the head.[22] Five months after that, an enormous shrapnel-filled bomb proved a newspaper horoscoper wrong about "Chicken Man" Testa ("With Neptune in exact conjunction with his retrograde Jupiter, no matter what's going on, Testa will come out in a better position than he started"),[23] demolishing the front of his house, and him, as he returned for the evening.[24] At this writing, more than a dozen slayings have rocked Philadelphia gangland, along with a handful of unsuccessful attempts, one on Testa's son Salvatore, about whom Welch's LCN expert Gino Lazzari remarked, "He wants to be a bad guy in the worst way—and Lord knows he's got the breeding."[25]

On May 7, 1982, a full six years after FBI agents had obtained the evidence at Frank's Cabana Steaks, Strike Force attorneys finally used the tapes from that operation to convict six organized crime figures, none of them a significant power.[26]

> QUESTION What personal knowledge do you have of COINTELPRO files and activity in the Detroit office?
> ANSWER Shortly after my arrival in the Detroit office I made it perfectly clear to the security supervisors that no counterintelligence programs or activities were to be initiated while I was SAC. If there were any such programs before I arrived, I am not aware of them.[27]

By mid 1976, the Bureau's investigation of Welch's missing files had moved from embarrassment to backfire.

It had started nicely. A sharp-eyed Bureau prober had found the incriminating notation "Too late!"[28] scrawled on a

Bureau memo ordering Detroit to retain its files indefinitely, and the experts had agreed that it was Welch's handwriting.

Smoking gun!

What explanation could Welch possibly have for that?

"Since the Bureau had previously approved an optional file destruction policy," Welch responded innocently, defusing the charge, "I simply meant that by the time we received that memo, it was 'too late' for files previously destroyed."[29]

Grinding their teeth, the probers had continued to dig, seething that their case somehow seemed uncertain, even though Welch freely admitted his crime to anyone who asked. "We destroyed the files when we moved to our new office," he acknowledged, unconcerned, "the way you might clean out your garage."[30]

Actually, it had been more the way you might put out a fire, the Bureau investigation revealed, and that discovery had further complicated the probe. Welch had assembled his agents in a bucket brigade for the exercise, and the files had been passed man to man to destruction. Each agent could offer only a fragmentary account of the entire operation ("My job was to rip out page six in each file and pass it on—I don't know what the agent on my right or my left did"),[31] and the investigators could not find any agent who would testify what Welch's role had been. Still, the determined Bureau probers might have discovered that themselves by piecing the fragments together—except for Welch's wholly unanticipated counterattack.

There were no missing files at all, Welch contended.

Copies of every document they were searching for were contained in headquarters files. Indeed, the nonexistence of the Detroit documents had been discovered as a result of the Bureau sending identical documents to the Detroit office, each marked "Follow suit." And "Follow suit," Welch charged ominously, was Bureau code instructing each field office to *retroactively* classify the indicated document, thus making it unavailable to congressional investigators.[32]

(The Bureau had other stratagems to stymie congressional scrutiny. The Senate Judiciary Committee had attempted for years to obtain a copy of Chapter 87 of the FBI *Manual of Instruction*—the rules for internal security probes—and had encountered a series of ingenious Hoover runarounds. Finally out of patience, the committee authorized a subpoena for the material. That same night, before the subpoena had actually been received at headquarters, agents labored through the night, completely rewriting Chapter 87, the new version of which was obediently delivered to the committee the following day. Completion of the deception then necessitated a series of meetings in field offices around the country in which Bureau officials replaced the old Chapter 87 with the new version, explaining emphatically—with a wink—that "nothing has changed.")[33]

By the time Welch observed, in answer to a Bureau question, that retroactive classification was "a highly questionable legal maneuver," enthusiasm for questioning Welch had been replaced by concern that Congress might see his answers. The inspectors were summoned back from Detroit, and urgent telex questions to Welch in Philadelphia slowed, then stopped.

The probe quietly died.

Died, Welch grumbled, before he even had an opportunity to try his ultimate defense: "I cleared the file destruction program with Hoover."

(In 1977, after reviewing the Bureau's charges against Welch in connection with the Detroit file destruction, the Justice Department formally confirmed that there was "no evidence of any deliberate wrongdoing.")[34]

Bureau antipathy toward Welch, however, did not die with the probe, though it turned more passive. "We don't care what Welch does," an assistant director had sniffed with testy complacence when a field agent praised a Welch innovation during in-service training. "What Neil Welch does is *not* the policy of the FBI."[35]

That complacence would be undone, ironically, by the 1976 revelation that what Clarence Kelley said was apparently not FBI policy either. Retracting his prior assurances that illegal FBI burglaries had ceased in 1966, Director Kelley conceded that bag jobs had continued until at least 1973, adding, astonishingly, that there was "obviously someone or some people who have deceived me."[36] Kelley declined to say who his deceivers might be (reinforcing the impression that he was neither master of deceit nor of the Bureau), but the holdover Hoover loyalists at headquarters were natural suspects. They had bitterly resisted Kelley's determined efforts to modify Hoover policies and would, in the end, diminish his record of accomplishment.

Neil Welch might be exiled in Philadelphia, but it was increasingly apparent that he and Director Kelley had common enemies in Washington.

Philadelphia cops and robbers was complicated, as Detective Martin Stasiak demonstrated in November 1977, when he showed that one person could be both.[37]

It was an unwelcome complication, because from the beginning Neil Welch's relationship with the Philadelphia Police Department had been less than harmonious. He had ordered Mayor Frank L. Rizzo's photograph removed from the FBI office, offending friends of the former police commissioner, and had neglected to pay the normal courtesy call on then-Commissioner Joseph O'Neill. When Rizzo and O'Neill had demanded fifty thousand federal troops to counter feared demonstrators at the Bicentennial celebration, Welch had first toyed with the request (Perhaps it should be one hundred thousand? Or maybe thirty thousand would suffice. Should they be airborne? Would they need special weapons?), and then, at a Washington meeting, he had told Deputy Attorney General Harold R. Tyler that he anticipated perhaps two or three busloads of demonstrators—half of whom were likely to be police or FBI informants.[38]

The troop request had been denied, provoking an O'Neill complaint that Welch "really let us down," and the Bicentennial was celebrated without incident.[39]

It was the Stasiak case, however, and a handful of others like it, which most seriously impaired the FBI-police relationship in Philadelphia.

During a routine investigation into the death of Harold
Atkinson, a recluse whose decomposed body had been found
in his shabby home on Ontario Street, Stasiak discovered
several unexpected items—bank books showing $100,000 in
deposits, a $100,000 check payable to Atkinson, and nearly a
half-million dollars' worth of negotiable securities. Actually,
there was more—Atkinson's carefully written inventory catalogued over $870,000 in securities, and bank records re-
vealed a total of $670,000 in deposits—but what Stasiak had
found would be enough. With three coconspirators, Detective Stasiak systematically looted the estate of Harold Atkinson, stealing the money and liquidating the securities
through phony accounts around the country.[40]

Police misconduct was not new, but Welch's remedy,
which he had developed in Buffalo and Detroit, was.

Customarily, charges against police which reached the FBI
had been informally disposed of in a friendly telephone call,
SAC to commissioner, a law enforcement courtesy allowing
allegations from police brutality to corruption to be quietly
pressed, or passed, in-house. When Philadelphia agents in
1975 brought their new SAC a tip that police were receiving
stolen merchandise, he had immediately reached for the
phone, seeming to understand the custom. But instead of
calling Joe O'Neill, Welch had called Kirk Rohn, supervisor of
his surveillance squad, and ordered undercover agents to
penetrate the crime. They arrested two officers with merchandise in hand and set the pattern for Welch's police
probes. O'Neill was informed of FBI investigations only
when arrests were imminent, except in police brutality cases,
which O'Neill and his top brass learned of when agents delivered their subpoenas to appear before the federal grand jury.

The commissioner was furious. He demanded a meeting
with Welch.

The two Irishmen met, speaking different languages.
O'Neill asked why the FBI would resort to subpoenas of
fellow law enforcement officers in brutality cases. Welch replied that the subpoenas would stop if the police showed any
inclination to probe those charges themselves. Welch asked

who had promulgated the Homicide Division policy in which detectives routinely dragnetted the area at a murder scene, holding hordes of people in custody until someone gave a statement. O'Neill responded that it was a district attorney's policy, which sounded impressive until he added that the district attorney in question had served more than three decades earlier and that the policy had not been reconsidered since. O'Neill demanded to know how he was supposed to conduct police radio operations, when the communications tapes on which calls were recorded were all in the federal grand jury. Welch suggested that he buy more tapes.

Finally, O'Neill requested immediate notification of any police corruption charges, followed by a joint FBI-police investigation, and Welch flatly refused.

"I've seen police corruption in New York and Detroit," Welch said, "where an entire precinct systematically shakes down the prostitutes, gamblers, after-hours places. Cop cases are never just one cop—it's the captain, the lieutenant, the inspector, the sergeants, the whole pad, as they say in New York.

"And I've seen what happened here in Philadelphia, at Harold Atkinson's house.

"I will always inform you in time for you to announce that you cooperated in the investigation," Welch continued. "But I am not going to tell you what cops tell us about corruption" —he paused, glaring directly at O'Neill—"because the cops who tell us would not want me to."[41]

Welch's point was confirmed, indirectly, a short time later. Forced into a high-speed chase to capture a fleeing suspect, the FBI undercover surveillance team flashed past a Philadelphia police cruiser, which immediately gave chase to the chasers. The suspects were captured, and police and agents returned to the station house to do the paperwork. There, with sudden recognition, an officer turned on the casually dressed agents and pointed accusingly.

"You're the guys! You are the FBI agents who have been working undercover to bust cops!"

Electric silence.

"That's right," one of the agents conceded, tensing for action.

Police move.

"Well, keep it up, goddamn it," a cop finally growled, "and clean those fucking crooks out of this outfit."

He walked across the room and shook hands with the agents—and the other officers followed.[42]

In 1978, former Detective Martin Stasiak pleaded guilty to interstate transportation of stolen property, wire fraud, and conspiracy. He was sentenced to two years in federal prison, followed by two years' probation.[43]

15

Washington

Any Bureau official who took vacation in July 1976 would have been certain, on his return to headquarters in August, that there had been a coup d'état.

Director Clarence Kelley was in a hospital in Kansas City.[1]

Associate Director Nicholas Callahan had retired, with encouragement, effective July 16.[2]

Empty desks dotted the security section—the veteran supervisors who had occupied them had vanished.

And Philadelphia SAC Neil Welch was barking commands from a large headquarters office, impartially peppering field offices and Bureau supervisors with orders—orders purporting to be from the Director of the FBI.

Which in fact they were, which meant that Welch was actually directing a countercoup.

Stung by the Senate Select Committee, which had critically noted his office's fifty-year irrelevance to FBI intelligence operations, Attorney General Edward Levi had issued stringent domestic security guidelines and ordered FBI Director Kelley to implement them immediately.[3] Each of the FBI's 21,414 open investigations—which ran the gamut from Communists to Weathermen—were to be reviewed for compliance with the AG guidelines. Only cases which involved actual criminal conduct or clear and present national danger would remain open—all others were to be closed.[4]

Director Kelley had given the orders.

But his Hoover-trained assistants knew better. The orders might be in the Director's name, but they were the Attorney General's orders, a clear attempt to interfere in the Bureau—which had five decades of institutional experience in thwarting such interference.

The exercise was conducted with practiced agility. Extensive memoranda were written. Urgent telexes were sent. Conferences were held. Memos memorializing the conferences were circulated with sufficient copies so that every official at headquarters—and Justice—would be aware of the status of this priority activity. Every field office was ordered to review every case subject to the guidelines, and when the responses were collected, they reflected the meticulous attention to detail for which the FBI was legendary.

> Captioned case has been reviewed in accordance with instructions and criteria set forth in referenced communication. As a result of this review, it has been determined that investigation of captioned individual meets the standard of investigation established in referenced communication for reasons set forth below and it is therefore recommended that this investigation remain in a pending status.

In the end, although thousands of ancient or inactive cases were closed, 4,868 were not—in direct defiance of Levi's guidelines.[5]

The Attorney General was not pleased, which had been expected, but Clarence Kelley went into a furious rage, which had not been—though it should have, because the domestic intelligence fiasco was the second embarrassing public demonstration of his impotence at Bureau headquarters. Several months earlier, Kelley had created an Ad Hoc Committee of top Bureau officials to probe allegations that Hoover-era officials had profited from transactions with the sole supplier of Bureau electronics equipment, United States Recording Company, and had obtained personal services from other Bureau suppliers and had misused the funds of the FBI Recreation Association. Whitewash was the only word to describe the Ad Hoc Committee's conclusions. An angry Attorney General Levi had rejected the FBI report and instead ordered an investigation by the Justice Department Criminal Division, assisted by FBI agents handpicked *from the field.*[6]

Kelley's patience was gone. Leaving for hospital treatment of a recurring back problem, he decided to follow Levi's example and bypass his own headquarters chain of command. His instructions were unambiguous. He ordered Associate Director Richard Held, a highly respected former SAC who had replaced Callahan, to find the "meanest, toughest sonuvabitch in the FBI" and get those domestic security cases closed.[7]

A search of personnel files was not required. Held called Neil Welch, who, having no idea why he was being summoned, immediately flew to Washington. Held briefed him on the assignment, assuring Welch that he and Kelley were fully behind him—actually several hundred miles behind, as it developed that Held, too, was departing Washington at once, for several speaking engagements. But before he left, Held escorted Welch through the executive section of the building and summarily informed the assistant directors— who included bitter Welch enemies—that they were to follow Welch's orders.

His first one transferred the security section chiefs out of the office.

With Held gone, it was an order no one planned to follow.

Wily, recalcitrant veterans, the security section chiefs had effectively killed Kelley's first compliance effort, and they had new tactics ready for the second. They arranged for the Administrative Division to advise Welch that a number of technical bureaucratic requirements precluded any immediate transfers. With new wariness, however, it was added that the matter could certainly be more fully reviewed, and perhaps a comprehensive written statement of Welch's plans and objectives would be helpful.

Welch liked the idea of a written statement.

He summoned a stenographer into his office and dictated immediate transfer orders for the security section chiefs—from the Director of the FBI.

They were gone—and the game was over.

Assisted by Special Agent Norm Rand, his close friend from Detroit who had been transferred to Washington, Welch plunged into the paper, reviewing every open domestic security case.

"Are these activities illegal?"

"Do we have an actual bombing case on this guy?"

"How does this organization meet AG guidelines?"[8]

He scrawled his questions on the previous responses (the same distinctive scrawl which had become familiar to the Bureau handwriting experts in the Detroit file fiasco) and fired them back to the field, ordering immediate replies. When a West Coast SAC advised him by phone that he had eight hundred priority security cases which he intended to keep open, Welch said he would be there in the morning to close them all. Reconsidering, the SAC closed all but a handful.[9]

When Welch was finished, of the 4,868 original investigations, 626 had been justified and remained open.

4,242 cases were closed.[10]

It took about a week.

It took somewhat longer for the Attorney General's task force to resolve the allegations that FBI officials had improperly profited from the Bureau's transactions with United States Recording Company and others. On January 10, 1978, the Justice Department issued its report, which stated that the receipt of government goods and services by FBI officials personally constituted a violation of federal criminal law. Nicholas P. Callahan and John P. Mohr—formerly associate director and assistant director, respectively—were found to have engaged in such activities. Prosecution was barred by the statute of limitations. Former Director Hoover, the Justice Department further reported, had used FBI employees to paint his house annually, to build a portico, deck, fish pond, shelves, telephone stands, cabinets, tables, and an oriental fruit bowl, to service his home appliances, to replace his sod twice a year, to polish his silver, to provide his firewood—and to prepare his federal tax returns.[11]

Perhaps because the Director's commitment to law enforcement remained beyond question, it was not stated in the Justice Department report whether those tax returns reflected any taxes paid by J. Edgar Hoover on his extensive fringe benefits.

For the dwindling band of Hoover loyalists at Bureau headquarters, events of the mid 1970s justified both their hopes and fears. The unprecedented interference of Congress and the Attorney General in FBI affairs represented a dangerous power shift—that was undeniable—and the Attorney General's public suggestion that Callahan, Mohr, and Hoover had committed federal crimes was unthinkable. Moreover, Kelley's unwillingness—or inability—to control FBI agents in the field threatened to completely erode the foundations of Hoover's empire. Neil Welch, the most resented example, appeared to have been given total freedom to pursue his own priorities. In January 1977, he announced that his Philadelphia Organized Crime and Corruption Program, whatever that was, had produced 317 major convictions in its first year, more than one every working day.[12] Worse, Kelley had clearly been seduced by Welch's success, describing Philadelphia's accomplishments in detail to congressional committees (a welcome relief from defending past practices) and promising to replicate them in other cities.[13]

But Kelley's weakness offered encouragement as well. If a tough veteran agent like Kelley—who had mastered a big-city police department—could not assert command over the headquarters hierarchy, then his announced departure held no threat; no successor would be any more effective. Field agents might create occasional irritation—as Welch had with the domestic security cases, and others had with the United States Recording probe—but Hoover's men would, in the end, inherit the Bureau.

Indeed, until June 13, 1977, they still had a flicker of hope that one of them might actually be named Director, though they were practical men and understood that was not likely. Failing that, they would be satisfied with a Director who would make speeches, cut ribbons, testify before Congress— leaving the real power and control over the FBI with the Bureau bureaucracy, Hoover's legacy. Indeed, the bureaucracy was so entrenched and intransigent that the identity of the Director had become nearly irrelevant. It was difficult to imagine any potential Director who might successfully impose his own will on the Bureau and more difficult to imagine —assuming that such a person existed—that he might be recognized by the panel of citizens named by President Carter to find a new FBI Director.

16

Beth

"I was asleep.

"It was after midnight when I received a call from Special
Agent Tom Dolan, who told me that a twenty-three-year-old
newlywed had been kidnapped in State College, Pennsylvania. Two armed men had dragged her from her parents'
home, bound and gagged, leaving her mother tied to a bed.
They had demanded a $150,000 ransom, paid according to
detailed instructions they would give over a CB radio channel—and had warned the family not to call the FBI.

"I called Tom Crane immediately and told him to hand-
pick our sixty best agents and order them to State College at
once. I told them to bring a full arsenal of weapons, electronic and photographic surveillance gear, and all the office
equipment they would need to conduct a field investigation
for up to one month.

"Deer season opened the next day, and hunters would

flood State College. I instructed our agents to wear hunting
clothes, and to buy their gasoline with cash—not FBI credit
cards. I imposed total radio silence.

"It was spitting snow when I left Philadelphia shortly after
midnight."[2]

> "Do you have the CB turned to Channel 7?"
>
> "OK. But what if something goes wrong with that
> channel?"
>
> "If we lose contact, go to the number I just called
> and wait for us to call and give you further instruc-
> tions. Now I want you to go to the Bald Eagle Res-
> taurant in Milesburg. You go underneath Route 80
> and it's on the right about a quarter of a mile. You
> understand?"
>
> "The Bald Eagle Restaurant. OK."
>
> "I want you to sit in the parking lot with the dome
> light on in your car . . ."
>
> "Is Beth all right?"
>
> "Yes. There is no problem. I cannot let you talk to
> her, it would cause a lot of problems at this time. I
> will be able to give her to you one half hour after we
> get the money."
>
> "You said 5 P.M."
>
> "Yes, but we have to wait till dark to make the
> pickup. I'll give you your instructions at the Bald
> Eagle Restaurant, Channel 7."[3]

"After a treacherous four-hour drive, much of it on icy
mountain roads, our task force assembled at the State College Sheraton before dawn. I organized the agents into small
teams and assigned investigative priorities to each.

"By this time, I had ordered in two surveillance aircraft
from Harrisburg—we had everything we needed to conduct
a sustained surveillance, by air or on the ground. So far, there
had been no leaks, no press inquiries, no radio traffic on the
local police channel.

"But time was against us. The temperature was below
zero, raw sleeting weather—if Beth was outside, we had to

find her within hours. We copied her wedding pictures—she was a beautiful girl—and distributed copies to every agent.

"We knew what she looked like but did not have a single clue where she was."[4]

> "Breaker to Domelight."
> "This is Domelight."
> "Go to Channel 12."
> "I'm going to 12."
> "Are you on the way to the mall?"
> "I'm on the way to the Nittany Mall where Penn Traffic is."
> "Go to the main entrance, turn left. There are two pay phones on the left . . . or on the wall, I mean. Is that right?"
> "10-4. 10-4."
> "Wait for one of them to ring."
> "I heard you."
> "Follow instructions."[5]

"We immediately asked the telephone company to 'trap' all calls to Don Meyer's home or business, so we could trace the origin of each call.

"Unfortunately, we discovered that the ransom calls were being made from a number of different public telephones. After several calls, however, we were able to plot the locations on a map, and we narrowed it down to a small area. Then we flooded that area with agents, some dressed casually like Penn State students, others in hunting gear.

"We waited.

"Finally, one of the kidnappers returned and made the next call—while FBI agents pretended to talk on the phones on each side of him. Then he hung up, unsuspicious, and our agents did the hardest thing they would have to do: They let him walk away free.

"We had no choice.

"We still did not know where Beth was, but we knew the kidnapper at the phone bank had a partner—who might murder her at any second. So we watched him walk away."[6]

"Go up the hill."

"I'm turning up . . ."

"Turn left up the hill!"

"I did turn—I turned left up the hill."

"Go up to the turn of the hill and turn left. Are you listening to me Domelight? Do you hear me? Do you hear me?"

"I heard you."

"Top of the hill . . . When you come to the crest of the hill about one hundred feet, there'll be a cornfield. Stop in the road. Open the door. Put the briefcase out on the ground and then continue on down that road. Do you understand?"

". . . I read you."[7]

"Our surveillance agents crawled through those cornfields and spotted the kidnappers picking up the ransom money. Then they followed them.

"The surveillance team stayed with the kidnappers through the mountains, down isolated dirt roads, over the countryside. By using the plane, we thought we had stayed far enough behind to avoid detection—we could never have tracked them without it.

"By this time, we had identified both kidnappers—they had previously threatened Don Meyer—and had them within range.

"But we still had no idea where Beth was, and I made a snap decision: Our best chance of finding her alive depended on convincing them that they had gotten away with their crime."[8]

"Mr. Meyer?"

"Yes."

"You blew it."

"I didn't blow it, what are you talking about?"

"You had a plane on us."

"I did not have a plane on you!"

"How do they know then?"

"How do they know what? I delivered the money. Where is Beth?"

"We have been going round and round because the police are after us."

"There are no planes. What are you talking about? Nobody. Where is Beth?"

"You wait at that number and I'll call you in one hour. This is being hard on both of us, but you'd better call them off right now or I'm not . . ."

"Nobody knows anything. Nothing."[9]

"We knew we would not have any second chances.

"They called the local airport to ask if one of their planes had been circling overhead. The man who answered said yes, we're taking advantage of the foul weather to qualify some trainee pilots on instrument flying.

"That man was one of our agents."[10]

"Mr. Meyer, please."

"This is Mr. Meyer."

"I'm sorry to have taken so long but we had to get rid of the police. Why did you notify the police?"

"I didn't notify the police. I don't know what you're talking about. Where is Beth?"

"OK, listen very carefully. Do you have a pencil?"

"Yes."[11]

"We raced to the quarry.

"She was supposed to be in an abandoned farmhouse near an old limestone quarry.

"You never know what you're going to find. Your mind races ahead, imagining the worst.

"It was dark by now, and we fanned out, flooding the area with powerful search lights. Her father was with us—and we were all holding our breath.

"She had been chained like a dog. We finally found her in a remote corner of the farmhouse, chained in a crouched position, unable to sit or stand. They had left water for her, but it was beyond her reach—and frozen solid.

"Beth had suffered severe exposure and would have been dead in a few more hours. But she was alive—and suddenly safe in her father's arms.

"There wasn't a dry eye on the entire rescue crew.

"We raced her back to the Sheraton, where her doctor was waiting, and I simultaneously ordered the arrest team to pick up the kidnappers. When we got them, we discovered that they had sophisticated electronic gear and had been monitoring all police radio traffic—but our communications, as they learned too late, were automatically scrambled and secure.[12]

"Once we had them in custody, I ordered the bar at the Sheraton to stay open all night."[13]

A scant twenty-four hours had elapsed from Beth Ferringer's kidnapping until motorcycle mechanics George and Gary Young were arrested and charged with the crime; the paperwork, however, consumed nearly a week. Welch was determined to deliver the suspects, and the case, to local authorities in a perfect package, with every detail complete. His mobile fingerprint lab assembled all prints, the ransom team recovered the money and painstakingly compared serial numbers with the cash originally issued, and other agents took statements from witnesses and prepared evidence for trial. FBI clerks and stenographers had been ordered into State College at the first alarm, and they had come armed with office equipment, everything from typewriters to the petty-cash box. Welch sequestered the entire task force in the Sheraton Hotel and refused to permit anyone to return to Philadelphia until everyone's work was perfect.

In public statements, state and local police were credited with important cooperation and assistance, but the case was classic FBI—and trademark Welch. He could have moved cautiously, awaiting developments, but he decided to create them instead. It was a high-stakes strategy. Split-second decisions had crackled out of his command center, and a girl's life depended on every one being right. Every one was. *Kidnap!* had triggered an instant FBI blitzkrieg, and, as Welch commented later, his agents could not have performed more superbly if they had practiced for a year.

In a sense, however, they had practiced half a century. Neil Welch's tactics had been brilliant, his execution fearless and flawless, but it was unarguably J. Edgar Hoover who had made kidnapping such a paramount priority that the FBI institutional response had become, over the years, almost reflexive. Welch's success was Hoover's success, the sort of triumph which had for fifty years set the FBI apart from all other law enforcement agencies.

It was fitting, then, that when the call came from Washington eight months later, Welch was finally located in a State College courtroom, where he was attending the sentencing of Beth's kidnappers.[14] The message, on June 13, 1977, was that Neil Welch had been selected by President Carter's blue-ribbon committee as one of five candidates—and the only unanimous choice—for Director of the FBI.

17

Choosing

I told the President my only allegiance was to the
law.

I had been trained by the Jesuits. I understood
what a crime was. I knew what burglary was.

And if the occasion arose, I would be happy to
walk into the White House with my handcuffs, to
arrest anyone there who had committed a federal
crime.

-Special Agent
Neil J. Welch[1]

The forces which put Neil Welch in Jimmy Carter's White
House in July 1977 had their origins, inevitably, with Hoover,
but they also reflected the vacillating political preference
between an FBI fearless and incorruptible or one toothless
and tame (at least around Washington).

Hoover's genius, of course, had been evident in that his
FBI had seemed to be both at once, simultaneously comforting, for different reasons, to taxpayers and to politicians. But
even prior to his death, lawmakers had sensed his control
slipping and moved to assert their own. Taking a timid first
step in 1968, Congress had required that the FBI Director be
appointed by the President and confirmed by the Senate (a
precaution which, had Hoover lived, would likely have had
the ironic effect of permitting him to choose his successor).[2]

The confirmation requirement had eventually eliminated L. Patrick Gray as Director, but new charges of abuse had refuted any notion that the FBI was under control and had triggered new congressional demands for change.

As members approached the task, however, it quickly became apparent that their rhetoric was more confident than they were. Wary veterans remembered their former colleague from Missouri, Senator Edward Long, who in the mid 1960s had asked Hoover to turn over specific records on a handful of questionable FBI electronic surveillances. Ominously cooperative, Hoover had volunteered instead to make public full transcripts of *all* FBI surveillances. They would be of particular interest to the distinguished senator, Hoover had confided, because his name was mentioned on several of them. Long, of course, hastily canceled his request.[3] But the lesson was indelible, and it reinforced the uneasy suspicion that serious congressional scrutiny of the Bureau was likely to be reciprocated.

Groping for the appropriate action, some members favored adoption of an FBI charter, a comprehensive new statute specifying precisely what agents could—and could not—lawfully do. After extensive hearings, the FBI charter would finally drift, unenacted, into legislative limbo. But FBI reform proved simpler when directed at the Director rather than at the institution he headed, and proscriptions were more obvious than prescriptions. Agents should not destroy evidence or spy on innocent citizens, lawmakers agreed, but they were less certain about what the FBI *should* do. Their perplexity was, if anything, increased by Director Kelley's definition of the FBI mission in testimony before the Senate Judiciary Committee in 1974.

> SENATOR BYRD . . . Have you formed an opinion as to what the role of the FBI should be in today's society?
>
> MR. KELLEY Yes sir, I have.
>
> SENATOR BYRD Would you state it?
>
> MR. KELLEY I feel, Senator, that the FBI certainly

should perform its duties as an investigative
agency as well as possible, and that it should at
all times make itself responsive to the needs of
the citizens to the fullest extent provided by
law.[4]

It was the problem and the solution. Kelley's response
confirmed that the most concrete conception of the FBI role
was still Hoover's, which was at once an unsettling reminder
of the potency of his afterlife but also an encouraging indicator that FBI problems might go away if Congress could simply outlaw the existence of another Hoover. Limiting the
Director's term to a fixed number of years should have that
effect, the lawmakers agreed in 1974, although their debate
over the right number reflected more faith in numerology
than democracy.

Brandeis University Professor John Elliff, a former Brookings Institute fellow who specialized in FBI research, testified in favor of fifteen years, the term of the comptroller
general of the United States (who, it was understood without
saying, had generally done what Congress wished, in an independent sort of way).[5] Senator Robert Byrd, untroubled by
hobgoblins, introduced legislation proposing, variously, that
the FBI Director serve four, seven, or ten years, and when
Clarence Kelley suggested nine, Byrd retorted, "Why not
eleven?"[6] The lawmakers finally settled, uncertainly, on ten,
but the only number between four and fifteen without pro-
ponents was thirteen, an inadvertent intimation that legislative mastery of the FBI might depend heavily on luck.

The executive branch, however, was unwilling to rely entirely on the number's magic, and when Clarence Kelley
announced his retirement in 1977, the Carter administration
unveiled a talisman of its own: a specially created search
committee which would presumably Hoover-proof its choice
for FBI Director. Headed by DuPont chief executive officer
Irving Shapiro, the panel included a Southern judge (who
happened to be a woman) and a big-city mayor (who happened to be black), a mix apparently premised on the notion

that if reform was contagious, the Bureau might catch it from the committee.

But there were also two more tangible reasons to expect that a panel-picked Director would reshape the FBI, and they were named Charles Morgan, Jr., and F. A. O. Schwarz, Jr. Between them, they were uniquely experienced in dissecting FBI activities—Morgan as longtime Southern field director of the American Civil Liberties Union, Schwarz as recent chief counsel to the Senate Intelligence Committee— and their inclusion on the committee sharply improved the prospects that it would find as well as search.

Daniel J. Flood was a beloved figure in Pennsylvania coal country and a familiar eccentric in Washington. A flamboyant former Shakespearean actor, the veteran congressman favored black shirts and white ties, a combination entirely harmonious with his finely twirled villain's mustache and trademark red-lined cape. He generally rode in a white Cadillac convertible (joined, on occasion, by his wife, their parakeet, and goldfish in a bowl)[7] and gave cigars wrapped in twenty-dollar bills to Capitol Hill policemen at Christmas.[8] But his quirks did not diminish his clout. As potent chairman of the appropriations subcommittees which funded health, education, and defense, Flood had dotted his district—in which hard times had replaced hard coal as the dominant economic reality—with more than its fair share of hospitals, schools, and bases. His grateful constituents had reciprocated by making his reelection automatic, a biennial certainty which translated into durable power on Capitol Hill.

Indeed, like most masters of pork-barrel politics, Flood was invincible at home, omnipotent within his sphere of interest in Washington, and widely unknown throughout the rest of the country.

The major exception to his national anonymity had occurred during the devastation of hurricane Agnes in 1972. Television viewers had been struck by the frail, spectacled sixty-eight-year-old figure who, having commandeered a military helicopter to race to the inundated city of Wilkes-Barre, surveyed the surging water and pronounced, imperiously, "By God, it's Flood against flood!"[9]

It was a memorable line, snapped off with an actor's timing, and what followed was unforgettable. Driving himself to exhaustion, Flood had beaten back his namesake, skipping meals and sleep as he directed evacuation and relief efforts for his desperate constituents. He had muscled federal agencies unmercifully, unraveling red tape into impotent threads, demanding—and getting—an eye-opening array of assistance for his district. When a doctor friend suggested that Flood was pushing himself beyond endurance, the congressman replied, simply, "My people need me, Murph."[10]

Later, back in Washington in the Congressional Hotel where Flood resided, Flood aide Stephen B. Elko told lobbyist Deryl Fleming that the fatigued Flood needed "something to calm him down." Fleming handed the congressman an envelope containing one thousand dollars. The remedy seemed to work. Flood shoved the envelope into his bathrobe pocket and calmly padded next door to his room to sleep.[11]

It was a small crime which seemed certain to go unpunished, even when, five years later, Fleming turned up as a prosecution witness in a federal bribery case in California. By then, Fleming's regimen as a Washington lobbyist had taken its toll, and the acuity of his memory was in doubt. Seeking to establish his credibility, he testified that he rarely had a drink before noon and generally had twelve or fifteen bourbons before lunch—an apparent impossibility which suggested that any brain cells not drowned in whiskey had been at least saturated into hopeless confusion.

But Fleming insisted, under questioning, that his memory was "quite good." He could explain. The Democratic Club bar at the Congressional Hotel where he lived and drank did not open until eleven forty-five, and he usually lunched at two-thirty. Having resolved that, he proceeded to recall other things as well. He remembered clearly that defendant William Fred Peters, seeking federal accreditation for his West Coast Trade Schools, had repeatedly passed him cash to

give to Steve Elko. And Elko, Fleming recalled on the witness stand, had priced political assistance in terms of "long
underwear" (one thousand dollars) and "short underwear"
(one hundred dollars) and had left no doubt that the political
intervention of Chairman Flood would, whatever the
weather, require a comfortable supply of long underwear.

Fleming's memory proved adequate to convict Fred Peters of bribery in early 1977, but even the certainty that
prosecutors would attempt to move the corruption probe
eastward and upward did not seriously concern Flood. He
had already taken steps to make certain that the probers
would not be armed with the more volatile recollections of
Steve Elko.

Anticipating the Peters indictment, Flood had met, in the
office of his Washington lawyer, with Elko and his girl friend
during June 1976. The widening West Coast Trade Schools
investigation dictated that Elko resign as Flood's chief assistant, all had agreed, and simple prudence required that he
depart happily. An unhappy Elko might brood about his mis-
fortunes, which would certainly include, for example, the
$180,000 payoff he had never received, even after Flood had
added $14.5 million for Philadelphia's Hahnemann Hospital
to the 1975 Community Services Act appropriation at the
request of Congressman Joshua Eilberg. But there was no
cause for concern, Elko assured those at the meeting, because money could do what Fleming's alcohol had not—
namely, make him forget.

Flood had, at first, not seemed to hear. He urged Elko and
his friend, Patricia Brislin, simply to trust him, reminding
them that his close association with their families extended
back to Brislin's grandmother. Brislin responded brusquely
that her grandmother was dead, and Elko needed $3,100 per
month. Reluctantly facing the problem, Flood mumbled reservations about several suggested money sources. Finally
Elko proposed Phillip Medico. Stabbing the air with a bony
finger, the old actor had agreed, "That's it."

Known to Elko as Uncle Phil, Medico was known to Wilkes-
Barre area residents as one of five brothers who had built

Medico Industries into a thriving mini-conglomerate, buoyed by a dependable supply of army defense contracts.[12] Dan Flood had used the Medico Industries private box at Pocono Downs Race Track and had a close personal relationship with the family.[13] Medico was perfect. The problem was solved, the meeting confidently adjourned.

Those present would have departed with less assurance had they understood that their precautions would, inadvertently, bring Flood to the attention of Neil Welch. Even before Elko and Flood had agreed on Medico, Welch had taken an interest in him, since he had been named by the Pennsylvania Crime Commission as a capo in the Bufalino organized crime family.[14] And because of his recognized expertise in official corruption investigations, Welch would soon be asked to take an interest in Elko as well.

Even so, it was difficult to imagine how Welch—in the Philadelphia field office—could have any significant impact on the investigation of Flood. California FBI agents had developed the case and would probably forward any allegations about the congressman to the Washington field office, which had historically been dependably incurious about the activities of powerful committee chairmen in Congress.

"They asked a lot about Hoover.

"For my generation of agents, he was a father figure, just a year or two younger than my own father. And I thought he was a genius in many respects—but he should have retired in 1960.

"Still, even with his mistakes in the last few years, he continued to do some important things right. Until the day he died, for example, Hoover rigidly limited Bureau headquarters to 475 agents—an implicit recognition that headquarters agents are essentially nonproductive in fighting crime.

"Less than five years later, that number had jumped to over 900, a full 10 percent of all FBI agents sitting around Bureau headquarters like drones.

"I told the committee—and Clarence Kelley was sitting there—that the explosion of headquarters staff was Kelley's worst mistake. The Bureau wanted huge buildings, miles of fingerprint files, dozens of agents firing tracer bullets from submachine guns . . . and it was really all for the tourists.

"Everyone knew those machine guns had never been fired in anger—we called that Bureau operation Disneyland East.

"But even though Hoover would have been furious to find 10 percent of his agents inside it, the new FBI building with his name on it was a perfect monument. It dominates Pennsylvania Avenue, imposing and intimidating from the outside, a Byzantine maze inside. Like the man himself, his building is complex and controversial—and unique."[15]

Maneuvering to break Hoover's dead man's grip on both his building and his Bureau, the search committee had declined the convenience of FBI background checks on candidates under consideration, and it met in a nearby Guest Quarters Motel instead of a Bureau conference room.[16] There, after screening 235 resumes, the panel narrowed the list to 48 and then conducted the interviews which would cut the field to five.[17] To fix the FBI's future, they probed its past, questioning each candidate who had Bureau experience about bag jobs and abuses, and automatically disqualified any interviewee tainted by involvement in questionable FBI techniques.

(Candidate candor produced some uncomfortable moments. After one stony-faced veteran acknowledged participating in both black-bag jobs and COINTELPRO activities, panel member Charles Morgan, groping to fill the awkward silence which followed, asked, good-naturedly, "You . . . uh . . . never left a piece of tape on a door latch, did you?" Unblinking and unsmiling, the official replied, "Not an ash from a cigarette . . . and not a print from a finger." *My God*, Morgan thought to himself, *I just found the only poet in the FBI.)*[18]

But as the interviews progressed, it became evident that it was easier to dismiss the participants in past abuses than the questions raised by them, and the panel recognized that judging the men who appeared before it also required a judgment about one who did not, namely former Special Agent John J. Kearney. A former supervisor of New York's Squad 47, which had targeted the violent Weatherman underground, Kearney was indicted (even as the search committee searched) in April 1977 for alleged wiretaps, break-ins, and mail openings.[19] The illegality of his actions was not at issue, but the next Director's task would be shaped by whether Kearney had given orders or followed them, and the committee's pointed questions about FBI policies and problems were always counterpointed by Kearney.

"I thought it was a mistake.

"Sergeants don't make policy. The Justice Department Civil Rights Division had immunized the agents who actually did the wiretaps and bag jobs, to get their cooperation against Kearney, who was only a first-level supervisor. It was like immunizing privates to testify against their sergeant—and far from getting at the generals who had actually given the orders.

"When the CIA had similar problems, Vice President Nelson Rockefeller was named to head a presidential commission of fact finders, which recommended institutional reforms, not criminal indictments.

"But for the FBI, they unleashed those notorious bumblers from the Civil Rights Division, who found no fault at all with the Presidents and congressional committees and Justice Department officials who had encouraged and monitored Bureau counterintelligence activities for decades—instead, they put the total responsibility on one miserable supervisor in New York.

"But the unfairness of the indictment did not change my views on COINTELPRO. That whole domestic intelligence program had been wrong from the beginning. When headquarters asked why I refused to participate in their crazy schemes, I said that if I was going to be sued for being stupid, I wanted to think up my own stupid plan—I wasn't going to execute theirs.

"I don't think the FBI has any damn business fooling

around with people's political beliefs. And I've never thought radical violence in this country was much of a threat —there's more violence in any big city any Saturday night than all of the radicals from coast to coast have ever managed to produce.

"Who cares what books their neighbors read, which political leaders they admire? I don't—and those factors never impacted on the FBI mission as I saw it.

"Our business is enforcing federal law . . . period."[20]

In the end, the committee concluded that a liberal's conservative might be the perfect outsider's insider. Appearing before the panel in a somber pin-striped suit, strong and serious, Neil Welch was a cookie-cutter copy of a Hoover-trained agent—until he spoke. And even then, his words came deliberately, building sentences with police-report circumspection, but what he said was innovative, original, and refreshingly simple. In the tangle of proposed guidelines and charters, Welch argued persuasively that the FBI should be governed only by the Constitution and existing federal law, and he offered a career of accomplishment to prove it was possible.

Hoover would have instantly understood, in the circumstances, that Bureau praise would damage Welch far more than criticism, but his heirs did not. Instead, they offered dozens of Welch defects to the search committee, omitting only the one which would have reversed the panel's conclusion; Welch had not engaged in improper domestic intelligence activities, the officials reluctantly agreed, and their agreement convinced the committee to make Welch the standard against which other candidates would be judged.[21] The next Director, it was evident, would have to overcome the headquarters bureaucracy to set a new FBI course, and the nine distinguished citizens who assembled around a folding metal table in a Washington motel were ultimately most impressed by the fact that Neil Welch had already fought that battle—and won.

"I think the Bureau viewed Welch as exactly the kind of

person I figured he was," panelist Charles Morgan said, "a tough sonuvabitch who was going to do his duty, what he thought was right—and it did not much matter who got in the way. That made Welch frightening to a number of people —but we were not interested in picking the great American wishywash to run the Federal Bureau of Investigation."[22]

Jimmy Carter, however, was the man who would actually do the picking, and his primary interest seemed to be in replacing Clarence Kelley at the earliest possible date. Underscoring his sense of urgency, Carter denied, without explanation, his search committee's request for a thirty-day extension and announced instead that the panel's task was successfully completed. Displaying no favorites, the President pronounced all five finalists "superbly qualified," said he would probably name one of them Director, and scheduled personal interviews to decide which one.[23]

Ignoring the line of waiting players, two men jumped into a golf cart and motored off across the fairway, jarring the dignified tournament protocol of Foxhill Country Club, a transgression mitigated—or perhaps compounded—by the fact that they had no golf clubs.

Steve Elko and his attorney had not come to play. A California grand jury had indicted Elko for bribery in the West Coast Trade Schools case a month earlier,[24] and a key figure in the defense strategy was located, as they would discover, on the fairway of the suburban Wilkes-Barre course. Uncle Phil Medico had agreed to help pay for Elko's defense and his silence, which made him a central figure in defense strategy. When Elko finally caught up with him, Medico's vague comments about friendship and loyalty (and the "bastards" in Washington chasing Elko because he had "balls") did not, at first blush, seem to justify the effort made to receive them, although on reflection the attorney opined that each Medico sentence had three meanings. One of them, inescapably, was that Elko should not talk.

Three months later, shortly after Elko's October 1977 conviction in California, Elko returned to Wilkes-Barre with some disturbing news for Medico: Federal prosecutor John Dowd had proposed to place Elko in the Witness Protection Program, trading leniency at sentencing for Elko's coopera- tion. Medico listened silently, remarked prudently that Elko should simply tell the truth—and then pointed to the loca- tion outside his window from which the FBI was conducting surveillance. After several other meetings in Wilkes-Barre, it was decided that Elko would enter the Witness Protection Program for the purpose of learning how much the govern- ment knew—but he did not plan to tell the truth.

Lacking tea leaves, Bureau-watchers watched their watches on July 7, 1977, and concluded that Neil Welch's sixty-five minute interview with Attorney General Griffin Bell meant that he was the front-running candidate for FBI Director.[25] (Others had met with the AG much more briefly.) The assessment was, at the time, probably accurate, even though Bell had mentioned the die-hard Bureau opposition to Welch ("Neil, they're just afraid you'll destroy the whole thing over there")[26] and had refrained from mentioning the intense political pressures Welch's Pennsylvania probes were generating, particularly from Congressmen Eilberg and Flood.

Leaving the Justice Department, Welch was escorted by Deputy Attorney General Peter Flaherty to the White House and ushered into the Oval Office,[27] where he was received by the President with cautious politeness (a marked improve- ment, nevertheless, from his Washington reception as a rookie agent twenty-six years earlier and four blocks east). The interview began slowly, with Vice President Mondale more observer than participant. President Carter masked any sympathy he might have had for either side in the bitter Bureau-Welch battle which had erupted after Welch's selec- tion as a finalist.

"To improve federal law enforcement," Welch had ob- served, lobbing the first shell, "the best thing you could do would be sandbag Bureau headquarters and rip out the phones."[28] And if someone had, smoke signals would have sufficed nicely for the boiling Bureau officials. Two angry puffs: Stop Welch.

"If he gets it, there won't need to be a housecleaning— most of the brass will pass him on their way out as he comes into the building,"[29] a veteran FBI official had shot back, incredulous that Welch was the unanimous choice of the blue-ribbon panel. Indeed, it had quickly become apparent that unanimity was something the search committee and Bureau brass had in common, for and against Welch, respectively, and a hubbub of official whispers had offered Welch's flaws to anyone interested.

Short fuse was one solemn warning of Welch's shortcomings, one backed up by Thomas Kennelley and Edward Rye. A former Strike Force attorney in Buffalo, the slightly built Kennelley told reporters that, but for his rescue by another agent, he "would still be in orbit," into which Welch had threatened to punch him ten years earlier in a dispute over evidence.[30] (Having fervently wished a similar fate on the entire Strike Force, however, Bureau officials could not protest too much.) Rye's mistaken-identity shoot-out with Detroit agents in 1971 had not involved Welch at all, until in its aftermath he called Rye "stupid and lucky." This, while indisputably at least half true, was nevertheless, Bureau officials had piously warned, suggestive of recklessness.[31]

Even if Welch had a short fuse, however, fifty years of history suggested that might be a professional prerequisite for the position of FBI Director, and it had proved difficult to document any defect more serious. Welch's wholesale closing of domestic security cases signaled softness on subversives, Associate Director James Adams was sure,[32] but a careful review of his shutdown orders had not proved it, and the military crispness of Welch's words undercut any claim that his actions spoke louder. Similarly, the sinister specter of "missing" Detroit files had fizzled, simply another anti-Welch rumor which, as a Justice Department official charged, "could only have come from people in the Bureau."[33]

It was uncertain which whispers Carter had heard from the Bureau, but he listened attentively to Welch's views on law enforcement and the Director's position, interjecting only an occasional question or comment. The interview lasted twenty-five minutes (ten minutes longer, observers noted significantly, than the President's interview with another candidate the same day)[34] and ended as it had begun, with noncommittal politeness. The President graciously showed Welch to the door.

Welch was convinced it was over. He would not be President Carter's choice for Director. Mentally replaying the interviews and his previous discussions with Attorney General Bell, Welch concluded that his liabilities with the Bureau old guard had not been seriously damaging—but that his inherent assets had. Bell had made clear that the Administration wanted an FBI firmly under the Attorney General's control[35] (undeterred by the fact that Pat Gray's had been), and control, Carter's expression had communicated eloquently, did not include the possibility of an FBI Director walking into the White House with handcuffs to make an arrest. The President did not share his search committee's enthusiasm for Welch's success against white-collar crime and political corruption. The textbook FBI probes which had recently toppled the powerful Democratic Speaker of the Pennsylvania House of Representatives, along with a bipartisan bag of lesser figures, went unmentioned in the interview. And even though a Federal Election Commission probe which forced Pennsylvania Governor Milton Shapp's abortive presidential campaign to repay $299,000 had also revealed abundant grounds for a federal criminal probe,[36] Attorney General Bell had made it unmistakably clear to Welch that the Carter administration did not desire a vigorous FBI investigation.[37]

(Characteristically, Welch launched one anyway, and several months later Bell told him bluntly that he would not permit any Republican United States Attorney to prosecute indictments arising out of the investigation of the Shapp campaign. Since Pennsylvania, at the time, did not have any other variety of federal prosecutor, Bell's action effectively killed the case, with only a handful of convictions of fringe figures.)[38]

Carter hesitated.

Finally, apparently stymied by the certainty that he could not control the only candidate for Director who might control the Bureau, Carter decided he could not decide.

By the end of July, the new FBI Director had not been named, and the appointment had apparently, for unexplained reasons, lost its presidential urgency. It would be another six months before the Chief Executive, who had refused his committee a thirty-day extension, would nominate his Director—which would necessitate a somewhat embarrassing request to Clarence Kelley, the man marked for immediate removal, that he please postpone his retirement.[39]

Carter was more decisive in November 1977 when he was contacted by Philadelphia Congressman Eilberg—who was by then himself a subject of criminal investigation linked to the Flood probe. Eilberg urgently requested the President to fire Pennsylvania United States Attorney David W. Marston, coauthor of this book, whose office prosecuted the corruption cases built by Welch. It was a demand which Attorney General Bell had repeatedly refused.

Asking no questions, Carter agreed.

He called Bell and ordered him to fire Marston.

Bell did.

Several months after his interview with President Carter, Welch received a telephone call from Washington.

It concerned Steve Elko.

Washington FBI agents had interviewed Elko repeatedly —with minimal success. The savvy Elko wove tangled webs, candidly describing crimes only if the statute of limitations had expired, stubbornly yielding facts only as a last resort.

But the FBI grapevine whispered that Welch had trained several agents as specialists in the interrogation of subjects in complex corruption cases. Would he detail them to Washington to conduct the Elko interrogation?

Welch would.

By then, the Flood-Eilberg probes had become a Welch priority, and his agents were meticulously reconstructing the corrupt activities of the two Pennsylvania congressmen. Compliance with the request from Washington would be automatic.

Furious opposition from the Bureau was equally automatic. In mid interrogation, rumors that Welch's agents were secretly operating nearby (indeed, within pistol shot) filtered back to Bureau headquarters. Officials there were apoplectic. Ordered to supply an immediate explanation, Welch charged that headquarters knew all about it. He had notified them by telegram, which, he asserted, was probably unread and buried in some supervisor's IN box—which, on investigation, proved to be the case. The incident sparked a vintage Welch rage ("We're busting our asses to make cases and you sons of bitches provide nothing but harassment—why don't you read your own goddamn mail before you raise hell with me?"), which diverted the Bureau's attention from his agents in Washington, who successfully completed the interrogation of Steve Elko.[40]

Elko's testimony, together with other evidence developed by Welch's agents, would in time make Flood and Eilberg former congressmen and convicted felons.[41] The House Committee on Standards of Official Conduct, after making its own investigation of Flood, reported that his criminal conduct was a pervasive pattern: On twenty-four separate occasions, the committee charged, Flood had demanded or received money to influence government officials.[42]

The national attention generated by those two cases, however, overshadowed a more significant development. Neil Welch had revolutionized the FBI's investigative techniques in political corruption cases, and the sophisticated undercover methods he had pioneered were being quietly—and unofficially—adopted in FBI field offices around the country. And while it was not yet apparent, Welch's innovations would soon allow the FBI, for the first time, to attack patterns of official corruption instead of isolated cases—with dramatic success.

Back in Dan Flood's coal country, Elko's allegations against Flood were widely disbelieved—a corrupt fixer accusing a revered public servant to save himself. It was a phenomenon which Welch had witnessed before and which he would address—in ABSCAM—by creating indisputable videotaped evidence.

Even so, it is doubtful whether such evidence would have changed the sentiment of Dan Flood's "people." The mayor of Wilkes-Barre proclaimed March 16, 1978, as "Dan Flood Day,"[43] in honor of the beleaguered congressman. The local Lion's Club named him "Citizen of the Year."[44] In a newspaper interview, Mrs. Flood, somewhat less ceremoniously, named Steve Elko "that mucko."[45]

On January 19, 1978, Attorney General Griffin Bell announced the nomination of a federal appeals court judge, William H. Webster, to be Director of the FBI, and the Senate promptly confirmed the nomination.[46]

On August 4, 1978, Director Webster, describing Neil Welch as his "most effective field commander," announced his promotion to director in charge of the three New York field offices. This meant 850 agents and the heaviest caseload in the country, and the New York operation was widely regarded as the model FBI office.[47]

"I plan to take this office apart brick by brick and reassemble it," Welch said, accepting the appointment and giving notice that he had a different model in mind. "I want to do here what I've done elsewhere."[48]

18

NYO

Straddling Park Avenue, the Pan Am Building soars skyward out of a solid clump of short squat buildings, its dominance of square neighbors nourished, perhaps, by the surplus sunlight collected by its graceful six-sided shape. Unlike Grand Central Station and the Helmsley Building, which huddle cautiously at its base, Pan Am's business is the sky, and the tenants who share its tower also share its lofty perspective. None of them, it seemed certain, would have any interest in an incident which occurred in a blood-spattered meat-packing house across town in early 1977. Certainly not the former Attorney General of the United States, who, on the fifty-second floor, behind a rich wood door confidently set off by a faded oriental carpet, presided over the prestigious law firm of Rogers & Wells.

It had started with a subpoena, and the two FBI agents who had come to serve it on meat packer Pat "Patty Bones" Collarusso appeared to have nothing in common except an employer and a problem. DiSimone and Brookings were white and black, stocky and slim, cocky and careful, and, working their first assignment together, they were suddenly in the center of a silent circle of men with meat hooks, who made their living using them.

DiSimone glanced quickly at the men who surrounded them and then at his new partner; Joe Brookings, who had executive gray hair, a perfectly tailored suit, and twelve tough years on the street as a New York beat cop, sensed the question and answered quietly.

"I'm not going anywhere."

Taking two fast steps across the sawdust-covered floor, DiSimone whipped his .45 automatic from its shoulder holster and jammed it into Collarusso's mouth, which opened obligingly, like a fish being fed, while Brookings pulled his own gun and covered the room.

"Look, Pat," DiSimone said slowly, forcing Collarusso's head back, "I don't know what you and your bozos have planned here, but you're the first motherfucker to go." He paused, punching it in a little further, gunmetal grating frozen teeth. "I just thought you should know that."[1]

No one moved.

A meat hook clanged to the floor.

Another.

Then the rest, an odd cacophony of surrender, as the men who had held them melted away, leaving their shaken boss alone to accept service of the subpoena which Tony DiSimone handed him. It had been alleged that Collarusso paid five thousand dollars to Staten Island Congressman John M. Murphy to obtain Social Security benefits for his mother,[2] and the agents had been ordered to investigate.

The packinghouse clamor did not carry as far as the fifty-second floor of the Pan Am building, of course, and it would be several months more before anything was heard there which gave cause for concern. FBI probes in the meat-packing district did not generally penetrate Park Avenue, and if an odd one did, it could be countered with weapons more potent than meat hooks. It did not become apparent until the summer of 1978, then, that the case DiSimone and Brookings were working had indeed taken some odd twists. And even then, there was no particular sense of urgency until August 14, when DiSimone, without warning or prior approval, served the ambassador.[3]

The reaction from the Pan Am Building was furious and immediate, and less than twenty-four hours later Special

Agent Anthony P. DiSimone met his new SAC under less than ideal circumstances.

"You're DiSimone, aren't you?"

"Yes sir."

"Did you serve a subpoena on the former Iranian ambassador yesterday?"

DiSimone hesitated, feeling a fear which had been absent when he faced Collarusso's henchmen.

"Yes sir," he finally answered.

"Did you know he is represented by William P. Rogers, who has served as both Secretary of State and Attorney General of the United States?" the SAC demanded.

"I do now, sir. Mr. Rogers called and ripped into me. He said I was completely out of line, Ambassador Zahedi was a very important person with prior diplomatic immunity, I had no business serving him, and I would be disciplined for doing it."

"And what did you say to Mr. Rogers?"

DiSimone swallowed miserably, knowing the prior questions had only been groundwork for this one.

"Well, sir, after the conversation went back and forth a couple times, I finally told Mr. Rogers to go fuck off."

The SAC glared down at the young agent, his lips set in a tight line.

"You are going to have a problem with me, DiSimone," he finally said deliberately, "if it ever takes you that long again to tell someone interfering with an FBI investigation where to go. Next time a lawyer tries that," he added, "subpoena him.

"And one more thing—I'm going to work this case along with you and Brookings. Keep me advised at every step."[4]

From that day, the extraordinary case being developed by DiSimone and Brookings would also be worked by Neil Welch, who, in addition to being New York SAC and assistant director, was still regarded as one of the best street agents in the FBI.

The investigation was UNIRAC, FBI-short for union racketeering, a probe spawned by an aborted extortion on the

Miami waterfront.[5] The intended victim had led the FBI
undercover, penetrating the perennially suspect international longshoremens' union, and UNIRAC had rambled up
the coast like a tropical storm, unpredictable and dangerous,
battering some port cities and sparing others. After dissipat-
ing into a swirl of unfocused allegations in the middle Atlantic states, UNIRAC had tentatively regathered its strength in
New York and ripped into the Brooklyn waterfront. There,
its chief victim would be powerful longshoremen union
leader Anthony M. Scotto—who had campaigned with President Carter, socialized with establishment New York,[6] and
raised, by his count, almost a million dollars for the recent
reelection of New York Governor Hugh Carey.[7]

But Neil Welch thought the probe might reach further.
After reviewing evidence with DiSimone and Brookings, he
agreed that veteran Congressman Murphy was an obvious
target but instructed them also to run out all leads which
seemed to implicate another important official.

That official, who, like Scotto, counted Presidents and congressmen among his personal friends and the blue-chip firm
on the fifty-second floor of the Pan Am Building as his counsel, was the Shah of Iran.[8]

While NYO fit neatly within its box on the Bureau organizational chart as a field office identical to others, it had never,
since its origin in 1924, been comparably confined in reality.
New York Office was unique. The unchallenged FBI flagship
in the field, it had been the scene of some of the Bureau's
most memorable triumphs and most unforgettable disasters,
both the result, headquarters had always suspected, of its
characteristic indifference to Washington's rules.

Bureau inspectors had perennial difficulty in New York, in
part because there were simply too many agents there, but
also because of the inventive measures employed to thwart
them. One legendary NYO agent specialized in undercover
work, in violation of Hoover's prohibition, and kept his
secrets secure by keeping his notes in Yiddish.[9] Most of the
graves in Brooklyn, it was rumored, held Communist Party

members (since the tombstones provided all that was needed to open a subversive file—name and birth date), and, despite its obsession with Communists, headquarters never could distinguish the living from the dead.[10]

A day which started routinely at NYO might end anywhere. In 1959, during the state visit of Nikita Khrushchev, a New York agent was invited by a friend in the State Department security section to attend a reception for the Soviet leader. There, the agent demonstrated that he was one of the few Americans who could consume vodka in the volume, and with the gregarious enthusiasm, customary with the Russians, and they promptly requested his assignment to the official security delegation. Weighing the intelligence possibilities against the chance for some unforeseen disaster, the Bureau reluctantly agreed. And for the next few days the agent lived with his new Russian friends, presumably imbibing their secrets along with their hospitality.

On Khrushchev's departure date, the agent went to the airport with his comrades, and then, to the horror of watching Bureau officials, boarded their plane. Vividly imagining Hoover's reaction to an agent defection, they stared dumbly as the plane's engines started—then, seconds before takeoff, the agent suddenly emerged. Back on the ground, he was instantly surrounded by a protective circle of senior Bureau officials who, certain they had an intelligence bonanza, began debriefing on the spot.

What had the Soviets tempted him with on the airplane? A farewell drink.

What had he learned about Russian strategic objectives? The agent seemed lost in thought.

They waited expectantly.

Someone repeated the question.

He looked puzzled.

"How should I know?" he finally demanded groggily. "I've been drunk for a week!"[11]

By the time Welch reported in 1978, the New York FBI had spilled into three separate field offices with more than thirteen hundred[12] employees. Even before reviewing active cases, he knew that demographics alone guaranteed better Bureau business. The city harbored the nation's major financial markets and most potent organized crime families, a mutually inexclusive mélange which made quality crime reliably rampant. In addition, the United Nations contingent of diplomats and spies required priority attention to foreign intelligence, a specialty which accounted for close to half of the NYO agent resources. (FBI foreign intelligence activities are not treated in this account.) It was the same busy kaleidoscope which Welch had studied twenty-five years earlier, and he expressed his enthusiasm at an introductory press conference to be "returning to the scene of the crime."[13]

But two things had changed.

The FBI's war against the Weatherman underground, Welch soon discovered, had been won by La Cosa Nostra. Responding to Washington pressure for results, New York had transferred its best undercover agents from the organized crime unit to Squad 47, which targeted the violent Weatherman underground, and the move had produced triple failure. The Weathermen (and women) remained at large, members of Squad 47 had been disciplined and indicted for their illegal tactics (and Welch's immediate predecessor, SAC J. Wallace LaPrade, had been fired by Attorney General Griffin Bell in the controversy), and FBI penetration of New York's crime families had disappeared.[14]

Agent morale had plummeted everywhere. Even agents who had no affection for former Assistant Directors W. Mark Felt and Edward S. Miller thought that their Civil Rights Act indictment, along with former Director Pat Gray's, was upside down; it named relatives of the Weatherman underground fugitives who had declined to assist the FBI search as *victims.*[15] Agents had marched on Washington, standing on the courthouse steps in bitter silent protest while the three officials were arraigned inside.[16] The indictments were, on balance, far less remarkable than the agent demonstration, but neither could have happened in Hoover's FBI, and both offered vivid evidence that the FBI had no leader. Nowhere was the agent malaise as acute as in New York, Welch found, and he knew immediately that rebuilding agent morale was one of his most pressing priorities.

(Despite Welch's efforts, however, the widespread belief that FBI agents had been treated unfairly inspired formation of the FBI Agents Association, a national lobby group for G-men—and G-women. While it has not yet received major public attention, the FBIAA is unquestionably the most significant structural reform of Hoover's FBI to date.)[17]

Welch was startled at the extent to which the diversion of agents from organized crime to the Weatherman fugitives had devastated the FBI's capability against the crime families. The steadily expanding FBI penetration of the LCN, which had originated under Robert Kennedy, had been abruptly reversed in the early 1970s, dwindling to nearly pre-Apalachin impotence by 1978. Veteran Manhattan District Attorney Robert Morganthau had raised the question immediately after Welch's arrival: What had happened to the FBI's organized crime intelligence, which had been indispensable to local prosecutors?[18] A few days later, Special Agent Paul Cummings, Welch's old friend from Mississippi days, supplied the incredible answer.

"When I leave, Chief, you can turn out the lights," Cummings told Welch, announcing his retirement, "because I'm the last agent in New York with any member informants in La Cosa Nostra."[19]

Welch's second surprise came from United States Attorney Robert B. Fiske, Jr., who told him during an early strategy session that he would not find the sort of political corruption in New York which had made Welch's reputation in Philadelphia and Detroit.[20] A highly respected trial lawyer, Fiske went on to explain that New York officials were more sophisticated and that their corrupt activities were generally covered with a veneer of legality, applied by shrewd lawyers. He was anxious to develop more corruption prosecutions, Fiske emphasized, but complaints were rarely made to his office.

Welch listened thoughtfully and concluded that Fiske's comments said more about the priorities of his office than the practices of corrupt officials. Historically the premier federal prosecutor's office in the country, New York's Southern District had recently come under increasing criticism from agents, who contended that its chief interest was in providing basic trial experience for young lawyers fresh from the city's best firms rather than in building sophisticated criminal prosecutions. Most Southern District prosecutors stayed only two or three years before returning to their firms, which precluded continuity in complicated cases, and agents suspected a reluctance on the part of these young prosecutors to pursue targets represented by the firms which were their once and future employers.[21]

Moreover, the Southern District had disbanded its Organized Crime Strike Force, a move which provoked criticism from law enforcement experts, including Professor G. Robert Blakey, whose harsh assessment was that the Southern District had not "conducted a major corruption prosecution in the last ten years."[22] And the absence of complaints, Welch knew from experience, did not reflect any decline in corrupt activity, but rather a resigned public's shrugging acceptance of the potency of corrupt officials and the impotence of law enforcement, both unchangeable facts of life.

It would require a number of months to accomplish, but the public would eventually realize, several hours after it became evident to a stunned assortment of public officials, that Welch had changed the facts of life. In the beginning, however, only his agents had any inkling of Welch's plans, and even they, seeing only the fragments which fitted their need-to-know, would underestimate the scope of his strategy.

He moved three small units out of the office to secret sites in the New York area and imported Special Agent Len Vernier from Philadelphia as his personal supervisor of their activities. The sites were stocked with state-of-the-art cameras and communications equipment, including infrared equipment for nighttime photography and a camera mounted behind pepper-shakerlike holes in an attaché case for filming business meetings. A bewildering potpourri of vehicles suddenly appeared—panel trucks, motorcycles, and New York taxis rolled into the sites—along with two Vernier acquisitions from the Drug Enforcement Administration—a white, soft-top Lincoln Continental "pimp mobile" and a thirty-five-foot cabin cruiser (both previously confiscated from drug dealers). Finally, Vernier added his favorite personal touch—a magician's mix of wigs and disguises, ingredients for instant dockworkers or doctors, bartenders or priests.

Back on East Sixty-ninth Street, Welch roamed his tenth-floor FBI office restlessly, as unpredictable as Hoover but with a strikingly different agenda. He ordered three carefully chosen agents to investigate the FBI itself, to evaluate critically the weaknesses and strengths of its efforts against the organized crime families. It was an unprecedented assignment which the agents half expected would result, somehow, in their dismissal. After assurances from Welch, however, they attacked the project with enthusiasm and eventually documented the astonishing dimensions of the FBI's intelligence failure: Even though crime remained a young man's business, existing Bureau files did not identify any crime family member under the age of forty-five.

Welch had an even more unorthodox assignment for several other agents, ordering them to enroll as students in the Greenwich Village Shade Tree School. They thought they had misunderstood. Shade Tree was an antiestablishment action group, a free-form assemblage of radical thinkers and critics. Surely the SAC had intended that they infiltrate the school or covertly discredit it.

No.

They would be students.

The FBI would pay their tuition.

And after they graduated, they would gradually realize why a school which would likely have been investigated by Hoover's FBI was instead schooling Welch's investigators.

Matching agent skills with investigative priorities, Welch made hundreds of other reassignments. Bureau approval was not required, and only in retrospect would the headquarters

officials who had smiled tolerantly at his intention to reassemble the New York office "brick by brick" realize that agents
were his bricks. Even then, there was no immediate compre-
hension of what he had accomplished, because the NYO telex
to the Bureau on May 26, 1978, three months before Welch's
arrival in New York, had been routinely approved and forgotten.[23]

It had been an application for approval of a national undercover operation aimed at organized crime figures who dealt
in rare art and counterfeit securities. Headquarters had not
investigated sufficiently to learn, as its files would have revealed, that the proposed informant had previously been
terminated for committing felonies while working for the
FBI.[24] His name did not, at the time, ring any bells at the
Bureau.

It was Melvin C. Weinberg.

Welch did not know where the investigation might lead,
but he was certain that organized crime was inseparable
from political corruption.

"Every time we set up a camera and turn the lights on a
stage aimed at the mob," he told an agent as they reviewed
the operation which was code-named ABSCAM (short for
Abdul Enterprises, Inc.-scam), "politicians appear immediately. I defy anyone to investigate organized crime apart
from political corruption—the actors play on the same
stage."[25]

The ABSCAM drama had been meticulously casted and
scripted. A fabulously wealthy Arab sheik would seek to
make investments in the United States and would be steered
—by Weinberg and other corrupt middlemen—through the
maze of officials and fixers whose assistance might be helpful.
If payoffs were required, they would be paid. The sheik's
payoff money was sufficiently authentic that the government
would later sue some bribe-taking officials to get it back, but
his investments were imaginary—as was he. Though they
wore carefully chosen Arab dress, the sheik and his entourage were all FBI agents.

After reviewing the ABSCAM operation, Welch made a

decision which would, in the end, determine its success. Having been alerted that political corruption was difficult to detect in the Southern District of New York, Welch turned his attention to the Eastern District. There, an aggressive prosecutor named Thomas Puccio presided over the Brooklyn Organized Crime Strike Force, an office staffed for the most part with ambitious street-smart lawyers who had *not* received job offers from New York's best firms. Like Welch, however, Puccio and his assistants were itching for an all-out assault on official corruption.

Welch transferred nearly one hundred FBI agents from Manhattan to Brooklyn—and in doing so, radically refocused the ABSCAM operation.[26]

The stage was set.

19

Shah and Sheik

Running down their last lead in East Orange, New Jersey, DiSimone and Brookings were prepared to quit.

Collarusso had denied making payoffs to Murphy, and other allegations involving the congressman seemed to hold more smoke than fire. The two agents had established, for example, that Murphy had for years combined business and politics with friends high in faraway places, notably Nicaragua and Iran[1]—but the leads went cold at the water's edge. They knew that the maritime lobby had given him a contribution of nearly $10,000 as his powerful Merchant Marine Committee conducted hearings on a multimillion dollar maritime subsidy[2]—and this more than a year prior to any election—but dozens of other politicians had enjoyed similar largess. And they had learned that he served on the board of the Shah's New York–based Pahlavi Foundation, but even the specific allegations made by disappointed bidders on the foundation's Fifth Avenue headquarters building had not been backed by proof.[3]

Each of the three contractors who had bid unsuccessfully on the Iranian project had told the agents a similar story. They had lost, they contended, because they had been unwilling to make the two illegal payments demanded—a $250,000 kickback to the Iranian officials and a comparable payoff to Congressman John Murphy.[4]

The successful bidder, Frank Briscoe Company of East Orange, would undoubtedly deny the allegation, and the probe would be ended.

"We're here to talk about payoffs on the Pahlavi Foundation construction project," Brookings started, deciding to try a bluff, "and you might as well tell us straight, because frankly we already have the whole story."

His words settled in the room.

A Briscoe officer glanced at the company lawyer, who nodded, and excused himself. A moment later, he returned to the room and handed the agents a canceled check for $250,000, payable to Kenna Holding Company.

Brookings and DiSimone were astounded.

They examined the check incredulously, struggling to contain their excitement.

The Briscoe officials seemed not to notice. They patiently explained that, after the award of the Pahlavi contract, their now-deceased company president, William Kelly, had been instructed by foundation official Nasser Sayyah to prepare the check, as agreed, and fly to Teheran. There, he had met Sayyah, who had laundered the check through an Iranian casino with the assistance of a South African expatriate named Noel Anthony Souter.

The agents could not take notes fast enough.

Who was Souter again?

An associate of Sayyah's, Kelly had said, who had a shell company on the Isle of Man.

It was named Kenna Holding Company.

Remembering more details, the Briscoe officials produced telex messages sent by Kelly from Teheran.

THIS COUNTRY IS FANTASTIC—BOOMING, WITH GREAT CULTURE . . . I EXPECT TO BE HOME LATE NEXT WEEK. NASSER COMING U.S. END OF MAY.

NEGOTIATION SEEMS TO BE COMING WELL. I LIKE THE PEOPLE.

And as the agents tried to absorb it all, the company officials recalled one more detail: When he had met Sayyah in

Teheran to launder the check, Kelly said that Sayyah had been accompanied by Congressman Murphy.

The next few weeks were a frenzy of activity.

Trace the money.

To their surprise, Brookings and DiSimone experienced no official difficulty in booking a flight to the Isle of Man, an Irish Sea tax haven midway between England and Ireland, and to their amazement they found Souter without difficulty. He knew Sayyah, remembered the check, and confirmed the details.

Pin down Sayyah.

Nasser Sayyah lived in a glass house, the exclusive Olympic Tower on Fifth Avenue, a sleek skyscraper with smoked-glass sides across the street from the solid stone grandeur of St. Patrick's Cathedral. Its apartment entrance was unmarked, and it was well guarded by a muscular doorman who had orders to bar any FBI agents. He was unsuccessful. On the eleventh floor, DiSimone and Brookings rapped on Sayyah's door until he grudgingly opened, then served him with a subpoena. Sayyah seemed undecided how to react—then abruptly invited them in.

A powerful man in his fifties, Sayyah wore a gray sharkskin suit, a white shirt with black buttons, and black alligator shoes. He exuded confidence.

"You know, I am a very important man in the law," he confided smoothly, smiling indulgently at the young agents. "I am the Shah's representative in the United States of America. Do you understand that before we start talking?"

DiSimone was not impressed.

"I am with the FBI," he replied. "I am the President's representative. Do you understand that?

"And by the way," DiSimone continued, seeing Sayyah's wife within earshot in the next room, "there are a few people who told me to say hello."

He started down a list of female names. Sayyah, no longer smiling, cut him off.

"What do you want from me?" he asked coldly.

The agents asked questions. Sayyah knew Congressman Murphy, a friend. He denied ever paying him for anything. Yes, he did remember a check that William Kelly had brought to Iran—but vaguely. If the check was for him, it must have been consideration for construction work Sayyah would find for Kelly in Iran.

Suddenly impatient, he refused to answer any more questions until he was called to the grand jury.

He had already been called, but he never went. Instead, his attorney, William Rogers, promptly contacted the United States Attorney's office and vigorously protested the conduct of the FBI agents.

It was the kind of complaint Neil Welch relished. In his experience, the immediacy of a major case break was always signaled by the vehemence of defense counsel objections to agent activities—and the significance of pending developments increased with the eminence of complaining counsel. (And often, angry defense protests were the first indication the agents themselves had as to their case's overall implications, as in the Agnew probe, where investigators had focused exclusively on other targets until the Vice president called twice to demand that the case be closed.)

Welch took personal command. He ordered his agents to report breaking developments at once. He contacted his own investigative sources, piecing together new leads, and as they quickly multiplied, he unconsciously shed his title and plunged into the case. He was no longer the assistant director in charge; he was the same New York brick agent he had been twenty-five years before, senses taut, adrenalin racing. Acting on a tip, he went with his agents to interview an Iranian living on Eighth Avenue; there, the FBI men were urged to immediately contact the Khaibar Khan.

They knew the name—and were skeptical. A longtime enemy of the Shah, Khaibar Khan lived in exile in Las Vegas. For years, he had charged that millions of dollars in U.S. foreign aid to Iran had been systematically kicked back to American government officials and business leaders, and he claimed that bank records from the Shah's secret "blue book," obtained by his agents in Iran, documented his contention. The charges had been published in a detailed 1965 *Nation* article by Fred J. Cook and had been periodically recirculated since.[5]

Despite his doubts, Welch concluded that the possibility of Khaibar Khan producing the blue book was not significantly less than that of Briscoe officials obligingly handing over the payoff check—and DiSimone and Brookings flew to Las Vegas.

As instructed, they checked into the Las Vegas Hilton and waited in their room. Hours passed. Finally, at 11 P.M., there was a knock on the door. Three people entered. The first was a slinkily exotic young lady ("like Dragonlady from Steve Canyon," DiSimone thought); next, a huge bodyguard; and finally an older man dressed in white pants, white silk shirt, white leather jacket, white alligator shoes, and white Panama hat, cocked to the side. It had to be, thought Brookings, a Forty-eighth street pimp; but it was, in fact, the Khaibar Khan.

Within the next few days, however, Brookings would conclude that his first impression had been more accurate. Khaibar Khan presided over a series of clandestine meetings, each at a different location, each attended by his full retinue. At every rendezvous, he promised to deliver vital information about the blue book at the next. As he talked, his hands shook, sometimes violently. (Brookings wisecracked, "What's he saying with his hands?" and the demonstrative DiSimone whispered back, "I dunno—different dialect.") The drama quickly wore thin. The agents became convinced that he had no new information and that his old documents were probable forgeries. As was, in a sense, the seductive Dragonlady, who, they were mildly disillusioned to see as they departed, worked as a clerk in a local gift shop.

From the witness stand, Governor Carey called him "trustworthy, energetic, intelligent, effective, and dedicated."[6]
John Lindsay testified that "his word was always good."[7]
A parade of other public officials offered comparable acco-

lades, all character witnesses for Anthony Scotto, and all apparently equally unimpressive to the federal jury which convicted him of bribery in November 1979 after hearing two months of testimony from the UNIRAC probe.

"The Governor does not deal with Anthony Scotto as a Mafia figure," an aide to Governor Carey later explained. "He deals with him as a labor leader and a civic leader."[8]

The distinction was apparently more obvious to Carey than others. The Justice Department had identified Scotto as a captain in the Gambino crime family as far back as 1969,[9] and as Mayor Edward Koch—one of the few public officials who declined to be a Scotto character witness—observed wryly, "A capodecina is not a cup of coffee."[10] That was the only humor in the situation. Scotto's criminal actions spoke for themselves, and his official friends spoke louder, suggesting a dangerous convergence of organized crime and political corruption, buttressing Welch's hypothesis that the actors in both played on the same stage.

There were other ominous indicators of the pervasiveness of LCN power. Welch's internal critique of the FBI's effort against organized crime spotlighted a pattern of establishment financing and support for crime family enterprises. LCN's massive economic muscle had bought respectability in the marketplace, and its access to conventional credit, the FBI study showed, had permitted expansion far beyond the traditional crime family businesses. (Ironically, LCN's overall impact on the economy was magnified by the coincident stagnation of private sector activity, attributable, in part, to commercial bank interest rates which would have embarrassed a loan shark.) Mob infiltration of "legitimate" business had mushroomed, sometimes dominating entire industries. Welch's analysts reported, for example, that in the carting industry the LCN controlled ". . . both the industrial employees (through a union) and also the companies employing the workers (through a trade association)."

"Organized crime is like weeds in your garden," Welch told agents. "You cannot eliminate them completely—but either keep them cut way back, or they take over the whole garden."

Welch flooded new personnel into his organized crime and political corruption units. Reversing the Weatherman debacle, he ordered undercover agents to infiltrate the LCN families, and the criminal intelligence they amassed would soon permit energetic pruning of crime family growth. Officials— governmental and union—were prosecuted with impartial efficiency. Welch directed the intensive FBI investigation which resulted in the conviction of Nassau County Republican leader Joseph M. Margiotta on fraud and extortion arising out of insurance kickbacks. (Margiotta later claimed he was convicted "because [he'd] been a successful political leader.")[11] Welch also charted the probe which led to the conviction of powerful teamster official John Cody on labor racketeering charges.[12]

The most extraordinary accomplishment recorded under Welch's command in New York, however, was one which he had actually shaped during the two decades prior to his assignment there. The miscellaneous unmarked vehicles Welch had secretly assembled in Buffalo starting in the mid 1960s was part of it—though by 1979, the FBI fleet, matching the attainments of its LCN targets, included a lavish cabin cruiser in Florida, a Lear jet in New York, and a ready supply of Lincoln Continental limousines (rented as the occasion required). Videotape cameras and microphones were also essential components, carefully concealed in a New Jersey condominium, a Washington town house, and a plush Philadelphia hotel suite, all documenting corruption as relentlessly as those first installed by Welch in Detroit's run-down Anchor Bar, eight years before.

The sum of the parts was ABSCAM, the culmination of every undercover investigative technique which Welch had pioneered, starting with his development of Mario as a mob informant in the late 1950s. Before it was concluded, ABSCAM would deceive a number of important officials, including, not incidentally, many at Bureau headquarters. There, the general understanding was that it was an operation aimed at art thieves,[13] a misperception which was itself a classic Welch technique.

Monitoring the probe's progress, Welch was awed by the agile inventiveness of his agent-sheiks. After promising to pass $100 million to several public officials to finance a secret titanium venture, the undercover agents were pressed to make immediate payment. They stalled. More pressure. Finally, the agents arranged for bank verification of a $1 million transfer, and the public officials immediately demanded more. Having exhausted their authority with the bank, the agents solemnly explained that the sheik, regrettably, was limited by Islamic law. Tribal approval was required for each payment, and no single payment could exceed $1 million. Unfortunately, tribal approval could only be obtained at a desert convocation of all of the sheik's tribes, after appropriate feasting and dancing. Such matters took time.

But it was a practice prescribed by Islamic law.

The officials understood completely. They wanted to be certain, they reverently assured the agent-sheiks, that they did nothing in violation of Islamic law.[14]

It was clear from the outset, however, that those being deceived were themselves eager deceivers. When the sheik first met several New Jersey politicians aboard his cabin cruiser in Florida, it was explained that he did not speak or understand English. His authenticity was unquestioned, however, as he and his entourage had arrived at pier side in a fleet of Lincoln Continental limousines. (Having arranged Hoover's travel for years, agents joked, it was simple to satisfy the needs of a lesser potentate.) The sheik simply sat and smiled beatifically as his subordinates discussed business with the politicians, who quickly relaxed in his presence, comforted, no doubt, by the gleaming gold inlays which adorned his teeth.

After a few minutes, the entourage abruptly departed from the boat to confer among themselves, leaving the beaming sheik alone with the politicians. They immediately began conspiring to defraud him. They would extract a secret $3 million profit from the Atlantic City real estate trans-

action being arranged on his behalf; and when he smuggled
his vast fortune out of his kingdom, as planned, they would
take it and give him counterfeit certificates of deposit in
return.

He would be back driving camels, they agreed, by the time
the sharp guys from New Jersey were finished with him.

The sheik smiled.[15]

Welch thought he had a breakthrough. The Shah's government appeared to be toppling, near collapse, and there was
only one attorney in New York who, despite occasional prior
differences with the FBI, might be able to help resolve the
Iranian payoff allegations. He had agreed to see Welch. Tall
and gaunt, the lawyer was a Lincolnesque figure, face etched
with concern for the causes he championed. From his appearance, though, Welch would not have guessed that he was
a former Attorney General of the United States. But the
evidence was there in his office, cluttered with the indicia of
an impressive international practice.

After summarizing the allegations and evidence the FBI
had sifted through, Welch asked bluntly whether he thought
it possible that millions in U.S. foreign aid to Iran had been
kicked back to American officials.

The lawyer was thoughtful, deliberating.

"There are some things," Ramsey Clark finally replied quietly, "which are too obvious to be skeptical about."

Would he assist the FBI in producing the proof?

Clark stood up, hands in the pockets of his faded blue jeans,
reflecting.

"Of course," he agreed. "I'm your best hope."[16]

When Ramsey Clark and the Ayatollah Khomeini met in
Paris in January 1979, the whim of history had invested each
with real power which they had not had days before, a rare
sort of power which flowed not from any official position
(which neither man held) but rather, simply, from who they
were.

Shah Mohammed Reza Pahlavi had finally given up on

January 16, fleeing Iran for Egypt after months of turmoil.[17] If the caretaker government which followed fell as expected, the force of Khomeini's fanaticism, violently evident in Teheran even while he remained in Paris exile, would forge his nation's future shape. And Ramsey Clark was the only significant public figure in America who had supported the Iranian student movement in opposition to the Shah—and thus emerged as the only person with cordial access to the Ayatollah Khomeini.

Clark's unique entree with Khomeini made him the focus of numerous efforts, public and private, to communicate with the post-Shah Iranian leadership, and he would preserve his entree, as he had created it, by declining to represent interests contrary to his personal beliefs. But he was personally committed to answering the same question which Welch's agents had been probing for months, and it was high among the messages he took to Paris in January: Where was the evidence that millions in U.S. aid to Iran had been kicked back to American officials? If Khomeini should assume power, Clark advised strongly, that evidence should be secured at once.[18]

Events accelerated wildly.

On February 1, Khomeini returned to Iran. He announced his intention to form an Islamic republic and threatened to arrest the caretaker Prime Minister if he did not resign. After a tumultuous week of frenzied street riots, the Prime Minister stepped down in favor of Khomeini's designee, Mehdi Bazargan.[19] Bazargan formed a government. The U.S. embassy was held hostage for two hours on February 14, then freed by Khomeini supporters. And back in Washington, when Khomeini followers assumed custody of the Iranian embassy, one of them announced the discovery of account records showing payments to American officials, but gave no specifics.[20]

In April, Ramsey Clark flew to Iran, with one primary purpose. He urged Khomeini to immediately create a commission, with powers to seize all documents which detailed corrupt payments under the Shah, before the evidence disappeared. In a separate meeting with Bazargan, Clark made an extraordinary suggestion: Once recovered, the evidence of corruption should not be showcased in a press conference, but rather turned over to the FBI for use in criminal prosecutions. Such action, Clark contended, would advance Iran's international relations by demonstrating respect for the laws of another country and would assure the prosecution of those guilty. Bazargan agreed.[21]

But it did not happen. In August, Ramsey Clark was back in Iran, and he made one last effort, but by then it was too late. Events were spinning out of control, and official access, even for Clark, was fast diminishing. Any flicker of hope that Iranian officials might yet produce the records was extinguished three months later, one of many casualties of the seizure of the U.S. embassy by Iranian students.

Neil Welch closed what might have been the biggest case in FBI history.

Ramsey Clark offered a personal explanation. "The irony, of course, was that insiders in both governments, Iran's and ours, frustrated the investigation. God knows what price humans paid for that."[22]

Welch had one more mission with the Shah.

After the Shah's stay in a New York hospital, the FBI was ordered to secretly transport the ailing exile to the airport, without detection by the massive international press contingent which had the entire area under intense observation. Welch gave the assignment to Vernier's surveillance squad. Agents drove a battered delivery van into a basement loading area, hustled the Shah inside, and drove out.

The operation did not entirely escape the attention of the press, but the agents had anticipated that possibility, stationing cars along their route which could be moved into position as roadblocks. When a television camera crew was spotted in pursuit, an agent in the van radioed an FBI backup car, requesting that it "neutralize" the pursuers.

At that word, a wan smile flickered across the Shah's pale face, and he seemed to feel at home.[23]

At 7:30 P.M. on Saturday, February 2, 1980, FBI agents went to the Georgetown home of New Jersey Senator Harrison A. Williams, Jr.[24]

At approximately the same time, other agents contacted Congressmen Richard Kelley, Raymond F. Lederer, Michael O. "Ozzie" Myers, John W. Jenrette, Frank Thompson, and John M. Murphy.

Camden Mayor Angelo Errichetti, Philadelphia City Council President George X. Schwartz, Councilmen Harry P. Jannotti and Louis C. Johanson, New Jersey State Senator Joseph A. Maressa—and a number of private citizens—also received surprise visits from FBI agents on that cold winter Saturday.[25]

After the agents departed, Senator Williams came to the door and told a crowd of waiting reporters, "This is the first time I've learned of this. I really don't know any of the facts so I don't feel I can comment."[26]

The most tantalizing of the facts unknown to Williams—and to the others—was precisely which of their criminal acts might have been captured on FBI videotape. Even as the senator faced reporters on his doorstep, cascading disclosures around the country were rushing ABSCAM into sharp focus, revealing that a string of officials had taken money from agents posing as Arabs and that the FBI had pictures to prove it.

Reaction rained. Watergate-scarred Republicans immediately called for a congressional investigation into corruption,[27] while some Democrats demanded a probe of news leaks and FBI tactics.[28] House Speaker Tip O'Neill mourned that "the institution has been hurt,"[29] and polls confirmed it —public approval of Congress plummeted to 19 percent.[30] State Senator Maressa said, "It was like *Arabian Nights* . . . It almost became patriotic to take their money . . . You know, let's get some of that OPEC oil money."[31] The American-Arab Relations Committee took sharp exception, complaining that ABSCAM "perpetuates the traditional prejudicial view of the Arabs." ("Couldn't the FBI have used a waspish character, nondescript, or an oil-rich Venezuelan, Nigerian, or an Israeli businessman to pose as the corrupting agent?" the committee protested to the Attorney General.)[32]

Prior to seeing the FBI tapes, however, most of the officials in question hid behind ritual denials. Mayor Errichetti "categorically denied"[33] any wrongdoing. Congressman Murphy said, "I am not in violation of any laws."[34] His colleague from South Carolina, Mr. Jenrette, asserted, "At no time did I engage in any improper activities."[35] More imaginative, Congressman Kelly explained, "This is what I've been doing since I came to Congress—getting the bleeding hearts off the back of the FBI. I've always been seen as a good guy with a white hat, and that's the way I still see myself."[36]

Every citizen with a television set, however, would soon see the ABSCAM defendants quite differently, and even the most fervent of their denials fell unpersuasively into limbo while the public awaited the chance to compare it with the pictures. By the time the ABSCAM prosecutions reached court, pretrial review of the videotaped evidence had forced most defendants to drop their denials and to argue instead that the government had entrapped them into doing what they had done. But the tapes were still there, always more tapes, playing relentlessly on a bank of courtroom television sets, and the defendants watched helplessly as their own words answered every contention their lawyers made in court.

In the end, the conclusion was inescapable that the Honorable Ozzie Myers had been, unknowingly, speaking for all of the indicted officials when he had confided the following, on camera, to FBI agent Kambir Abdul-Rahman: "I'm gonna tell you something real simple and short. Money talks in this business and bullshit walks. And it works the same way down in Washington."[37]

All officials indicted in ABSCAM were convicted, and their convictions were upheld by the United States Supreme Court.

The convictions did not, however, close the case. The sting still stung in Congress, where members remained understandably angry that it was considered front-page news when one of their number, Senator Larry Pressler of South Dakota, *declined* a bribe.[38] A half century of congressional affection for the FBI had been abruptly spurned, and congressmen wanted to know why. The Senate Select Committee to Study Undercover Activities of Components of the Department of Justice was created to discover the answer.

In the J. Edgar Hoover Building, officials debated the unpleasant choices. Certainly Bureau headquarters could not have been ignorant of an FBI operation which lasted twenty-three months, involving hundreds of agents and nearly a million dollars—but neither could the Director march to Capitol Hill and announce that he had targeted for investigation the congressmen who would decide future FBI appropriations. There had to be some middle ground.

After taking extensive testimony, the Senate Select Committee filed its report on December 15, 1982, and in it concluded: "The investigative focus of ABSCAM began to shift in September and October 1978 from property crimes to political corruption, in large part as a result of Weinberg's conversations with suspects. FBI special agents knew of at least some of Weinberg's conversations in that regard sometime before November 16, 1978, *but failed to inform FBI HQ* . . ."

The conclusion was arguable, but the agent who had engineered the mysterious "shift" did not argue.[39]

"We never told Bureau headquarters when we were doing anything important in the field," Neil Welch agreed, "because we knew they would stop it."

20

Neil J. Welch

More than once during my three decades as a special agent, it occurred to me that the overlapping confusion of our law enforcement system could only have been created by a criminal mastermind.

Federal crime jurisdiction covers everything from shooting ducks out of season to treason, from international hijacking to interstate cattle theft. The *Federal Criminal Code* makes clear that almost any criminal act in this country can be defined as a federal case—and nearly every Congress tinkers with the *Code* a little more, steadily adding to the federal crime grab bag. Moreover, nearly all federal crimes, old and new, continue to be well within the constitutional reach of state and local enforcement efforts; as a consequence, the federalizing of these offenses simply expands the confusing morass known as "concurrent jurisdiction."

The net result is a criminal-justice system that overtaxes the taxpayers, frequently frustrates the best efforts of the professionals who serve in it, and indeed is most satisfactory from the viewpoint of the sophisticated criminals who operate under its supposed scrutiny. That is no exaggeration. The illegal profits of organized crime and official corruption amount to uncounted billions annually, and if the tens of billions that we invest in law enforcement has hampered their business, it is certainly not apparent by the bottom line.

That is a harsh indictment. But I make it not out of despair that we have done so badly—but rather out of conviction, based on my experience in the field, that we can do so much better.

The FBI success against kidnapping proves it. Before Hoover made kidnapping the top FBI priority, that crime was committed at the rate of one every day, hundreds of kidnappings each year. Then, suddenly, the crime virtually disappeared—kidnappings dwindled to a handful annually. Why? Because FBI agents had demonstrated to kidnappers that punishment for their crime was certain, and the sureness and swiftness of justice proved to be the most potent deterrent of all. If today's organized crime figures, corrupt officials, and white-collar criminals believed that sophisticated enforcement efforts like ABSCAM were ongoing at any meaningful level, a comparable certainty of justice would be created—and a comparable deterrent.

When I entered on duty in the FBI in 1951, I entered a very "special" world, as a special agent in a unique investigative agency. The FBI was devoted to the pursuit of justice. The people who were its life's blood were indeed special in their dedication to their responsibilities and in the discipline of their personal and professional lives. And for many of us, the official life of a special agent seemed the only life—there was simply no time for anything else.

The daily FBI experience was one of special challenge and opportunity. There were days of frustration, and some in which our efforts just plain failed. But these disappointments were more than outweighed by the many occasions in which we were spectacularly successful, and the complexity of the criminal challenges we faced made our victories all the more special. It was personally rewarding, usually fun, often funny, and frequently exciting—although as I went up in the ranks, the fun and excitement seemed to diminish.

Particularly in the early years, I always had a special feeling about being part of a unique corps of crime fighters. Almost every agent did. My confidence in the FBI, and particularly in its working special agents, was always sky-high. I saw daily evidence of that special ingenuity and near genius which repeatedly solved seemingly insolvable investigative problems. We all knew that our lives might depend on each other, and my personal trust in brother—and in later years, sister—agents was total. We felt privileged to work in an organization of uniformly high composite character. Retired and former agents often reported their greatest regret in subsequent careers was the lack of such high-quality working associates. The experience was, as we all learned, unique—as was the man who, until 1972, presided over it.

By all accounts, the organization which young J. Edgar Hoover inherited in 1924 was a national disgrace. Incompetent and corrupt, the Bureau was a wide-open patronage haven infested with political hacks.

Hoover cleaned house. He made all appointments based on ability and character, all promotions on merit—and no politics allowed. He infused the organization with his own legendary drive and attention to detail, and in a short while the remarkable results of his transformation were apparent. Hoover's Bureau was recognized as a highly dedicated and wholly professional agency, small enough to be highly mobile and flexible, but large enough to make a national difference.

It soon did. The untouchable "Public Enemies" of 1930s gangsterland were quickly collared, and the FBI success against gangsters was surpassed by its success against kidnappers and then wartime subversives and saboteurs. Most agents could recite from memory the precise dates and details of the big FBI cases of the 1930s. We were proud to belong to the organization that had made those cases. By the end of World War II, public esteem for Hoover and his Bureau was near universal; ironically, though, success itself had eliminated several of the factors which had made it possible. The FBI had grown enormously, and the Director who had prided himself on knowing every agent by name suddenly found that he knew mostly his subordinates at headquarters. By the 1950s, it had become a rarity for Hoover to visit any field office—regardless of circumstances. When he came to Boston during our Brinks probe, agents who had been labor-

ing round the clock on the biggest case in FBI history fully
expected a visit from our leader. He might berate us, or—less
likely—might inspire us, but we were certain that he would
appear.

We were wrong. Hoover stayed several days in a Boston
hotel, and never visited the field office. His apparent indifference to our actual work in the field made a lasting impression
on me.

Moreover, as the headquarters bureaucracy gradually separated Hoover from his agents, it also came between FBI
field agents and their work. Indeed, the fundamental structural weakness of the FBI gradually became as obvious as its
name, although for years, agents were the only ones who
recognized the unfortunate legacy of the agency's christen-
ing. "Federal" was understandable, and "Investigation" indeed its business, but "Bureau," with its connotation of stag-
nant bureaucracy, was a terrible mistake. And unfortunately,
the outfit became universally known as "the Bureau," and its
agents, "Bureau agents." Most laymen never realized, when
they automatically said "Oh, you're from the Bureau" upon
meeting an FBI agent, what a negative reaction that comment evoked. After only limited experience, most agents felt
complete antipathy for the Bureau. Outsiders never understood that, while we would unhappily tolerate being called
Bureau agents, we were proud to be known as FBI special
agents.

This distinction may seem unimportant, to the outsider,
but as the years passed, the word "Bureau" captured everything which special agents felt limited their ability to perform effectively. "Bureau" meant bureaucracy, control for
control's sake, statistics, quotas, and endless paperwork—all
of which, agents realized instinctively, did not contribute
one iota to the solution of any actual case. Individual energy
and ingenuity solved cases, and most of the Bureau's requirements seemed aimed at curtailing those qualities. But despite the endless demands from headquarters, agents quickly
recognized one fundamental truth: *No case was ever solved
unless an agent in the field solved it.*

Once that truth was understood, field agents came to regard the demands from Washington as simply one more impediment to be overcome. There was plenty of creativity and initiative among field agents—all we wanted from our agents in charge was enough insulation from headquarters so we could exercise it. And later, when I became an agent in charge, I counted each day a success if I was able to stand off the Bureau enough so my agents could get their work done.

Hoover did not live to see the FBI occupy the building with his name on it, which was perhaps fortunate. I believe that in his final years he had come to regret the FBI's uncontrolled growth and even lamented the planned move from the Justice Department fifth floor (which he shared with the Attorney General) to a dramatic new FBI building. Perhaps he sensed, as every field agent knew, that the building which would be his monument would inevitably be filled to the brim with an even larger and more stifling headquarters bureaucracy.

Most knowledgeable observers of today's FBI believe that the agency has overcome the shocks of the 1970s and is again performing at high levels of excellence. The uniformly high quality of agent effort in individual targeted cases is undisputed. More important, the organization has made the transformation from reactive, case-by-case investigation of separate offenses to developing in its place a space-age assault on sophisticated patterns of criminal conduct. Elaborate undercover investigations of organized crime and governmental corruption have yielded dramatic results; the historic flaw in such prosecutions, the tarnished credibility of middleman witnesses, has been largely eliminated by videotape techniques which have moved covert criminal conduct out of the shadows and onto every family's television set.

These new techniques have raised questions, as indeed they should, and the federal courts had responded with answers. At this writing, the FBI's new undercover techniques, most notably utilized in ABSCAM, have been fully supported and upheld by the courts, including the United States Supreme Court.

Congress—and the Justice Department—have been less enthusiastic. Working FBI agents sensed that the congressional probes which followed ABSCAM were aimed more at the investigators than at the corrupt officials under investigation, and the guidelines which resulted really amount to an implicit OFF button. The message is clear: Sophisticated undercover operations are not favored in official Washington, and agents who develop them are taking a chance with their careers. Certainly there has been little post-ABSCAM that could be characterized as an official ON button, an affirmation that undercover techniques are effective and valuable, that the agents who used them so successfully should be commended, that ABSCAM-style operations should be multiplied.

Because the official reaction to any innovative assault on corruption and white-collar crime is to reach for the OFF button, the overall effectiveness of our criminal-justice machinery is marginal at best. The dollar cost of crime to society —and to American commerce and government—is staggering. The actual cost is even higher. Crime produces human suffering, ravaged lives, inflated prices, and—often overlooked—America's damaging international reputation as the world's most criminal society.

It almost seems as if we have deliberately constructed the most inefficient system possible, and perhaps we have. A few years ago, an FBI official was testifying before the Senate Judiciary Committee on the need for a major computer system. In response to sharp demands from the chairman, Senator Sam Ervin, as to why the requested expenditure was necessary, the flustered FBI official finally replied, "It is needed, Senator, to make the FBI more efficient."

Ervin, a former North Carolina Supreme Court justice and highly regarded expert on constitutional law, had a ready reply. "Son, the United States Constitution does not require the FBI to be efficient."

The senator was undoubtedly correct—and indeed, based

on the record, he might have even said that the Constitution does not appear to *permit* efficient law enforcement.

The Attorney General has under his command a generous array of crime-fighting agencies: FBI, Drug Enforcement Administration, Immigration and Naturalization Service, Bureau of Prisons, Border Patrol, and all of the bureaus and divisions within the Justice Department itself. All of these entities are highly specialized, each with its own distinct bureaucratic turf. Following the pattern set by Hoover, all employ almost exclusively career personnel.

Yet their efforts are almost totally uncoordinated.

Moreover, the political orientation of the Justice Department—nearly all Attorneys General have been active politicians—unquestionably influences enforcement priorities. Equally damaging, the Justice Department leadership changes with each national election—officials retire from government service approximately when they have finally started to understand the problems. Continuity in the direction and oversight of FBI efforts is, as a result, almost nonexistent. And in the one area where every Attorney General was in fact actually involved—approval of FBI domestic intelligence activities—the Justice Department simply pointed the finger at the Bureau, thus escaping actual, as well as legal, liability.

It is surprising to me that the Justice Department has not been the focus of critical scrutiny by law enforcement experts. The American Bar Association, which has offered constructive proposals on criminal justice generally, with special attention to the debilitating influence of partisan politics on the office of United States Attorney, has not made any recent comprehensive analysis of the Justice Department itself. Other professional groups have been comparably negligent.

But it has been clear, since at least 1967, that the overall leadership supplied by the Justice Department would determine the outcome of any war on crime. In 1967, President Johnson empaneled a national commission to make a comprehensive study of crime in America. One of the commission's key recommendations was for increased coordination of state law-enforcement efforts as part of a national anticrime strategy. Unfortunately, despite the subsequent federal allocation of more than $8 billion into state enforcement activities, most of it under the Law Enforcement Assistance Administration program, the national strategy largely failed —and the Justice Department leadership must accept major blame for the failure.

There are serious problems within the FBI as well. Performance is spotty. Quality varies widely in different states, different offices. Investigating minor crimes for easy statistics is still irresistible to some, and backsliding away from the quality case program is chronic. The agency is having trouble keeping its best people—first-class veterans are retiring at the earliest possible opportunity. And—for the first time— dissatisfied working agents have formed an association to lobby Congress and the public.

Part of the problem, in my view, is that the FBI today has too much to do—or, stated differently, has the comfortable option of doing innumerable easy little things, none of which has particular impact on significant criminal conduct. The *Federal Criminal Code* has been steadily expanded, often in response to special-interest pressure aimed at getting the FBI to provide security for some particular industry, and efforts to comprehensively revise and streamline the *Code* have been stalled for more than a decade.

The result for law enforcement is clear confusion, because there is no answer to the most basic question: Who is responsible for what?

In such uncertainty, bureaucracy thrives. The perennial "crime wave" justifies higher appropriations, more jobs, bigger buildings—state and federal—while the failure to assign fundamental responsibilities precludes any effective evaluation of the results achieved—or, more often, not achieved. In short, the congressional mandate that the FBI do much has created an ideal bureaucratic environment for it to do little, and there is no meaningful accounting for the billions it spends.

J. Edgar Hoover understood the problem, but not the solution. He strove for efficiency and was near genius in devising methods to measure individual and group effort, time and productivity. Unfortunately, many of his systems were defeated by equally ingenious agent stratagems. The result was a bureaucratic stalemate which generated bushels of statistics without much meaning.

I am certain that today's FBI retains the basic desire to achieve efficiency and excellence. As much as is possible in any human institution, the FBI heart is pure, the spirit is willing, but the quality control is nearly nonexistent. Given the vast differences in local circumstances throughout the nation, uniformity in federal law enforcement remains elusive. New York's priority may be unimportant in Seattle, and FBI headquarters has yet to devise any meaningful system for measuring performance in the field—mainly because its basic accounting principle, the notion that bigger is better, is wrong.

That notion pervades our system. More arrests are better, as are more convictions, which means that more agents must be desirable in order to make more arrests. Rarely does any federal appropriations request for law enforcement offer Congress any alternative to simple numerical increases, such as improved methods. Happily, the recent increase in undercover operations is an exception to this rule, and the dramatic undercover successes clearly demonstrate that better methods accomplish more than bigger budgets.

I am convinced that by radically restructuring our methods we can cripple organized crime and corruption—without major new expenditures.

In 1980, a national conference was held at the University of Southern California to develop a national strategy to fight organized crime. The event itself defined the problem. One would have supposed that some basic plan of attack already existed.

It did not.

There was no such plan in 1980.

And there is no such plan in 1984.

The FBI bureaucracy does not need a battle plan, but the public interest demands one, and the crime fighters in the front trenches deserve one.

In those trenches there are literally millions of police, agents, prosecutors, court personnel, correctional institution employees, and similar professionals, and they are working without any fixed plan or long-term objective. It is no wonder that their results are haphazard at best.

We must adopt a criminal-justice battle plan. Such a plan would match resources with enforcement priorities, eliminate duplication, and permit businesslike management of the overall effort. I expect that those whose performance would not measure up would oppose this proposal vigorously. There would be legitimate objections as well. Would a law enforcement plan somehow jeopardize individual freedoms? Is there more danger in efficiency than there is in crime? Is it more than coincidental that this proposal is made in 1984?

I share these concerns, but I remain convinced that we can have both law enforcement efficiency and constitutional security, with full protection of individual freedoms. Indeed, the real threat to freedom is in our present system. Organized crime is a fundamental threat to democracy not because it is crime—we don't really feel endangered by office football-pool betting, even though it is technically a crime—but because it is organized. In competition with our free institutions, La Cosa Nostra has created its own national government, imposing its own values and meting out rewards and punishment with ruthless efficiency. Its economic resources are enormous, and its ability to corrupt legitimate institutions reflects that financial muscle.

This is not some vague menace that may strike in the indefinite future. It is the current reality—today. The combination of organized crime and official corruption have created an atmosphere in which pervasive criminal conduct is openly accepted. There is no stigma in dealing with institutions that are crime-controlled—they pay their bills promptly (though sometimes in cash). Except in isolated instances like the Scotto case, where an actual criminal conviction occurs, the biggest companies and the best lawyers in America often have no embarrassment about doing business with the underworld.

After all, they say, you have to be realistic.

That sort of realism has made organized crime an awesome reality. It is not an enemy which might be accidentally defeated without any plan.

Once the plan is in place, it will be possible for the first time to critically assess the effectiveness of law enforcement. Every enforcement agency could be held to a new standard of accountability, with results measured against the objectives of the national plan.

The measuring of those results, however, should no longer be performed exclusively by the FBI. Hoover always favored "safe" employees. As a consequence, he siphoned off investigative strength, assigning agents to noninvestigative specialities. Laboratory scientists, librarians, linguists, financial experts, and public relations specialists were all drawn from agent ranks because Hoover did not want to risk engaging outsiders. More significantly, the same concerns have operated to deprive the FBI of critically needed expertise from the academic, business, and financial communities. We can no longer afford to keep our law enforcement records off-limits to the best minds in the nation.

In addition to measuring FBI effectiveness, academic experts—with full access to Bureau files—could use the FBI's vast reservoir of information to address broader questions.

> Why are crimes committed?
> How can we have better protection?
> Can the opportunities for specific crimes be eliminated?
> Have new crime trends developed?
> Under what circumstances do particular investigative techniques succeed or fail?

The possibilities are endless. The necessity is obvious. And indeed, such analysis may reveal that the best methods to combat certain crimes may not be traditional law enforcement techniques at all. Education, financial incentives, medical-psychiatric services, strengthened family life, and improved social conditions will, in the long term, reduce many kinds of criminal conduct far more dramatically than the prosecution and jailing of individuals. The Attorney General, as commanding officer of the war on crime, has in my view needlessly restricted his weapons, relying largely on investigators, lawyers, and jailers. The basic strategy has been legalistic, case by case, and it is difficult to demonstrate that the scales of justice have been balanced by the results.

To the wise old bureaucrat who counseled me, early in my career, that "it's too late for anything new," I can now respond with certainty: "It is far too late, and too expensive, to continue our old approach."

President Reagan took an important first step in establishing a National Commission to Study Organized Crime. Not that the problem itself requires more study—we have been regularly "rediscovering" organized crime about once every decade, as it has grown enormously in scope, profits, and influence on politics, commerce, and other vital elements of American institutions. The focus at this point must be on finding solutions. To this end, the following structural reforms are, in my view, essential.

Given the multitude of overlapping law enforcement departments and agencies, federal and state, there is an urgent need for coordination of policy and operations, which could best be accomplished through creation of the National Criminal Justice Council.

Leadership of any enterprise as large and complex as our criminal-justice system actually has two basic elements—inspiration and organization. In trying to make sense out of the clear disorganization of our current system, the framework used by the national-defense intelligence agencies offers a useful model.

Defense intelligence—like criminal intelligence—is the product of a multitude of departments and agencies. The departments of State, Defense, Army, Navy, and Air Force, along with the Central Intelligence Agency, the Defense Intelligence Agency, the National Security Agency, and others, all participate. These agencies all have differing missions and various priorities, and indeed the quality most common to them (as in the criminal-justice system) may be an intense sensitivity to any threat to bureaucratic turf. Nevertheless, our national requirement for coordinated defense intelligence and effective foreign policy has dictated creation of the National Security Council, an entity with clear authority to reorder the activities of all intelligence agencies, to mold them into efficient and coordinated operation.

Similarly, the National Criminal Justice Council would bring new efficiency and coordination to the task of law enforcement and, even more important, make excessive zeal and abuse of citizens' rights accountable at the highest politically responsive level of government.

The National Criminal Justice Council would be composed of representatives from the major segments of the criminal justice world, both federal and state, and would serve as a national board of directors, setting priorities and coordinating operations in our war against crime. The need for such leadership and coordination is undeniable. In addition to the criminal-justice agencies under direct control of the Attorney General, the departments of Treasury, Transportation, and Commerce all have important criminal-justice functions, as do numerous other entities, including, most significantly, the Securities and Exchange Commission. It is a patchwork creation which has proved far more efficient at producing duplication and jealousy than at providing uniform criminal justice.

The National Criminal Justice Council would, for the first time, permit central planning, research, and development of enforcement and prevention techniques, allow the coordination of multifaceted operations, and unify critical audit and accounting activities. This council should have its own professional staff, allowing it to operate independently from its constituent agencies. And the council would have the authority to set and to change the priorities of participating agencies, to insure maximum efficiency in deployment of law enforcement resources.

The ultimate success of the council, however, will depend largely upon the commitment and the composition of its membership. For that reason, I would urge that participation be mandated at the highest levels of the federal government. The Vice president would perhaps be a natural choice for chairman, and the Attorney General might serve as vice-chairman or in another leadership capacity. The other cabinet members should also be active participants, but their subordinate officials should not be. The organization must not be permitted to deteriorate into a roundtable for federal bureaucrats. In addition, general membership would be drawn from the Congress (probably the judiciary committees), bar associations, other criminal-justice organizations, and civil liberties groups, and it would also include the top criminal-justice experts from our colleges and law schools.

I believe the funding required to establish and operate this council has already been appropriated within the budgets of the various agencies that would participate. Virtually all of these departments and bureaus include funding for planning, research, and general administrative purposes; a simple transfer resolution could shift these monies to the National Criminal Justice Council.

Once established, the council should immediately take the following actions:

> Adopt a comprehensive strategy for a national war on crime, and communicate specific policy objectives to each agency involved: FBI, DEA, Secret Service, prosecutors, local police, and others. In short, establish a crime-fighting master plan and make certain that each team involved understands its specific assignment.
>
> Ensure that all plans and expenditures proposed by the respective agencies are in accordance with the master plan.

Monitor all law enforcement operations conducted pursuant to the plan, measuring productivity; obtain expert evaluation of efficiency.

Sift through operational reports to identify effective new techniques, and mandate their adoption
throughout the law enforcement establishment.

Make recommendations to consolidate operational activities of respective agencies, streamlining
organizations to eliminate waste and duplication,
and to combat the stifling stagnation of ever-ex-
panding bureaucracy.

Establish an internal, publicly accountable system
for policing itself and its constituent agencies, especially in areas in which there are threats to civil
liberties or the potential for political manipulation.

Operating under the umbrella of the National Criminal
Justice Council, the Multiagency Strike Force unit would be a
potent new weapon against carefully selected criminal
targets.

Prior experience with Organized Crime Strike Forces has
proved that multiagency efforts can be tremendously effective. But the existing Strike Forces have suffered from a lack
of central coordination and bureaucratic resistance from the
agencies involved. The council would have the power to
eliminate these difficulties and to assemble the best talent
from each agency into the Multiagency Strike Force units for
deployment wherever the extent and complexity of criminal
activity dictated.

The Multiagency Strike Force would be composed of personnel drawn from federal and state agencies who have
demonstrated the vital personal qualities of motivation, exceptional intelligence, experience, and that special extra
spark which I call entrepreneurial genius. The reservoir of
such talent is in perennial short supply, and it would require
the resources of the council to make certain that this small
pool of unusual talent is focused against the challenges of
sophisticated high-profit crime.

The Multiagency Strike Force concept would provide a new career challenge for the top talent of the various agencies. If properly directed, it would soon be recognized as the elite corps of crime fighters at the federal level. Perhaps even more important, deployment of the Multiagency Strike Force would inevitably stimulate competitive responses from enforcement agencies already at work in the area, and the result would be improved performance by enforcement agencies across the board.

Another necessity is the "de-federalization" of federal crimes that simply clog the system. The preoccupation of many enforcement agencies with minor offenses and the severe caseload backlog which is crippling the federal court system both have a common cause—the uninterrupted federalization of state crimes by Congress.

As previously noted, virtually every criminal case is—or could be—a federal case.

If we are to improve the efficiency of the criminal-justice system, we must reverse that process, and there is a simple way to do it. State court prosecutors could be permitted to try certain designated federal offenses in the state court system. For example, there is no inherent reason why crimes such as auto theft, forgery of Social Security checks, or even routine bank robberies must be tried in a federal court.

But federal law is better, critics will contend—and indeed it is.

My proposal is to retain the benefits of federal law, by continuing to use it as the basis for criminal charges, while permitting the investigation, prosecution, and trial of those charges to occur in the state court systems. Congress clearly has the authority to empower various courts to enforce federal law, much as it can legislate the appointment of special prosecutors, and I suggest that such a "de-federalization" could result in a more efficient utilization of federal justice resources. A pilot program, developed, implemented, and evaluated by the National Criminal Justice Council, would provide concrete answers as to the feasibility of this concept.

The best investigative system in the world, however, is

only as effective as the prosecutors who try its cases in court. Although the Justice Department and United States Attorneys offices have many capable trial lawyers, agents repeatedly see months of investigative effort wasted in major cases because the federal prosecutors are simply outgunned. In any important prosecution, it is a safe bet that the defense counsel will be more experienced (and certainly better paid) than the government prosecutor, and experience in criminal trial work, as in brain surgery, has an inescapable impact on the outcome.

Moreover, agent frustration at this disparity is aggravated by the fact that most top-notch criminal-defense counsel received their original training as federal government prosecutors. FBI agents routinely assist in the education of rookie prosecutors, tolerating their "practice" runs in minor cases, only to see them quit the government for private practice as soon as they acquire "top gun" status. The taxpayers, in effect, are paying for the training of some terrific criminal defense attorneys.

There is an obvious answer.

The British legal system, from which we have borrowed so much, does not have a Crown (or government) prosecutor as such; instead, private attorneys are simply retained and paid to conduct criminal prosecutions. The result: Both prosecution and defense are represented by private counsel, of comparable experience and ability.

I strongly advocate the adoption of such a system for federal criminal prosecutions in this country, limited, in the beginning, to major cases. Again, the National Criminal Justice Council could devise the program and evaluate the results.

I know that I speak for most FBI agents when I state that we welcome the courtroom battles which test the quality of our work—but believe that the sides should be more evenly chosen.

Today, lawyers in criminal practice—and the firms they belong to—rise to fame and fortune only by serving as effective defense counsel in spectacular cases. Think, for a moment, of the effect not only on law enforcement, but on the entire community of the law if the sort of public recognition a private lawyer or law firm now attracts with successful criminal defense could be gained by effective criminal prosecution.

In another area, it is cliché wisdom that hitting where it hurts the most is generally in the pocketbook, and yet we have made only the most tentative efforts to incorporate that truism into federal criminal law. Imprisonment remains the reflex remedy for every serious crime, and while jail is undoubtedly punishment, it rarely results in either rehabilitation or deterrence. Moreover, experts believe that only 15 percent of the total prison population is truly dangerous; the other 85 percent are there because they thought that committing crimes would be profitable.

We must take the profit out of crime.

When a single illicit transaction can make a drug dealer rich for life, it is obviously important to chase the riches as well as the dealer.

While recent statutes allow confiscation of the proceeds of a criminal enterprise, I believe we should go further. We should assess convicted criminals with the expenses of investigation and prosecution, and should impose treble damages for punitive purposes. Moreover, prosecutors should be empowered to trace the expenditure of ill-gotten gains, and to seize any assets thereby acquired.

The integrity of our justice machinery absolutely dictates that investigation and prosecution of crimes by government officials be a permanent priority. The opportunities for public officials to profit by breach of the public trust seem limitless—and enforcement efforts are often thwarted by the fact that corrupt officials can manipulate the justice system itself. Politicians have, can, and will obstruct justice for their own benefit, and no perfect method has yet been devised to make the machinery of law enforcement "fix-proof." The Watergate-inspired special prosecutor was an appropriate first step, but a National Criminal Justice Council should consider further steps.

The public confidence which is, in the final analysis, the bedrock foundation of our criminal justice system will go on being dangerously eroded unless we are able to make certain that there is, in fact, one standard of justice for all.

In reflecting on my FBI career, I find myself somewhat surprised that I ended my service feeling the same basic emotions that I felt that first day in the old Washington Post Office on June 25, 1951. I look to the future with enthusiasm, excitement, optimism—and confidence that right will prevail over wrong.

But, I am surprised, I suppose, because my three decades as an agent included my fair share of frustration and disappointment, and also because I know that many law enforcement professionals acquire a markedly different perspective as their careers continue. Perhaps because skepticism is a requirement of the job for agents and police, cynicism seems to be a common occupational hazard, and sometimes, in the end, bitterness arises.

But for me, the challenges of criminal justice are as exciting as they were three decades ago—and I believe the opportunities for meaningful progress are much greater than they were then.

We have made tangible progress in criminal justice in the second half of this century—and I feel privileged to have been a part of that. More important, I am certain that we have the capability to multiply our law enforcement successes, by applying the same American ingenuity and determination which have produced revolutionary accomplishments in agriculture, medicine, transportation, space travel, and computer technology.

One of the first lessons an agent learns is that crimes are solved by identifying persons who had the motive, the means, and the opportunity to commit them.

Today, criminal justice reform is the urgently needed solution. As a nation, we have a manifest motivation to achieve it —and we have the means, and, I believe, a historic opportunity.

Notes

PROLOGUE

1. Washington *Post,* June 14, 1977, p. A-1.
2. Washington *Post,* May 3, 1972, p. A-1.
3. Ibid., p. A-12.
4. Ibid., p. 1.
5. New York *Times,* May 3, 1972, p. 1.
6. Ovid Demaris, "The Private Life of J. Edgar Hoover," *Esquire,* September 1974, p. 75.
7. *Memorial Tributes to J. Edgar Hoover in the Congress of the United States* (Washington, D.C.: U.S. Government Printing Office, 1974), p. xvii.
8. Ibid., p. xxvi.
9. Washington *Post,* May 4, 1972, p. A-8.
10. *Memorial Tributes,* p. ix.
11. Ibid., passim.
12. Ibid., passim.
13. Washington *Post,* May 4, 1972, p. 1.
14. *Memorial Tributes,* p. 236.
15. "Ten Year Term for FBI Director," Hearing Before Senate Judiciary Subcommittee on FBI Oversight (S.2106), March 18, 1974, p. 17; Sanford J. Ungar, *FBI* (Boston: Little, Brown & Company, 1975), p. 62.
16. NJW.
17. TC Transcript, p. 26; Ovid Demaris, *The Director* (New York: Harper's Magazine Press, 1975), p. 74; Demaris, "The Private Life of J. Edgar Hoover," p. 160.
18. Don Whitehead, *The FBI Story* (New York: Random House, 1956), pp. 104, 106.
19. Demaris, "The Private Life of J. Edgar Hoover," p. 160.
20. NJW Transcript, pp. 240–41.
21. J. Edgar Hoover, "Memorandum for Mr. Tolson," April 21, 1967.

22. NJW Transcript, X-9; Oakland *Press*, January 14, 1974, p. 6.
23. NJW.
24. J. Edgar Hoover, "Memorandum for Mr. Tolson," April 29, 1966.
25. "The FBI Five: A Closer Look," *Newsweek*, July 11, 1977, p. 22.

CHAPTER 1   HOOVER

1. Noel Behn, *Big Stick-Up At Brinks* (New York: G. P. Putnam's Sons, 1978), p. 2.
2. NJW Transcript, p. 35.
3. "J. Edgar Hoover Made the FBI Formidable with Politics, Publicity and Results" (obituary), New York *Times*, May 3, 1972, p. 52.
4. Ibid.
5. Ovid Demaris, "The Private Life of J. Edgar Hoover," *Esquire*, September 1974, p. 160.
6. Drew Pearson and Jack Anderson, "The Last Days of J. Edgar Hoover," *True*, January 1969, p. 99.
7. Demaris, "Private Life," p. 72.
8. Ibid.
9. Ibid.
10. *Memorial Tributes to J. Edgar Hoover in the Congress of the United States* (Washington, D.C.: U.S. Government Printing Office, 1974), p. 237 (quoting Washington *Star*).
11. New York *Times* (obituary).
12. Demaris, "Private Life," pp. 73–74.
13. New York *Times* (obituary).
14. Ibid.
15. "Hoover: Monument of Power for 48 Years" (obituary), Washington *Post*, May 3, 1972, p. C-5.
16. Ibid.
17. New York *Times* (obituary).
18. Demaris, "Private Life," p. 72 (quoting Jack Alexander *New Yorker* profile).
19. Ibid., p. 74.
20. William C. Sullivan, *The Bureau: My Thirty Years in Hoover's FBI* (New York: W. W. Norton & Company, 1979), p. 37.
21. *Memorial Tributes*, p. 230 (quoting Washington *Star*).
22. "J. Edgar Hoover Speaks Out," *Nation's Business*, January 1972, p. 48.
23. Constitution of the United States, Article I, Section 8.

24. *World Almanac and Book of Facts, 1980* (New York: Newspaper Enterprise Association, 1979), p. 196.
25. Samuel Eliot Morison, *The Oxford History of the American People* (New York: Oxford University Press, 1965), p. 883.
26. Ibid.
27. Will Durant, *The Age of Faith*, (New York: Simon and Schuster, 1950), p. 671.
28. Morison, *Oxford History*, p. 883.
29. Sanford J. Ungar, *FBI* (Boston: Little, Brown & Company, 1976), p. 43.
30. Morison, *Oxford History*, p. 883.
31. Ibid., pp. 883, 885.
32. Don Whitehead, *The FBI Story* (New York: Random House, 1956) pp. 51, 66.
33. Whitehead, *FBI Story*, p. 49; Ungar, *FBI*, pp. 42, 43.
34. Ungar, *FBI*, pp. 44–45; Morison, *Oxford History*, p. 884.
35. William Turner, *Hoover's FBI: The Men and the Myth* (Los Angeles, 1970), p. 192.
36. Demaris, "Private Life," pp. 72–73.
37. New York *Times* (obituary), p. 52.
38. Ovid Demaris, *The Director* (New York: Harper's Magazine Press, 1975), p. 54; Turner, *Hoover's FBI*, p. 192; Ungar, *FBI*, p. 48.
39. " ' Mr. FBI' and His 'G-Men': Near-Legends Since 1924," *Congressional Quarterly Fact Sheet*, December 22, 1969, p. 3.
40. Ibid., p. 2.
41. Ibid.
42. Ungar, *FBI*, p. 46.
43. Ibid., p. 45.
44. Ibid.
45. " 'Mr. FBI'," *Congressional Quarterly Fact Sheet*, pp. 2–3.
46. Demaris, "Private Life," p. 73.
47. Whitehead, *FBI Story*, p. 67.
48. Ibid.
49. " 'Mr. FBI'," *Congressional Quarterly Fact Sheet*, p. 5.
50. "J. Edgar Hoover Speaks Out," *Nation's Business*, p. 46.
51. " 'Mr. FBI'," *Congressional Quarterly Fact Sheet*, p. 5.
52. NJW.
53. "J. Edgar Hoover Speaks Out," *Nation's Business*, p. 46.
54. Demaris, *The Director*, p. 55.
55. NJW.
56. Demaris, *The Director*, p. 55.

57. *World Almanac,* p. 755.

58. NJW.

59. Whitehead, *FBI Story,* p. 108.

60. New York *Times* (obituary); Ungar, *FBI,* p. 261.

61. Whitehead, *FBI Story,* p. 108; Turner, *Hoover's FBI,* p. 75.

62. "J. Edgar Hoover Speaks Out," *Nation's Business,* pp. 39–40.

63. NJW.

64. Ungar, *FBI,* p. 264; Turner, *Hoover's FBI,* p. 76.

65. New York *Times* (obituary), p. 52.

66. Ungar, *FBI,* p. 255.

67. Turner, *Hoover's FBI,* p. 373 (quoting Hoover Estate Inventory, Appraisal and Re-Appraisal).

68. Seth Kantor, "Secret Trial of 'German 8'," Atlanta *Journal and Constitution,* July 5, 1980, p. 1-A.

69. Seth Kantor, "How Hoover Sold Out 'An Authentic American Hero'," Atlanta *Journal and Constitution,* July 4, 1980, p. 1-A.

70. Philadelphia *Inquirer,* July 6, 1980.

71. NJW.

72. New York *Times,* July 27, 1952, p. 1.

73. NJW.

74. "J. Edgar Hoover Speaks Out," *Nation's Business,* p. 41.

75. Senate Committee on Appropriations, *Departments of State, Justice and Commerce and the United States Information Agency Appropriations, 1955,* Part 1, p. 219.

76. New York *Times* (obituary).

77. Senate Committee on Appropriations, *Appropriations, 1955,* Part 1, p. 215.

78. NJW.

79. House Committee on Government Operations, *Inquiry Into the Destruction of Former FBI Director J. Edgar Hoover's Files and FBI Recordkeeping,* December 1, 1975, p. 38 (Helen W. Gandy testimony).

80. NJW.

81. NJW Transcript, p. 28.

82. Demaris, *The Director,* p. 74 (quoting 1937 *New Yorker* profile by Jack Alexander).

83. NJW.

84. NJW Transcript, p. 275.

85. NJW.

CHAPTER 2 SPECIAL AGENT

1. ML Transcript, p. 13.
2. TC Transcript, pp. 12–15.
3. Greg Walter, "Exit Neil Welch—A G-Man's G-Man," Philadelphia *Inquirer* Magazine Section, September 17, 1978, p. 3.
4. Ibid.
5. Ibid.
6. GW Transcript, p. 299.
7. NJW.
8. NJW Papers.
9. FR Transcript, p. 4.
10. DWM Notes of FR Interview, May 11, 1981.
11. NJW.
12. CG Transcript, p. 12.
13. NJW.
14. NJW Transcript, p. 30.
15. Ibid., p. 32.
16. NJW.
17. Ibid.
18. Ibid., p. 25.
19. William C. Sullivan, *The Bureau: My Thirty Years in Hoover's FBI* (New York: W. W. Norton & Company, 1979), p. 196.
20. House Committee on Government Operations, *Inquiry Into the Destruction of Former FBI Director J. Edgar Hoover's Files and FBI Recordkeeping*, December 1, 1975, p. 70.
21. JS Transcript, p. 54.
22. Ibid., p. 5.

CHAPTER 3 NOVICE

1. Encyclopaedia Britannica, s.v., "Jerez de la Frontera—Liberty Party."
2. NJW.
3. NJW Papers.
4. ML Transcript, p. 3.
5. NJW Transcript, pp. 115–18.
6. NJW.
7. Senate Committee on Appropriations, *Departments of State, Jus-*

tice and Commerce and the United States Information Agency Appropriations, 1955, Part 1, p. 224.

8. NJW Transcript, pp. 237–38.

9. NJW Transcript, pp. 40–43.

10. Comptroller General's Report to the House Committee on the Judiciary, *FBI Domestic Intelligence Operations—Their Purpose and Scope: Issues That Need To Be Resolved,* February 24, 1976, as quoted in *FBI Oversight,* Serial 2, Part 2, p. 164.

11. Sanford J. Ungar, *FBI* (Boston: Little, Brown & Company, 1975), p. 61.

12. William C. Sullivan, *The Bureau: My Thirty Years in Hoover's FBI* (New York: W. W. Norton & Company, 1979), p. 36.

13. Senate Judiciary Committee, *Ten-Year Term for FBI Director,* 1974, p. 17 (Statement of John T. Elliff quoting Maj. Gen. Harry H. Vaughn).

14. James Q. Wilson, *The Investigators* (New York: Basic Books, 1978), p. 169.

15. Sullivan, *The Bureau,* p. 36.

16. Comptroller General's Report, as quoted in *FBI Oversight,* Serial 2, Part 2, p. 165.

17. Ibid.

18. Ibid.

19. Ibid., p. 166.

20. Ibid., pp. 166–67.

21. Committee on the Judiciary House of Representatives, *FBI Oversight: Hearings Before the Subcommittee on Civil and Constitutional Rights,* February 27, 1975, Serial 2, Part 1, p. 4.

22. Richard H. Rovere, *Senator Joe McCarthy* (Cleveland: World Publishing, 1960).

23. Sullivan, *The Bureau,* p. 267.

24. Rovere, *Senator Joe McCarthy,* pp. 124–30.

25. NJW Transcript, p. 42.

26. CM Transcript, September 24, 1981, p. 16.

27. FR Transcript, May 11, 1981, p. 4; TC Transcript, September 24, 1980, pp. 7, 10.

28. NJW Transcript, pp. 149–155.

29. Ibid., pp. 8–9.

30. CG Transcript, p. 24.

31. NJW Transcript, pp. 465–67.

32. Ibid., pp. 476–78.

33. CG Transcript, p. 40.

34. Ibid., pp. 40–41.
35. NJW.
36. NJW Transcript, pp. 243–44.
37. NJW.
38. TC Transcript, pp. 5–6.
39. NJW.
40. JFD (with SLH), "Tales About Nails" (poem).

CHAPTER 5   ACOLYTE

1. CG Transcript, p. 33.
2. *Department of Justice Building* (Office of Administrative Assistant to Attorney General, 1960), pp. 1–2.
3. New York *Times,* May 9, 1954, p. 1.
4. William Manchester, *The Glory and the Dream* (Boston: Little, Brown & Company, 1973), pp. 907–10; *Time,* December 31, 1956, p. 10.
5. "J. Edgar Hoover Made the FBI Formidable With Politics, Publicity and Results" (obituary), New York *Times,* May 3, 1972, p. 52.
6. CG Transcript, p. 43.
7. DWM Papers.
8. Ibid.
9. New York *Times* (obituary).
10. NJW.
11. NJW Papers.
12. NJW Transcript, pp. 413 et seq.
13. "J. Edgar Hoover Speaks Out," *Nation's Business,* January 1972, p. 32.
14. DWM Papers.
15. Ibid.
16. Ibid.
17. Ibid.
18. Ibid.
19. Ibid.
20. "The Conglomerate of Crime," *Time,* August 22, 1969, p. 19.
21. Joseph Bonnano with Sergio Lalli, *A Man of Honor—The Autobiography of Joseph Bonnano,* (New York: Simon and Schuster, 1983), pp. 70–71.
22. DWM Papers.
23. Bonanno, p. 71.
24. DWM Papers.

25. Ibid.

26. Bonanno, pp. 136–37; DWM Papers, September 17, 1975, p. 5.

27. DWM Papers.

28. *A Decade of Organized Crime, 1980 Report,* Pennsylvania Crime Commission, p. 156.

29. DWM Papers.

30. Ibid.

31. "FBI Keeps Lepke From Dewey Aides," New York *Times,* August 26, 1939, p. 32.

32. NJW.

33. New York *Times,* March 27, 1951, pp. 1, 23.

34. NJW Papers.

35. Ibid.

36. *The 1967 President's Task Force Report on Organized Crime* (Washington, D.C.: U.S. Government Printing Office, 1967), p. 8.

37. CG Transcript, p. 5.

38. NR Transcript, pp. 50–51.

39. NJW Papers.

40. CG Transcript, p. 13.

41. RB Transcript, pp. 4–6.

42. NJW.

43. Ibid.

44. DWM Papers.

45. New York *Times,* October 26, 1957, p. 1.

46. DWM Papers.

47. Bonnano, pp. 208–16.

48. Rand McNally World Atlas, (New York: Rand McNally, 1968).

49. DWM Papers.

50. NJW.

51. NJW Transcript, p. 72.

52. NJW Account.

53. *The 1967 President's Task Force Report on Organized Crime,* p. 6; Bonnano, p. 222.

54. NJW.

55. NJW Transcript, p. 463; Bonnano, p. 189.

CHAPTER 6 MISSIONARY

1. J. Edgar Hoover, "The FBI's Role in the Field of Civil Rights," U.S. Department of Justice, reprinted with permission from *Yale Political Magazine,* New Haven, Connecticut.

2. "J. Edgar Hoover Speaks Out," *Nation's Business*, January 1972, pp. 35–36.

3. Don Whitehead, *Attack on Terror: The FBI Against the Klu Klux Klan in Mississippi* (New York: Funk & Wagnalls, 1970), p. 20.

4. "Tear Gas is Used: Mob Attacks Officers—2500 Troups are Sent to Oxford," New York *Times*, October 1, 1962, p. 1; "Enrolling of Meredith Ends Segregation in State Schools," New York *Times*, October 2, 1962, pp. 1, 24.

5. "Birmingham Bomb Kills 4 Negro Girls in Church; Riots Flare; 2 Boys Slain," New York *Times*, September 16, 1963, p. 1.

6. "Mississippi Campaign Heads Fear Foul Play—Inquiry by FBI is Ordered," New York *Times*, June 23, 1964, pp. 1, 13; Whitehead, *Attack on Terror*, p. 35, pp. 51–52.

7. NJW Transcript, pp. N-10–N-11.

8. NJW.

9. NJW Papers.

10. NJW.

11. "The Faith to Be Free," Remarks of J. Edgar Hoover Upon Receiving the Criss Award in Washington, D.C., December 7, 1961, p. 5.

12. NJW Transcript, p. 422.

13. Sanford J. Ungar, *FBI* (Boston: Little, Brown & Company, 1975), p. 658.

14. Whitehead, *Attack on Terror*, p. 67.

15. Ibid., p. 64.

16. Ibid., pp. 37, 64.

17. NJW Transcript, pp. 430–31.

18. Ibid., p. 426.

19. Ibid., pp. 426–27.

20. Whitehead, *Attack on Terror*, pp. 95–96.

21. NJW.

22. WD Transcript, p. 9.

23. Ibid., p. 1.

24. Ibid., p. 6.

25. NJW Transcript, pp. 156–57, 376–77, 429 et seq.

26. WD Transcript, p. 11.

27. Ibid., p. 1.

28. WD Transcript, p. 6; DWM Interview Notes.

29. NJW Account.

30. Ibid.

31. Ibid.

32. Ibid.
33. Ibid.
34. NJW Transcript, pp. 137–39.
35. Whitehead, *Attack on Terror*, p. 133.
36. WD Transcript, p. 20.
37. WD Transcript, p. 13.
38. "Hoover Assails Warren Findings," New York *Times*, November 19, 1964, p. 1.

CHAPTER 7 MEMORANDUM FOR MR. TOLSON

1. J. Edgar Hoover, "Memorandum for Mr. Tolson," April 29, 1966.
2. J. Edgar Hoover, "An Analysis of the New Left: A Gospel of Nihilism," *Christianity Today*, August 18, 1967.
3. William R. Manchester, *The Glory and the Dream* (Boston: Little, Brown & Company, 1974), p. 1266.
4. "Tolson Memorandum."
5. New York *Times*, March 14, 1964, p. 26.
6. Ibid.
7. New York *Times*, June 16, 1964, p. 1.
8. Ibid.
9. "Fright, Anger, Calm Courage Marked the Pursuit of Mosely," Buffalo *Evening News*, March 22, 1968, Section I–II.
10. "Tolson Memorandum."
11. Manchester, *The Glory and the Dream*, p. 1305.
12. *Tolson Memorandum*.
13. Niagara Falls *Gazette*, November 27, 1968, p. 13.
14. Samuel Eliot Morison, *The Oxford History of the American People* (New York: Oxford University Press, 1965), p. 900.
15. NJW.
16. Joseph Bonnano with Sergio Lalli, *A Man of Honor—The Autobiography of Joseph Bonnano*, (New York: Simon and Schuster, 1983), p. 96.
17. "The Conglomerate of Crime," *Time*, August 22, 1969, p. 19.
18. Niagara Falls *Gazette*, p. 13.
19. Ibid.
20. Bonnano, *A Man of Honor*, p. 291.
21. DWM Interview with Edwin Guthman, December 21, 1983.
22. NJW.
23. CG Transcript, p. 10.

24. TC Transcript, pp. 58–59; New York *Times*, May 22, 1963.
25. DWM Interview Notes with GW.

CHAPTER 8 SKEPTIC

1. CG Transcript, p. 28.
2. *The Budget of the United States Government for the Fiscal Year Ending June 30, 1965* (Washington, D.C.: U.S. Government Printing Office, 1964), Appendix, p. 570.
3. NJW.
4. NJW.
5. *World Almanac and Book of Facts, 1980* (New York: Newspaper Enterprise Association, 1979), pp. 446–47.
6. DWM Interview Notes with FR.
7. Ibid.
8. NJW Transcript, pp. 358–60.
9. Ibid., pp. N-71–N-72.
10. Photo in NJW Papers.
11. NJW Transcript, pp. 210–12, 215, 363–65.
12. Ramsey Clark letter to NJW, March 23, 1968.
13. NJW Account: taped August 7, 1982, Transcript Summary, p. 3; "Kitty's Killer Captured; 3 Hostages Safe," *Daily News* (New York), March 22, 1968, p. 48.
14. FR Transcript, p. 18.
15. "Fright, Anger, Calm Courage Marked the Pursuit of Mosely," Buffalo *Evening News*, March 22, 1968, Section I–II.
16. "Mosely Captured in Isle Apartment," Buffalo *Courier-Express*, March 22, 1968, p. 4.
17. "Hostage Tells of Ordeal With Rapist-Killer," *Daily News* (New York), March 22, 1968, p. 48.
18. Data from City Accessor's Office, Grand Island, New York, January 24, 1984.
19. "Kitty's Killer Captured; 3 Hostages Safe," *Daily News* (New York), March 22, 1968, p. 48.
20. NJW Account, taped August 7, 1982: Transcript Summary, p. 3.
21. "Fright, Anger, Calm Courage Marked the Pursuit of Mosely," Buffalo *Evening News*, March 22, 1968, Section I–II.
22. NJW Account, taped August 7, 1982: Transcript Summary, p. 3.
23. Ibid.
24. Ibid., p. 4.
25. Ibid.

26. Ibid., p. 5.

27. "4 Kew Gardens Residents Testify to Seeing Woman Slain on Street," New York *Times*, June 10, 1964, p. 50.

28. "37 Who Saw Murder Didn't Call the Police," New York *Times*, March 21, 1964, pp. 1, 38.

29. "Mosely Recalls Three Queens Killings," New York *Times*, June 11, 1964, p. 30.

30. "4 Kew Gardens Residents Testify," p. 50.

31. "Mosely Recalls Three Queens Killings," p. 30.

32. Ibid.

33. NJW Account, taped August 7, 1982: Transcript Summary, p. 6.

34. Ibid.

35. ML Transcript, p. 2.

36. NJW Transcript, pp. 353–54, 446–48.

37. Ibid., p. 362.

38. NJW.

39. "J. Edgar Hoover Speaks Out with Vigor," *Time*, December 14, 1970, p. 16.

40. NJW Transcript, p. 365.

41. Ibid., p. 216.

42. ML Transcript, p. 13.

43. DH Transcript, pp. 10–11.

44. "Coordinator of Roundup Is Tough Veteran of FBI," Niagara Falls *Gazette*, November 27, 1968, p. 25.

45. "Stefano: Arraignment in a Queen-Sized Bed," Niagara Falls *Gazette*, November 30, 1968, p. 1.

46. FR Transcript, p. 11.

47. NJW Transcript, p. N-72.

48. "Magaddino, 9 Others Charged in Gambling, Rackets Conspiracy," Buffalo *Evening News*, November 27, 1968.

49. NJW Transcript, p. 216.

50. FR Transcript, p. 11.

51. "Raid Yields Fortune in Loot," Buffalo *Courier Express*, December 5, 1967, p. 1.

52. "Police Arrest 4 Here, Find $150,000 Gems," Buffalo *Courier Express*, September 7, 1969, p. 1.

53. "5 Held in $7 Million Art Thefts," Buffalo *Evening News*, October 24, 1968, p. 1.

54. "Federal Agents Smash Gambling Ring Here," Buffalo *Courier Express*, February 21, 1967, p. 1.

55. "FBI Accuses 5 of Milking Vegas Flights," *Daily News* (New York), January 9, 1970, p. 4-C.

56. "Kidnapped Girl Is Found in Ontario—Patricia Ann Martin Is 'Alive and Well,' FBI Chief Reports," Buffalo *Evening News*, July 24, 1969, p. 1.

57. NJW Transcript, pp. N-6–N-10.

58. NR Transcript, p. 37.

59. NJW.

CHAPTER 10 HERETIC

1. NJW Transcript, p. X-1.

2. NR Transcript, pp. 73–74.

3. Ibid., p. 49.

4. DWM Notes from NJW Interview, November 10, 1982.

5. Ibid.

6. NR Transcript, p. 37.

7. Louis Heldman, "FBI Director Pays Detroit a Flying Visit," Detroit *Free Press*, June 13, 1972.

8. NR Transcript, p. 73.

9. DWM Notes from NJW Interview, November 10, 1982.

10. NJW Transcript, p. 329.

11. Ibid., p. 452.

12. NJW Transcript, pp. 372, 374, and X-13.

13. Berl Falbaum, *The Anchor, Leo and Friends* (Eugene, Oregon: JDW Publications, 1978), pp. 85–86; NJW Transcript, p. 372.

14. Detroit *Free Press*, May 7, 1971, p. A-3.

15. Ibid.

16. a. Jack Anderson, "Tough Guy Hoover Only an Image"
   b. Jack Anderson, "FBI Tactics Used to Reverse Prying," Grand Rapids *Press*, December 31, 1970.
   c. Anderson, "Tough Guy Hoover."
   d. Anderson, "FBI Tactics."

17. Detroit *Free Press*, December 11, 1970, p. 1-B.

18. Detroit *News*, January 18, 1971, p. 1; Detroit *Sunday News*, March 11, 1971, p. 21-A (by Louis Cassels, UPI Senior Editor).

19. Detroit *Sunday News*, March 11, 1971, p. 21-A (by Louis Cassels).

20. Detroit *Sunday News*, March 11, 1971, p. 21-A; Detroit *News*, November 17, 1970; Grand Rapids *Press*, November 17, 1970.

21. *Time*, December 14, 1970, p. 16 (as quoted in Montoya letter to Hoover, dated December 14, 1970).

22. Montoya letter to Hoover, dated December 14, 1970.

23. JEH letter to Montoya, dated December 15, 1970.

24. Senate Judiciary Committee, *Ten-Year Term for FBI Director,* March 18, 1974, p. 22.

25. Ibid.

26. Sanford J. Ungar, "The FBI File," *Atlantic Monthly,* April 1975, p. 45.

27. *Ten-Year Term for FBI Director.*

28. NJW.

29. Ibid., pp. 88–92.

30. Ibid., p. X-14.

31. Ibid., p. N-37.

32. Senate Intelligence Committee.

33. Ibid.

34. Ibid.

35. NR Transcript, pp. 29–30.

36. NJW Transcript, p. N-74.

37. NJW Transcript, p. 345.

38. Ibid., p. 346.

39. DWM Notes from NJW Interview, November 10, 1982.

40. NJW Transcript, p. 182.

41. NJW.

42. DWM Notes from NJW Interview, November 10, 1982.

43. NS Transcript, p. 2.

44. Ibid., p. 4.

45. Ibid., p. 9.

46. ML Transcript, p. 16.

47. Ibid.

48. Ibid.

49. ML Transcript, pp. 41–43.

50. Omnibus Crime Control and Safe Streets Act of 1968, P.L. 90–351, 82 Stat. 197 *et. seq.* (June 19, 1968).

51. NJW Transcript, p. 372.

52. NS Transcript, pp. 27–28.

53. NJW Transcript, pp. X-3, X-4.

54. Detroit *Free Press,* May 7, 1971, p. 1.

55. Ibid.

56. Detroit *News,* June 23, 1971, p. 1; NJW Transcript, p. 373.

57. Ibid., May 6, 1971, p. 1.

58. NJW Transcript, p. 324.

59. Detroit *Sunday News* (Cassels), April 11, 1971, p. 21-A.

60. McGovern Press Release, March 1, 1971.

61. Detroit *Free Press*, March 10, 1971, p. 1-B.

62. New York *Times*, April 19, 1971, p. 29.

63. Donald Janson, "FBI File Theft Stirs Rage and Joy Among 6,300 Residents of Media, Pa.," New York *Times*, March 29, 1971.

64. "Mitchell Issues Plea on FBI Files," New York *Times*, March 24, 1971.

65. NJW Transcript, p. N-49.

66. New York *Times*, April 19, 1971, p. 1.

67. Ibid.; Detroit *News*, April 20, 1971, p. 10-C.

68. "Congress Is Urged to Probe Charges of FBI Phone Taps," Detroit *Free Press*, April 8, 1971, p. 1-A.

69. Detroit *News*, April 20, 1971, p. 10-C.

70. Detroit *Free Press*, October 19, 1971, p. 2-A; Washington *Post*, November 18, 1971, p. 1.

71. *Atlantic Monthly*, p. 45.

72. NJW Papers.

73. NJW Transcript, pp. 84–86.

74. NR Transcript, p. 54.

75. NJW Transcript, p. X-5.

76. Ibid., p. X-4.

77. DWM Interviews.

78. Detroit *Free Press*, September 11, 1971, p. 1.

79. DWM Interviews.

80. NJW Papers.

81. NJW Transcript, p. X-13.

82. Ibid., p. 375.

CHAPTER 11   DEATH

1. NR Transcript, p. 40.

2. Washington *Post*, May 3, 1972, pp. 1, 12.

3. NJW.

4. New York *Times*, May 3, 1972, p. 1.

5. Ibid.

6. House Committee on Government Operations, *Inquiry Into the Destruction of Former FBI Director J. Edgar Hoover's Files and FBI Recordkeeping*, December 1, 1975, p. 65.

7. Ibid., pp. 35–36, 65.

8. NJW.

9. *House Inquiry Into Destruction*, pp. 34–48.

10. Washington *Evening Star,* May 3, 1972, p. A-7.

11. Bert Falbaum, *The Anchor, Leo & Friends* (Eugene, Oregon: JDW Publications, 1978), p. 150.

12. "J. Edgar Hoover Speaks Out," *Nation's Business,* January 1972, p. 40; NJW Transcript, p. N-50.

13. NJW Papers.

14. NJW Transcript, p. N-19.

15. "Nixon to Deliver Eulogy at Hoover's Funeral Today," Washington *Post,* May 4, 1972, p. 8-A.

16. Ibid.

17. NJW.

18. NJW Transcript, X-18 et seq.

CHAPTER 12   WHIRLWIND

1. DWM.

2. Ibid.

3. Ibid.

4. NJW Transcript, pp. 369–70.

5. ML Transcript, p. 24.

6. NJW Transcript, p. 370.

7. Louis Heldman, "FBI Director Pays Detroit a Flying Visit," Detroit *Free Press,* June 13, 1972.

8. Ibid.

9. Sanford J. Ungar, *FBI* (Boston: Little, Brown & Company, 1976), p. 264.

10. NJW.

11. Carroll Kilpatrick, "Interim FBI Head Selected," Washington *Post,* May 4, 1972, p. A-1.

12. Ibid., p. A-8.

13. House Committee on Government Operations, *Inquiry into the Destruction of Former FBI Director J. Edgar Hoover's Files and FBI Recordkeeping,* 1975, p. 187.

14. NJW Transcript, p. X-12.

15. "Flying Visit," Detroit *Free Press.*

16. Ibid.

17. NJW Transcript, pp. N-14, X-11.

18. Ibid., pp. N-17–N-18.

19. NJW Papers.

20. DWM.

21. "Ex-Aide Approved FBI Burglaries," New York *Times*, August 18, 1976, pp. 1, 22.

22. House *Inquiry into Destruction of Hoover's Files*, 1975, p. 43.

23. NR Transcript, p. 58.

24. "Gray Testifies That Dean 'Probably' Lied to FBI," New York *Times*, March 23, 1973, p. 1-A.

25. Ibid., March 2, 1973, p. 15-C.

26. NJW Papers.

27. House Inquiry Into Destruction, 1975, pp. 75–82.

28. NJW Papers.

29. "Detroit Links to NY Jewel Theft Probed," Detroit *News*, January 10, 1972, p. 1; "Gems in NY Hotel Loot Found Here," Detroit *Free Press*, January 10, 1972, p. A-3.

30. "Wyandotte Man Arrested in $502,000 Jet Hijacking," Detroit *News*, June 29, 1972, p. 1.

31. "Whisky Was Risky," Detroit *News*, March 1, 1972.

32. Louis Heldman, "FBI Nabs 3 in Plot to Steal Secret Ford Glass Process," Detroit *Free Press*, August 31, 1973, p. 1.

33. NJW Papers.

34. DWM.

35. Michael Graham, "FBI Calls Injured Depositor 'Stupid' in Bank Shootout," Detroit *Free Press*, November 16, 1971, p. A-3.

36. NJW Papers.

37. NJW Transcript, pp. N-62–N-63.

38. NJW Papers.

39. "Gray Quits FBI Under Fire for Role in Bugging Probe," Detroit *Free Press*, April 28, 1973, p. 1-A.

40. Ibid.

41. "Agents Want FBI Chief From Ranks," Detroit *News*, May 1, 1973, p. 11-A; NJW Papers.

42. "Ruckelshaus Calls Summit," *Daily Star* (Niles, Michigan), May 2, 1973, p. 2.

43. Rowland Evans and Robert Novak, "Watergate's Continuing Crisis for FBI," Tampa *Tribune*, May 23, 1973, p. 10-A.

44. NJW Transcript, p. N-62–N-63.

45. NJW Papers.

46. NJW.

47. "Nomination of Clarence M. Kelley To Be Director of the Federal Bureau of Investigation," Senate Judiciary Committee Hearings, June 19, 20, and 25, 1973.

48. "Changes at FBI—The Full Story," *U.S. News and World Report*, March 5, 1973, p. 22.
49. NJW Papers.
50. Anthony Marro, "Watergate: Justice Department Changes," New York *Times*, June 17, 1977, p. 1.
51. "Justice Swainson of Michigan Convicted of Perjury," New York *Times*, November 3, 1975, p. 16; "Ex-Governor Draws Sentence on Perjury," New York *Times*, January 27, 1976, p. 62.

CHAPTER 13 REASSIGNMENT

1. House Committee on Government Operations, *Inquiry into the Destruction of Former FBI Director J. Edgar Hoover's Files and FBI Recordkeeping*, December 1, 1975, pp. 158–70.
2. Ibid., p. 169.
3. Ibid., pp. 141–46.
4. Anthony Marro, "Aides to Bell Call for Indictments of FBI Officials Over Break-ins," New York *Times*, April 1, 1977, p. 1.
5. NJW Transcript, pp. P-10–P-11.
6. Ibid., p. P-2 et seq.

CHAPTER 14 PHILADELPHIA

1. "A Decade of Organized Crime," 1980 Report, Pennsylvania Crime Commission, p. 158.
2. Bob Schwabach, "The Quiet Man Ruled From His Rowhouse," Philadelphia *Daily News*, March 22, 1980, pp. 4, 20.
3. GL Transcript, pp. 11–12.
4. 1980 Crime Commission Report, p. 160.
5. TC Transcript, p. 34.
6. Ibid., pp. 37–38.
7. MR Transcript, pp. 6–10.
8. Ibid.
9. GL Transcript, p. 7.
10. NJW Transcript, pp. P-31–P-47.
11. Ibid., p. P-31.
12. Ibid., p. P-51.
13. Ibid., p. P-50.
14. LV Transcript, p. 21.
15. Ibid., p. 22.
16. NJW Transcript, p. 326.

17. Dick Cooper, "The Mob Tapes," Philadelphia *Inquirer,* May 16, 1982, Metro Section, p. 1.

18. GL Transcript, p. 17–18.

19. TC Transcript, p. 33.

20. "Bruno Slain," Philadelphia *Daily News,* March 22, 1980, p. 1 et seq.

21. "The Mob Tapes," Philadelphia *Inquirer.*

22. "Mobster Sindone's Body Found in Bag," Philadelphia *Daily News,* October 30, 1980, p. 1 et seq.

23. "Astro-Profile: The New Godfather," Philadelphia *Daily News,* March 31, 1980, p. 20.

24. "Bomb Blast Kills Testa," Philadelphia *Daily News,* March 16, 1981, p. 1 *et seq.*

25. Marguerite Del Giudice, "The 'Me Generation' Mob," Philadelphia *Inquirer,* September 5, 1982, p. 24-A.

26. "The Mob Tapes," Philadelphia *Inquirer.*

27. NJW Papers.

28. Ibid.

29. Ibid.

30. NJW.

31. NJW Transcript, p. N-12.

32. DWM Interview Notes with NJW, November 10, 1982.

33. NJW.

34. NJW Papers.

35. JS Transcript, p. 36.

36. "Kelley Deposition Raises Confusion Over Whether He Received the Reports on Recent FBI Burglaries," New York *Times,* November 19, 1976, p. 15.

37. 1980 Pennsylvania Crime Commission Report, pp. 173–174.

38. NJW.

39. NJW Transcript, p. P-59.

40. 1980 Pennsylvania Crime Commission Report, pp. 173–74.

41. NJW Transcript, pp. 342–44; pp. P-116–P-122.

42. Ibid., pp. P-131–P-132.

43. 1980 Pennsylvania Crime Commission Report, p. 174.

CHAPTER 15 WASHINGTON

1. NJW Transcript, p. P-61; New York *Times,* July 14, 1976, p. 47.

2. *The Department of Justice Report on the Relationship Between*

United States Recording Company and the Federal Bureau of Investigation, January 1978, p. 32.

3. "Levi's FBI Guidelines," New York *Times,* March 14, 1976, Section IV, p. 4; "Not Above the Law," New York *Times,* March 18, 1976, p. 41.

4. Senate Select Committee on Intelligence, "Statement of Clarence M. Kelley, FBI Director," September 22, 1976, p. 2.

5. Ibid.; see also NJW Transcript, pp. 104, 456, and X-25.

6. *Department of Justice Report,* p. 1.

7. NJW Transcript, p. P-62.

8. NJW Papers.

9. NR Transcript, pp. 52–53.

10. Kelley Statement, p. 2.

11. *Department of Justice Report.*

12. FBI, Philadelphia Division, *Year End Report,* released January 25, 1977.

13. Kelley Statement, p. 1.

CHAPTER 16   BETH

1. CB Transcript, p. 1.

2. NJW Transcript, p. P-69f. ("NJW/Beth")

3. CB Transcript, p. 2.

4. NJW/Beth.

5. CB Transcript, pp. 4–5.

6. NJW/Beth.

7. CB Transcript, pp. 9–10.

8. NJW/Beth.

9. CB Transcript, pp. 11–12.

10. NJW/Beth.

11. CB Transcript, p. 12.

12. NJW/Beth.

13. GL Transcript, p. 40.

14. NJW Transcript, p. P-88.

CHAPTER 17   CHOOSING

1. NJW/MP: DWM Interview Notes, Transcript.

2. Christopher Lydon, "Whoever Runs It, FBI Faces Problem of Political Control," New York *Times,* March 26, 1973, p. 30-C; Senate Judiciary Committee, *Ten-Year Term for FBI Director,* 1974, p. 2.

3. NJW Transcript, pp. 400, 439.

4. *Ten-Year Term*, p. 4.

5. Ibid., p. 30.

6. Ibid., p. 31, 36.

7. Myra MacPherson, "Dan Flood on the Spot," Washington *Post*, March 17, 1978, p. 1-B.

8. NJW Transcript, p. P-145.

9. House of Representatives, *Report of the Committee on Standards of Official Conduct: In the Matter of Representative Daniel J. Flood*, March 26, 1980, p. 213.

10. Ibid.

11. Ibid., pp. 42–43.

12. *A Decade of Organized Crime, 1980 Report*, Pennsylvania Crime Commission, pp. 238–39.

13. Ibid.

14. Ibid.

15. NJW Transcript, pp. 171–72, P-112–P-113, N-26, X-23.

16. CM Transcript, p. 14.

17. "The FBI Five: A Closer Look," *Newsweek*, July 11, 1977, p. 22.

18. CM Transcript, pp. 19–20.

19. "Ex-FBI Man Indicted by U.S. in Mail Openings," New York *Times*, April 8, 1977, p. 1.

20. NJW Transcript, pp. 173–75, 399.

21. "The FBI Five"; CM Transcript, pp. 14–15.

22. CM Transcript, pp. 16, 20–21, 26.

23. "The FBI Five."

24. House of Representatives, Report of the Committee on Standards of Official Conduct, p. 43.

25. Ronald J. Ostrow and Gaylord Shaw, "FBI Official in Front Rank of Race for Director Post," Los Angeles *Times*, July 9, 1977, p. 17.

26. NJW Transcript, p. N-27.

27. NJW Transcript, p. 172.

28. Anthony Marro, "Choice to Head FBI Still Eludes Carter," New York *Times*, July 31, 1977, pp. 1, 23.

29. "FBI Official in Front Rank."

30. "Ex-FBI Chief Hero With Maverick Image in Line to Head Agency," Buffalo *Evening News*, July 2, 1977, p. A-10.

31. "FBI Official in Front Rank."

32. NJW Transcript, p. P-67.

33. Saul Friedman, "FBI Panel: Is It Being Undercut?", Philadelphia *Inquirer*, July 7, 1977, p. 1-A.

34. "FBI Official in Front Rank of Race for Director Post," Los Angeles *Times*, July 3, 1977, p. B-1.

35. Anthony Marro, "Wanted: An FBI Chief All Things to All People," New York *Times*, June 19, 1977 (The Nation section).

36. NJW Account; Federal Election Commission, *In the Matter of Shapp for President Committee*, MUR 240 (76).

37. NJW Transcript, pp. P-125–P-126.

38. Ibid.

39. "Carter Sending Out Signals For New FBI Chief," San Jose *News*, November 30, 1977, p. 11-A.

40. NJW.

41. "Eilburg Pleads Guilty; Bargain Sets Penalty at Probation and Fine," New York *Times*, February 25, 1979, p. 1, 16; "Flood Enters Guilty Plea: Conspiracy Count a Misdemeanor—Pennsylvanian Is Placed on Probation by U.S. Judge," New York *Times*, February 27, 1980, p. 12; "Elko Disputes U.S. Aides on Flood-Eilburg Hospital Data," New York *Times*, March 15, 1978, p. 23.

42. House Committee on Standards of Official Conduct Report, pp. 5–16.

43. New York *Times*, March 12, 1978, p. 26.

44. Ibid.

45. "Dan Flood on the Spot," p. 3-B.

46. New York *Times*, January 20, 1978, p. 5.

47. "FBI Names Welch as New York Head," New York *Times*, August 5, 1978, p. 1.

48. "A Tough G-Man In A Tough Job," New York *Times*, August 6, 1978, p. E-3.

CHAPTER 18   NYO

1. DWM Interviews.

2. Ibid.

3. Ibid.

4. Ibid.

5. Wayne Barrett, "The Men Who Sold Scotto," *Village Voice*, November 26, 1979, p. 1f.

6. Anna Quindlen, "About New York—The Power and the Glory Fade to Prison Gray," New York *Times*, July 24, 1981.

7. Leslie Maitland, "Scotto's Dealings With Politicians are Subject of New Investigations," New York *Times*, December 17, 1979, p. 1f.

8. DWM Interviews; see also Ann Crittenden, "The Shah in New York," New York *Times,* September 26, 1976, Section 3, p. 1.
9. NJW.
10. Ibid.
11. Ibid.
12. "FBI Names Welch As New York Head," New York *Times,* August 5, 1978, p. 1.
13. Howard Blum, "Both 'An Innovator and a Doer'," New York *Times,* August 5, 1978, p. 44.
14. NJW Transcript, pp. NY-43–NY-44.
15. *U.S. v. Gray, Felt & Miller* (indictment).
16. "Gray and 2 Ex-FBI Aides Deny Guilt as 700 at Court Applaud Them," New York *Times,* April 21, 1978, p. 13.
17. NJW.
18. NJW Transcript, p. NY-43.
19. Ibid., p. NY-42.
20. NJW Transcript, June 1983, pp. NY-8–NY-9.
21. NJW; see also Wayne Barrett, "How Politicians Stay Out of Jail," *New York,* February 4, 1980, p. 32.
22. NJW quoting RB.
23. Senate Select Committee, *Final Report of Select Committee to Study Undercover Activities of Components of the Department of Justice,* December 15, 1982, p. 15.
24. Ibid.
25. NJW.
26. NJW Transcript, p. NY-53.

CHAPTER 19   SHAH AND SHEIK

1. Ann Crittenden, "Relation of Rep. Murphy With Iran and Nicaragua Under U.S. Inquiry," New York *Times,* October 26, 1977, p. 25.
2. "How to Buy a Bill," Washington *Post* editorial, September 1, 1977.
3. Ann Crittenden, "The Shah in New York," New York *Times,* September 26, 1976, Section 3, p. 1.
4. DWM Interviews; see also Wayne Barrett, "How Politicians Stay Out of Jail," *New York,* February 4, 1980, p. 32.
5. Fred J. Cook, "The Billion Dollar Mystery," *The Nation,* April 12, 1965, p. 380f.; Fred J. Cook, "New Twists to the Mystery," *The Nation,* May 24, 1965, p. 550 et seq.

6. "Governor Carey Says He Wasn't Told of Scotto Tactic," New York *Times*, December 17, 1979.

7. Edward Hoagland, "The Scotto Trial," *Village Voice*, November 26, 1979, p. 16.

8. Leslie Maitland, "Scotto's Dealings With Politicians Are Subject of New Investigations," New York *Times*, December 17, 1979, p. 1 et seq.

9. Ibid.

10. Ibid.

11. Arnold H. Lubasch, "Misuse of Patronage Was Focus of New York Trial," New York *Times*, December 26, 1981, p. 12.

12. Selwyn Raab, "Cody Sentenced to 5-Year Term As a Racketeer," New York *Times*, December 1, 1982, p. 1.

13. Senate Select Committee, *Final Report of the Select Committee to Study Undercover Activities of Components of the Department of Justice*, December 15, 1982, p. 16.

14. NJW.

15. NJW; see also Leslie Maitland, "FBI Bribe Probe Links Politicians," (New York *Times* News Service), Philadelphia *Bulletin*, February 3, 1980, p. 5.

16. DWM Notes from Interview with RC, March 21, 1983, p. 4.

17. *World Almanac and Book of Facts, 1980* (New York: Newspaper Enterprise Association, 1979), p. 918.

18. DWM Notes from Interview with RC, March 21, 1983.

19. *World Almanac, 1980*, p. 919.

20. DWM Notes from Interview with RC, p. 1, March 21, 1983.

21. Ibid.

22. Ibid., pp. 3–4.

23. LV Transcript, p. 14.

24. "Senator Williams Surprised, Baffled," Philadelphia *Bulletin*, February 3, 1980, p. 4.

25. Jan Schaffer and Donald Kimelman, "Three on Council Seen Taking Bribes," Philadelphia *Inquirer*, February 4, 1980, p. 5-A.

26. "Sen. Williams Surprised, Baffled."

27. Charles R. Babcock and George Lardner, Jr., "GOP, Ethics Panel Head Urge 'Sting' Probes," Washington *Post*, February 4, 1980, p. 1.

28. Ibid.

29. "The FBI Stings Congress," *Time*, February 18, 1980, p. 10.

30. Ibid.

31. Ibid., pp. 14, 19.

32. "An Arab Unit Protests FBI Undercover Cast," New York *Times*, February 4, 1980, p. A-15.

33. "City Suspects Aren't Talking," Philadelphia *Daily News*, February 4, 1980, p. 3.

34. Richard Lyons, "U.S. Allegations Prompt 3 Denials and the Tale of an Honest Senator," New York *Times*, February 5, 1980.

35. *Time*, p. 11.

36. "U.S. Allegations Prompt 3 Denials."

37. Bob Warner, "Myers Makes His TV Debut," Philadelphia *Daily News*, August 14, 1980, p. 3.

38. Martin Schram, "Senator Pressler: He Spurned the 'Arab' Offers," Washington *Post*, February 4, 1980, p. 1.

39. *Senate Select Committee to Study Undercover Activities*, p. 16.

Index